Lives of Hitler's Jewish Soldiers

Lives of Hitler's Jewish Soldiers

Untold Tales of Men of Jewish Descent
Who Fought for the Third Reich

Bryan Mark Rigg

UNIVERSITY PRESS OF KANSAS

© 2009 by the University Press of Kansas

Unless otherwise noted, all photographs and documents are from the Bryan Mark Rigg Collection, German National Archives (Bundesarchiv).

Published by the University Press of Kansas (Lawrence, Kansas 66045), which was organized by the Kansas Board of Regents and is operated and funded by Emporia State University, Fort Hays State University, Kansas State University, Pittsburg State University, the University of Kansas, and Wichita State University.

Library of Congress Cataloging-in-Publication Data

Rigg, Bryan Mark, 1971–
  Lives of Hitler's Jewish soldiers : untold tales of men of Jewish descent who fought for the Third Reich / Bryan Mark Rigg.
    p. cm. — (Modern war studies)
  Includes bibliographical references and index.
  ISBN 978-0-7006-1638-1 (cloth : alk. paper)
  1. Jewish soldiers—Germany—History—20th century. 2. World War, 1939–1945—Participation, Jewish. 3. Children of interfaith marriage—Germany—History—20th century. 4. National socialism. 5. Germany—History, Military—20th century. I. Title.

  DS134.255.R54 2009
  940.54'04—dc22   2008042553

British Library Cataloguing-in-Publication Data is available.

Printed in the United States of America

10 9 8 7 6 5 4 3 2 1

Do not judge thy comrade until thou hast stood in his place.

—Hillel, the Jewish Sage

This book is dedicated to Harvard Knowles and David Weber, two incredible teachers at Phillips Exeter Academy. They inspired me to write and explore the power of language. It is also dedicated to two fellow Yale students and friends, Kee Bong Kim and Stuart White, both of whom helped me to explore military history and the men who fought during World War II. It is dedicated to my Cambridge adviser, Jonathan Steinberg, who went beyond the call of duty to help me with this study. And finally, it is dedicated to my Starpoint TCU teacher Mary Stewart, who healed my soul and taught me how to read. After I failed first grade twice, she got me back on track and has been an angel in my life.

CONTENTS

Half Jew First Lieutenant Joachim Sonntag's grave on the Russian front. This picture was taken in November 1942 by Achim von Bredow, a "37.5 percent Jew" according to Nazi law.

In 1942 a former German soldier entered SS headquarters in Berlin. He walked uneasily. His civilian jacket was adorned with medals he had earned in battle. An SS officer asked what he wanted. Hugo Fuchs wished to know where they had taken his Jewish father. The SS officer, upset, said, "I would send you straight where your father is if you didn't have those medals!" Fuchs would never see his father again. He had been killed in the Sachsenhausen concentration camp.[1]

It was winter 1942 and Walter Gross ran for his life across snow-covered tundra on the eastern front in Russia. He heard the loud explosions of mortar shells and the whizzing of bullets as the enemy took aim at him. Things had gone wrong while he led a reconnaissance patrol. The enemy had killed everyone in his unit and he was desperately trying to make it back to his lines. As he reached the edge of the defensive trench, an explosion and shrapnel slammed his body against the earth. As he rolled over at the bottom of the ditch, he looked at his lacerated belly as his entrails poured out onto his legs. The warm blood soaked into his pant legs. With unbearable pain, he started to scream. One of his closest comrades, Joachim Schmidt, who had remained behind in the defensive trench, tried to shove his guts back into his body but he did so in vain. Gross and his comrade knew he was dying. Gross gave his friend a strange smile, shook his head, and said that this was a shitty war. He was dying for a country that had persecuted him and his family. He asked Schmidt to protect his Jewish mother. Schmidt promised. He knew that Gross was a *Mischling*. Blood continued to pour out of Gross. When his head slumped over and his body went limp, another Jewish soldier had died for the Fatherland. His mother committed suicide before her deportation to Auschwitz two months later.[2]

Fuchs and Gross were not alone in bravely serving their country while the Nazis murdered their families. During World War II, likely thousands of Jews and tens of thousands of partial Jews (*Mischlinge*) served in the Wehrmacht. A few even held high positions in it. Here follow some of their stories.

Knocked-out Russian T-34 tank with a dead body in front of it (top) and
Russian corpses on the battlefield (bottom). These pictures were taken on the
Russian front in 1943 by Achim von Bredow, a "37.5 percent Jew" according to
Nazi law. These were the types of tanks men like quarter-Jew Horst von
Oppenfeld, half-Jew Helmuth Kopp, and half-Jew Horst Geitner attacked
during their time in combat.

ACKNOWLEDGMENTS

Several of the men whose stories appear in the following pages—along with their families—offered support, advice, and often food and housing. Their help was critical for my research, and from the bottom of my heart, I thank them all.

Also, many historians, academics, and writers gave invaluable help. Foremost on the list is Michael Berenbaum. I cannot begin to express my gratitude to Michael Berenbaum of the University of Judaism for his constant support and willingness to help make my work stronger—it is not often that one has the help of one of the foremost Holocaust historians, and I am grateful for his support.

Next, Mark Bernheim of the University of Miami in Ohio was a tremendous help. He provided invaluable advice and feedback not only for this book, but also for my first book, *Hitler's Jewish Soldiers*. His insights and constructive criticism have made both works better.

Many thanks go to the lawyer Peter Schliesser, himself a "half-Jew" under the Nazis, for his extensive editorial help. His guidance and extensive editing throughout the writing of this book have been greatly appreciated. He is a true mensch. I would also like to thank the journalist David Seeley and author Michael Skakun for their comments.

Warm thanks go to my graduate advisor at Cambridge University, Jonathan Steinberg, who encouraged the exploration of such a project back in 1996. His years of guidance and help mean more than he knows. Author of *Frontsoldaten*, Stephen Fritz, and Günther Montfort, Bundesarchiv-Militärarchiv in Freiburg, provided useful feedback on the structure and content of the book.

James Tent, an expert on the *Mischlinge* (see his excellent book, *In the Shadow of the Holocaust*), of the University of Alabama at Birmingham has proven most helpful. His feedback during the editorial stage of this manuscript has greatly strengthened it. University of Virginia history professor Hans Schmitt, also a "half-Jew" during the Nazis years, gave me incredible feedback. His support and help these last few years have been tremendous. I also thank the late Andy Baggs at American Military University and Luftwaffe expert Horst Boog for their help. Baggs's comments and criticism, especially concerning military hardware, were greatly appreciated. Boog's insights on the Luftwaffe helped me greatly with my biographies of Wilberg and Milch. James Corum of Oxford University and Dennis Showalter of Colorado College offered their comments and words of support and have been an inspiration. Retired Brigadier General Charles Fred Smith and Howard Spiro of Yale Medical School gave me the honor of reading this work and provided helpful advice on its substance and style. To have such a group of historians behind me has added not only to my confidence but also to my sense of responsibility to do my best to live up to their expectations and examples.

Thanks also go to Lois Drew and Bryan Burg for their editorial comments. My colleague from the Phillips Exeter Academy Summer School, Robert Schur Jr., has provided helpful suggestions drawing on his knowledge of World War II and writing.

I profoundly appreciate the opportunity to work once again with the staff of the University Press of Kansas, especially editor-in-chief Michael Briggs and marketing manager Susan Schott, whom I consider both colleagues and friends. This book could not have happened without their support and help.

And last, I thank my wonderful mother, Marilee Rigg, and beloved wife, Stephanie Rigg, for their consistent encouragement throughout the years.

ABBREVIATIONS

AWOL   Absent without leave

DAK   (Deutsches Afrika-Korps) German African Corps

EKI   (Eisernes Kreuz Erster Klasse) Iron Cross First Class

EKII   (Eisernes Kreuz Zweiter Klasse) Iron Cross Second Class

Gestapo   (Geheime Staatspolizei) Secret State Police

KdF   (Kanzlei des Fuhrers) The Führer's chancellery (not to be confused with the same abbreviation used for Kraft durch Freude of the German Labor Front)

NCO   Noncommissioned officer

NSDAP   (Nationalsozialistische Deutsche Arbeiter-Partei) Nazi Party

OKH   (Oberkommando des Heeres) Army High Command

OKL   (Oberkommando der Luftwaffe) Air Force High Command

OKM   (Oberkommando der Marine) Navy High Command

OKW   (Oberkommando der Wehrmacht) Armed Forces High Command

OT   (Organization Todt) forced labor camps

POWs   Prisoners of war

RMI   (Reichsministerium des Innern) Reich Ministry of the Interior

SA   Sturmabteilung storm detachment, a Nazi Party paramilitary formation

SD   (Sicherheitsdienst) security and intelligence service of the SS

SPD   Social Democratic Party of Germany

SS   (Schutzstaffel) the most feared organization of the Third Reich: the Gestapo, SD, and the Waffen-SS were all part of the SS

Waffen-SS   Armed Forces of the SS

SS AND WEHRMACHT RANKS

SS and Waffen-SS	Wehrmacht	U.S. Army Equivalent
SS-Mann	Soldat/Funker/Kanonier/ Flieger/Schutze/Matrose	Ordinary
Sturmmann	Obersoldat/Oberschütze/ Oberfusilier	Private (Senior)
Rottenführer	Gefreiter	Private First Class
N/A	Obergefreiter	Acting Corporal
N/A	Stabsgefreiter/Hauptgefreiter	Administrative Corporal
Unterscharführer	Unteroffizier[a]/Maat	Corporal
Scharführer	Unterfeldwebel/Obermaat	Sergeant
N/A	Offiziersanwärter	Officer Candidate
N/A	Fähnrich/Fähnrich z. S.	Officer Candidate
Oberscharführer	Feldwebel/Wachtmeister/ Bootsmann	Staff Sergeant
Hauptscharführer	Oberfeldwebel	Technical Sergeant
N/A	Oberfähnrich/ Oberfähnrich z. S.	Senior Officer Candidate
Sturmscharführer	Stabsfeldwebel	Master Sergeant
N/A	Fahnenjunker/Feldwebel	Officer Candidate/ Sergeant
Untersturmführer	Leutnant/Leutnant z. S.	Second Lieutenant
Obersturmführer	Oberleutnant/ Oberleutnant z. S.	First Lieutenant
Hauptsturmführer	Hauptmann/Kapitänleutnant	Captain
Sturmbannführer	Major/Korvettenkapitän	Major
Obersturmbannführer	Oberstleutnant/ Fregattenkapitän	Lieutenant Colonel
Standartenführer	Oberst/Kapitän. z. S.	Colonel
Oberführer	N/A	N/A
Brigadeführer	Generalmajor/Konteradmiral	Brigadier General
Gruppenführer	Generalleutnant/Vizeadmiral	Major General
Obergruppenführer	General der Inf. usw./Admiral	Lieutenant General
Oberst-Gruppenführer	Generaloberst/Generaladmiral	General
Reichsführer	Generalfeldmarschall (field marshal)/Grossadmiral	Five Star General (general of the army)

Source: These ranks have been tabulated according to the *Handbook on German Military Forces,* ed. United States War Department Technical Manual (Washington, D.C., 1945), pp. 16–17; Hilde Kammer and Elisabet Bartsch, eds., *Nationalsozialismus. Begriffe aus der Zeit der Gewaltherrschaft 1933–1945* (Hamburg, 1992), pp. 204–5.
[a]Unteroffizier, although translated as corporal, was in reality more like a U.S. Army staff sergeant or a U.S. Marine Corps sergeant. This rank marked the beginning of a professional soldier for an enlisted man.

Prologue: A Brief History of the Wehrmacht

The men featured in this book served a war machine that accomplished some of the most successful feats in military history. Yet, to understand fully what these soldiers experienced, the history of the Wehrmacht must first be briefly explored.

In 1933, when Hitler took power, the German army numbered 100,000 men. In 1935, Hitler reintroduced the draft and did away with the Versailles Treaty, which was signed by the Allies at the end of World War I and restricted Germany's military. Many throughout the country praised Hitler's move and supported his desire for a stronger military. By 1945, nearly 18 million had gone through the ranks of Germany's military forces and they had devastated most of Europe.[1]

Hitler achieved amazing diplomatic successes using the Wehrmacht by remilitarizing the Rhineland in 1936 and integrating Austria and the Sudetenland into Germany in 1938 without war, a "triumph without bloodshed." He marched into these regions and declared them part of the German nation without firing a shot. Such achievements provided Hitler with "almost legendary standing" amongst the population. General Alfred Jodl, chief of military operations and Hitler's principal military advisor, said, "The genius of the Führer and his determination not to shun even a world war have again achieved victory without the use of force. One hopes that the incredulous, the weak, and the doubters have been converted, and will remain so."[2] The Wehrmacht fell under the spell of the Austrian private.

In the end, Hitler wanted to use his military the traditional way—by killing the enemy. His armed forces had grown from 100,000 in 1935 to 3.7 million in 1939.[3] And in 1939, his military started a major campaign of violence and destruction.

On 1 September 1939, Hitler triggered World War II by invading Poland. A few weeks into the campaign, Hitler sensed that he soon would achieve victory and exclaimed to an excited crowd at Danzig that "Almighty God" had blessed "our arms" with success. Poland would fall by the end of September. After securing his eastern border by defeating Poland, he turned his attention toward the west and attacked Norway and Denmark on 9 April 1940 and quickly occupied them. One month later on 10 May, Hitler invaded the Low Countries and France, conquering them in a few weeks. Although outnumbered and using inferior tanks, the Germans defeated the Allies in only a few weeks because the Allies depended on a World War I strategy of positional warfare that proved wholly inadequate to meet the new Blitzkrieg method of attack. General Wilhelm Keitel, chief of the Armed Forces High Command, declared Hitler in June the greatest military commander ever.[4]

The German population celebrated this quick and unexpected victory over the Allies in the west. Hitler's success made German officers more trusting of him and less critical of Nazism. Achieving such victories allowed Hitler to reach the apex of his popularity. "It has been suggested that at the peak of his popularity nine Germans in ten were 'Hitler supporters, Führer believers.'"[5] Clearly, many were drunk with the success of the Nazis.

Once securing his western border, Hitler paid hardly any attention to conquering England, thinking it would pose little threat to his next campaign against his arch foe, Stalin. Yes, he allowed his Luftwaffe to engage in a large air battle over the skies of Great Britain, but Hitler's true focus zoomed in on Russia.

The Soviet Union represented for Hitler "his object of conquest, the capstone of his efforts to establish the Third Reich as a racist Continental empire." This was indeed Hitler's main enemy. As he wrote in *Mein Kampf,* leaders of Russia "are common blood-stained criminals" and "are the scum of humanity." "The fight against Jewish world Bolshevization requires a clear attitude toward Soviet Russia. You cannot drive out the Devil with Beelzebub." He believed that 80 percent of the Soviet leaders were Jews, that they threatened to destroy civilization, and that he must act against this "pathetic country" quickly before it attacked Germany. He also believed that the Soviet military offered no real threat,

Hitler reviews his victorious troops in the streets of Warsaw on 5 October 1939. This photograph was taken by the German military. (Photo credit: U.S. National Archives)

saying that its "Armed Forces are like a headless colossus with feet of clay."[6]

And many Germans indeed believed Russia threatened their way of life and Western culture.[7] Countless *Mischlinge* related that although they did not agree with Hitler's racial policies, they definitely felt that the world should rise up and defeat the Communists.

In order to protect his southern flank before invading Russia and to bail out Mussolini from his disastrous campaign against the Greeks, Hitler invaded Yugoslavia and Greece in May 1941. After successfully defeating these two countries, he launched the largest invasion in world history when he attacked the Soviet Union on 22 June 1941. Over 4 million men, mostly German but also soldiers of countries allied with Germany, including Hungary, Finland, Italy, and Romania, poured across the Soviet Union's eastern border. The front spanned 1,500 miles and, after a few months of conflict, extended in depth to over 600 miles. Although most soldiers who "broke into Russia in June 1941" did so without "enthusiasm," the previous years of success gave them "a quiet confidence in victory."[8] Hitler would once again, they felt, lead them to triumph.

By this time, the Germans had become accustomed to one victory after the other. Even church leaders got behind Hitler with this invasion and praised him. Protestant clerics sent Hitler the following telegram on 30 June 1941:

> You, my Führer, have banished the Bolshevik menace from our own land, and now summon our nation, and the nations of Europe, to a decisive passage of arms against the mortal enemy of all order and all western-Christian civilization. The German nation, including all its Christian members, thanks you for this deed. The German Protestant Church accompanies you in all its prayers, and is with our incomparable soldiery who are now using mighty blows to eradicate the source of this pestilence, so that a new order will arise under your leadership.[9]

And sure enough, Hitler dealt the Soviet Union in 1941 one mighty "blow" after the other and many felt Russia would quickly collapse.

Only a few months into the campaign, after taking over most of western Russia and millions of Russian prisoners, Hitler's conquest seemed complete. Chief of the army's General Staff, Franz Halder, "noted in his diary that: 'the Russian campaign had been won in the space of two weeks.'"[10] This was an exaggeration on Halder's part, but the Wehrmacht accomplishments seemed to indicate that Russia would soon fall to its knees. The little country of Germany had taken over the equivalent geographic area of half the United States.

Hitler conducted the war against Russia without any regard to international law or ethics. General Halder observed that "the thing that most impressed me about Hitler was the complete absence of any ethical or moral obligation." And in keeping with his obsession with the Jewish danger, Hitler said in January 1942, still thinking Russia was defeated, "The war will not end as the Jews imagine it will, namely with the up-

rooting of the Aryans, but the result of this war will be the complete annihilation of the Jews." A few months later, Goebbels wrote in his diary,
"The prophecy which the Fuehrer made about [the Jews] . . . is beginning to come true in a most terrible manner. One must not be sentimen-
tal in these matters. If we did not fight the Jews, they would destroy us.
It's a life-and-death struggle between the Aryan race and the Jewish
bacillus." Then in September 1942, Hitler repeated himself, saying, "I
said that if Jewry started this war in order to overcome the Aryan people,
then it would not be the Aryans but the Jews who would be exterminated. The Jews laughed at my prophecies. I doubt if they are laughing
now."[11] Hitler's military aims included this program of extermination.
With this knowledge, the *Mischlinge*'s service is even more tragic.

In addition to Hitler's conquest of Europe, he conquered lands in
Africa. His Afrika Korps in 1941 and early 1942 under Field Marshal Erwin Rommel wreaked havoc with the British forces in Libya. Hitler had
sent his forces there to once again rescue Mussolini's forces from defeat.
It appeared that Hitler would soon rule all of Europe and even parts of
northern Africa. A few German generals believed in July 1941 that the
"war was as good as over." As historian Michael Geyer wrote, by late fall
1941, "Everybody agreed that the war was virtually won, and so it was,
at least in the eyes of almost all—and not just German—observers."
Hitler also conducted this war to implement his plan for a reordered
world. "National Socialist war was war for the sake of social reconstruc-
tion through the destruction of conquered societies."[12] In other words,
Hitler truly believed he was transforming the world for the better by
killing the people he deemed inferior and destroying nations he thought
weak.

Yet, Hitler's military glory was short-lived. His armies quickly got
bogged down in the heavy fall rains and winter cold of Mother Russia.[13]
The Nazis encountered their first major loss of territory outside of
Moscow in December 1941. Even though they had some local successes
during the summer and fall of 1942 with the attack on Stalingrad, the tide
turned decisively against the Germans. The supplies the Soviet Union received from the United States, the tenacity and overwhelming numbers
of the Russian fighting machine, and the brutal winter of 1941–1942 all
started to spell disaster for Germany by 1943. The defeat at Stalingrad in

the winter of 1943 "shocked" the German nation. It marked the beginning of the end for Hitler.[14] As Winston Churchill said in 1944, "It was the Russians who 'tore out the guts of the German Army.'"[15]

In the summer of 1944, the Russians pushed the Germans back to the borders of the Reich, and the United States and Britain launched one of the largest amphibious landings in history at Normandy on 6 June. Although the Allies had split Germany in half and decimated its army and navy, it was only in April 1945 when its leader, Hitler, committed suicide that Germany surrendered.

The men described in this book took part in almost every campaign during World War II in the European, Atlantic, and African theaters of operation. Many experienced combat for several months straight, if not for years on end. Their stories illuminate the difficult situation they found themselves in, serving a nation hostile to them as racially inferior beings. Several did so while serving in units deployed more widely and in constant combat than any other modern armed force has experienced. "For the *Landser*, combat consisted of a thousand small battles, a daily struggle for existence amid terrible confusion, fear, and suffering. Combat meant fighting in small groups, in sinister blackness or in cold, lonely bunkers, in crowded houses from room to room, on windswept steppes against steel monsters, with each unit and each man—confused men with a need for one another—fighting for their lives, longing to escape their fate, leaving a trail of torn, mutilated, and dead flesh in their wake."[16]

It was against this backdrop that the *Mischlinge* found themselves serving a nation that was conducting a nightmarish policy of "racial" extermination beyond these men's control or understanding. Half-Jew Richard Reiss said that having served, he felt "guilty, but logically I had no other choice. But I now think I did something I shouldn't have done . . . We were just not allowed to think under Hitler." There can be a "hermetically sealed" quality about studying war and the Third Reich at a distance, without feeling any of war's discomforts or any of the fear of living under a totalitarian state. Another German soldier, Guy Sajer, wrote,

Quarter-Jew General Fritz Bayerlein (right) with adjutant Kurt Kauffmann in Hungary, 1944. Fritz Bayerlein was the commander of the Panzer Lehr Division and was decorated with the Oak Leaves with Swords to his Knight's Cross (equivalent of three U.S. Medals of Honor). Not only was he partly Jewish, he was also bisexual, making his situation even more precarious as the Nazis persecuted homosexuals as well as Jews. Photo credit Patricia Spayd.

Too many people learn about war with no inconvenience to themselves. They read about Verdun or Stalingrad without comprehension, sitting in a comfortable armchair, with their feet beside the fire, preparing to go about their business the next day, as usual. One should really read such accounts under compulsion, in discomfort, considering oneself fortunate not to be describing the events in a letter home, writing from a hole in the mud. One should read about war in the worst circumstances, when everything is going badly, remembering that the torments of peace are trivial and not worth any white hairs. Nothing is really serious in the tranquility of peace; only an idiot could be really disturbed by a question of salary. One should read about war standing up, late at night, when one is tired, as I am writing about it now, at dawn, while my asthma attack wears off. And even now, in my sleepless exhaustion, how gentle and easy peace seems.[17]

Although Sajer's request for a reader to undergo war's discomfort is unrealistic, perhaps it will help the reader understand that what these men suffered and lived through goes well beyond what most experience in life. These men underwent such pain and anguish that few today can comprehend their mindset and behavior.

Often we can explain away what we see in movies as make-believe, but the decisions and death that surrounded these men in war were real and full of tragedy and pain. "The *Landser* lived in a complex world, one both physically unstable and emotionally chaotic."[18] For most, it represented the high-water mark of their lives, even though death threatened them from many sides. It seems that war makes one appreciate life more for having experienced that time of extreme hardship, compared with the "normal" life which, for a combat veteran, can seem so mundane and superficial. Through exploring the dramatic lives of several *Mischlinge* and Jews in Hitler's Wehrmacht, this book not only describes the many aspects of Nazi racial doctrine and practice, but also brings to life what it was like to serve in one of the most deadly war machines of all times controlled by one of the most evil men of history.

Introduction

People of Jewish descent were the most endangered group under Adolf Hitler. Yet probably several thousand Jews and over one hundred thousand partial Jews (or *Mischlinge*) served in the Wehrmacht (German armed forces). This fact has surprised many who considered themselves knowledgeable about World War II and the Holocaust.

How these men dealt with their situations is a fascinating and moving story. One partially Jewish soldier, Heinz Bleicher, observed that few today can understand the heavy emotional burden of partial Jews during the Third Reich. Every year they felt sucked deeper into an abyss with no escape.[1] Nevertheless, until at least 1941, the Nazis drafted many into the Wehrmacht during this time of trauma and confusion—a policy that seems contradictory, since Hitler called *Mischlinge* "blood sins" and "monstrosities halfway between man and ape."[2] Among them were career soldiers who, because Hitler had Aryanized them, were able to reach high rank, even though many of their relatives had to wear the yellow star and died in the Holocaust.

While lecturing from 2002 to 2008 about my books *Hitler's Jewish Soldiers* and *Rescued from the Reich*, I was often asked about the lives of those identified as Hitler's Jewish soldiers. How could they serve? Did they consider themselves Nazis or Jews? What did Hitler know about them? What did they know about the Holocaust? Did they feel guilty about serving? Many listeners found it difficult to accept that men of Jewish descent served in Hitler's armed forces, sometimes with great distinction. The biographies of these German Jewish soldiers give a clearer understanding of their personal and legal complexities.

Until recently, historians have not explored *Mischling* history. For some, these "victims of the Holocaust" represent "embarrassing leftovers from the trauma of Hitler's Germany."[3] These men often feel alone in their experience and harbor a fear that their testimony will be given "without an echo in the vast wasteland of war," the Third Reich, and the Holocaust.[4] Moreover, in general, German soldiers have really "nothing to celebrate and much, including dishonor, to forget."[5] So it is remarkable that Jewish and *Mischling* soldiers have shared their experience, when so often it is difficult for them to talk about serving in the military while they and their families were persecuted.

Mischlinge simply do not fit into neat categories of victim or perpetrator, Jew or non-Jew. Although a few of the men whose stories are presented here were Jews, most were *Mischlinge,* a category of people that never existed before the Nuremberg Laws. What unites *Mischlinge* is not only the discrimination they experienced, but also their anger, frustration, fear, and sense of inferiority.

The question of identity haunted many *Mischlinge,* not only those serving in the Wehrmacht. Most grew up as patriotic Christian Germans who suddenly learned after 1933 that their nation now viewed them as subhumans. The Nazis believed that being Jewish or partially Jewish made them unacceptable as full citizens. The German philosopher Immanuel Kant wrote that "government defines reality";[6] the Nazis violently upset the lives of millions by defining the new reality of this racial doctrine.

The nineteenth-century political philosopher John Stuart Mill described what happened to Jews and *Mischlinge* under the Nazis when he wrote: "Society can and does execute its own mandates: and if it issues wrong mandates instead of right . . . it practises a social tyranny more formidable than many kinds of political oppression . . . it leaves fewer means of escape, penetrating much more deeply into details of life, and enslaving the soul itself."[7] The men described here were persecuted by a system that issued "wrong mandates" about human value. They struggled to conform to the Nazi view of worthy Germans, though many of them failed to realize that their society had abandoned them. For example, Dieter Bergman wrote during the war that he represented what people wanted in a "good German." He was tall, blond, trim, kind, good-natured, and a "warrior type." Yet he realized that his destiny as a half-Jew hung from a pathetically slender thread in an environment without refuge and legal rights.[8] This perilous condition affected their perception of themselves and their behavior. They had to honor laws that eliminated their rights. The situation had the elements of a play in a Theater of the Absurd.

Jewish Identity: Definitions and Complications

In this book I use several Nazi terms to explain this history without implying any agreement with the Nazi racial theories that inspired their introduction. The book is organized according to the Nazi definitions for people of Jewish descent in order to simplify its structure. In sharp contrast to the Nazi racial laws, the men documented herein express a whole range of beliefs about who is a Jew and who is Jewish that follows neither Nazi classifications nor Jewish law. Such Nazi terms as "half-Jew," "quarter-Jew," "*Mischling*," "Aryan," and "non-Aryan" come from an evil system designed to eliminate people of "inferior" ethnicity from society. The Nazis introduced such vocabulary to abuse and dehumanize those they deemed *Untermenschen* (subhumans). The Nazi racial laws did not reflect the understanding of Jewishness prevalent in German society in the 1920s. The designation "*Mischling*" sounded just as foreign to the ears of *Mischlinge* as it does to ours. Bergman further explained, "half-Jewishness is a strange concept. It's like being half-circumcised—it doesn't exist . . . However, with Hitler, we had to try to understand what being a *Mischling* meant. Unfortunately, we were slow learners." Interpretations not of their making and events beyond their control beleaguered most *Mischlinge*. For example, Heinz Gerlach wrote Minister of Education Bernhard Rust in 1941 that "I cannot help it that I'm a *Mischling*. Also, no one should blame my parents for my situation. They married during a time without racial laws." Gerlach further clarified that his mother looked and acted like an "Aryan" and that his father's family never thought twice about accepting her. He wrote that she had proven her disapproval of Judaism by marrying a Christian, baptizing her son a Christian, and raising him to "love his Fatherland and the Führer."[9] Gerlach struggled with the Nazis' defining him as partially Jewish, a part of his background he had never accepted.

The lives of Jews and *Mischlinge* portrayed in this book show how the racial laws affected them on a personal level, the extent of their persecution, and the divided loyalties many struggled with during the Nazi years and afterward. They were put in the ludicrous position of serving in the military while the Nazis persecuted their family members.

Yet most did serve, and when one learns more about German society, this service does not seem so strange. Most *Mischlinge* grew up in an environment where their elders conditioned them to have a strong obedience to authority. They were taught to obey their parents, teachers, clergymen, and, most importantly, their government. A belief that the authority of superiors was based on "greater insight and more humane wisdom" was ingrained in German society. In the military, submission to authority was explicit. After the war, Gustav Knickrehm said, "The advantage of our armed forces lay in this monstrous training . . . You carried out all orders automatically . . . You acted automatically as a soldier." *Mischlinge* learned *Kadavergehorsam,* or slavish obedience, even if it infringed on their personal freedom and the human rights of their family. In other words, the Nazis imposed "political and ideological conformity" on all subjects under their rule.[10] Whatever Hitler ordered, they had to obey and they did so almost willingly because of their culture. Those who did not obey Nazi laws wound up in concentration camps or in front of a firing squad.

Also fundamental to comprehending the bizarre situation in which *Mischlinge* wore the swastika on their uniforms, while their relatives had to wear the Star of David, is an understanding of their religious identity. Most parents of *Mischlinge* did not raise them as religious Jews, and most *Mischlinge* did not consider themselves Jewish until Hitler persecuted them. But the Nazi racial laws considered them all Jewish to one degree or another.

On 14 November 1935, the Nazis issued a supplement to the Nuremberg Laws of 15 September 1935 that created the "racial" categories of German, Jew, "half-Jew (Jewish *Mischling* 1st Degree)," and "quarter-Jew (Jewish *Mischling* 2nd Degree)," each with its own regulations. These laws distinguished Germans from persons of Jewish heritage both biologically and socially. Full Jews had three or four Jewish grandparents, half-Jews had two Jewish grandparents, and quarter-Jews had one Jewish grandparent. If a person not of Jewish descent practiced the Jewish religion, the Nazis also counted him as a Jew. The Nazis resorted to religious records to define these "racial" categories, using birth, baptismal, marriage, and death certificates stored in churches, temples, Jewish Community Centers, and courthouses.[11]

The 1935 Nuremberg Laws provided the basis for further anti-Jewish legislation to preserve the purity of the "Aryan" race. The Nazis based their racial laws on the *völkisch* (ethnic in a racial sense) notion of the inherent superiority of the "Aryans."[12] These laws provided civil rights to those belonging to the Volk and having German "blood." This created a "new morality which, in terms of the old system of values, seemed both unscrupulous and brutal." The Nazis automatically denied Jews and *Mischlinge* citizenship privileges. However, under Article 7 of a supplementary decree of the Nuremberg Laws, Hitler could free individuals from the label Jew or *Mischling* by Aryanizing them with a stroke of his pen.[13] In fact Hitler allowed several high-ranking officers of Jewish descent to remain in the military by Aryanizing them.

But most *Mischlinge* did not receive this clemency, and the German authorities despised them as an unwelcome minority. Most Nazis considered *Mischlinge* predominantly Jewish and wanted them treated as such. Both the head of the SS, Heinrich Himmler, and SS General Reinhard Heydrich wanted *Mischlinge* exterminated just like the full Jews. But pressure on the SS and Nazi Party by "Aryan" relatives, prominent families, the military, and the government postponed the issue of how to deal with *Mischlinge* until after the war.

In addition to the racial laws, an essential element of this history explores Halakah (rabbinical law), which considers more of the men in this study Jewish (full Jews) than did the Nazi racial laws. Since the Nazis considered anyone who practiced the Jewish religion a full Jew, most *Mischlinge* were by definition Christians. However, according to Halakah, having a Jewish mother is the sole determining fact of Jewish identity, and based on this, the majority of half-Jews documented would be considered Jewish. Using this criterion, Halakah considers more than half of the half-Jews documented in this book as full Jews because they had Jewish mothers.

The conflicting terms of Nazi racial laws and Halakah make it difficult to understand the position of *Mischlinge*. Adding yet another layer of complication is the fact that many *Mischlinge* developed private connections to Judaism. Many developed Jewish identities, but the majority of those identities were born out of persecution rather than cultural or religious upbringing. Today, some *Mischlinge* "feel" Jewish, though their Jewish identity is private and complicated.

The following story illustrates the difficulties one encounters when identifying a Jew for the purposes of this research. After World War II, Wehrmacht veteran Karl-Heinz Maier decided to do something for his Jewish family. He traveled to Israel and fought in its War of Independence. Even after he became a major, the local authorities did not consider him Jewish because his father, rather than his mother, was Jewish. For twelve years, Maier explained, the Nazis persecuted him because he had a Jewish father, but the Israelis called him a *Goy* (a derogatory Yiddish term for gentile) because of his gentile mother. Although he could fight for the Israeli army, the government did not consider him Jewish.[14] The same type of identity crisis that Maier experienced also happened to tens of thousands of *Mischlinge* during and, for some, even after the Third Reich. So differences in religious belief, cultural background, ethnic makeup, historical experiences, and self-perception often make it difficult to answer the question, who is a Jew?

Until *Hitler's Jewish Soldiers* it was not widely known that probably a few thousand full and tens of thousands of half- and quarter-Jews, as classified by the Nazis, served in the German armed forces during World War II. It is conservatively estimated that, between 1870 and 1929, about 85,000 mixed marriages between Jews and gentiles took place in Austria and Germany, with approximately 75 percent taking place after the turn of the century. If every family had two or three children, according to the averages of those years, there should have been between 168,000 and 252,000 half-Jewish children of these unions. And some of these half-Jews would have later married gentiles and their children would have been quarter-Jews during the Third Reich. After examining assimilation records, birthrates, and mixed-marriage rates with mathematicians and statisticians, this study estimates that 60,000 half-Jews and 90,000 quarter-Jews served in the Wehrmacht.[15]

Some served as high-ranking officers, including generals, admirals, and even one field marshal. Full Jews who served did so with false documents. Their commanders believed them to be "Aryans." The estimated numbers of Jews and *Mischlinge* in the Wehrmacht have caused controversy because the assimilation records or definitions of Jewishness have not been carefully analyzed and deserve a closer look.

Christian Converts and Non-German Mischlinge

If one contends that *Mischlinge* were not Jewish because they had been born into Christian families, had converted, had not practiced Judaism, had not felt Jewish, or had only received this label from the Nazis, then one must also reevaluate the figure of 6 million Jews who died in the Holocaust. Tens of thousands of those exterminated did not consider themselves Jewish, but the Nazis labeled and treated them so. To comprehend this, a rudimentary understanding of the conversions going on in the lands Hitler controlled is needed.

Between 1800 and 1900, around 70,000 Jews converted to Christianity in Germany and in the Austro-Hungarian Empire. Most *Mischlinge* also had Jewish relatives who had converted to Christianity and did not view themselves as Jews until the Nazis came to power. The Nazis did not accept assimilation. Quite often, since Germans defined citizenship through Christian definitions, many Jews embraced the religion to escape discrimination and become more German. Hitler cynically described the conversion process: "If worst came to worst, a splash of baptismal water could always save the business and the Jew at the same time." The Nazis would make sure that "the ability to camouflage ancestry by changing religions will completely disappear."[16]

The reader will therefore not find it surprising that the Nazis deported countless converted parents, grandparents, and other relatives of the *Mischlinge* documented in this study to Hitler's death camps, even though, as Martin Gilbert wrote, "tens of thousands of German Jews were not Jews at all in their own eyes." For instance, the Nazis sent the philosopher Edith Stein to the gas chambers at Auschwitz despite her conversion to Christianity. Half-Jew Dieter Bergman said, "I lost over a dozen relatives in the Holocaust and most of them wouldn't have called themselves Jews—they'd converted to Christianity for Christ's sake." Half-Jew Hans Günzel, who lost fifty-seven relatives in the Holocaust, expressed his confusion about the Nazi definition of Jewishness when he claimed, "the sad thing about all of their deaths is that most had converted to Christianity and didn't consider themselves Jews." Even though an estimated 50,000 Jewish converts to Christianity lived in Germany in 1933, the Nazis treated them as racial Jews. They did so in other countries as well. For example, Chaim Kaplan, a distinguished principal of a Warsaw Hebrew school, took pleasure in 1939 in seeing that the Nazis treated Jewish converts to Christianity no differently than religious Jews. He wrote: "I shall, however, have revenge on our 'converts.' I will laugh aloud at the sight of their tragedy. These poor creatures, whose number has increased radically in recent times, should have known that the 'racial' laws do not differentiate between Jews who become Christians and those who retain their faith. Conversion brought them but small deliverance... This is the first time in my life that a feeling of vengeance has given me pleasure."[17] Obviously many Polish Jewish converts to Christianity had hoped their new religion would protect them, something that Kaplan described as painfully mistaken.

Furthermore, the Nazis labeled half-Jews in Poland and Russia as full Jews because they did not have "Aryan blood" and gentile relatives to protect them. Although most of these partial Jews had assimilated into their Christian society and converted to Christianity, the Nazis marked these non-German *Mischlinge* in the eastern territories for extermination. They died in the Nazi camps as Jews.[18] The Reich Security Main Office for the Eastern Territories stated in the summer of 1941: "In view of the Final Solution... anyone who has one parent who is a Jew will also count as a Jew."[19]

This policy for the occupied areas was clear: there would be no distinction between "half" and full Jews as in Germany. Hans Frank, the governor-general of occupied Poland, included *Mischlinge* in his plan of extermination in a report on 16 December 1941: "We have in the General Government an estimated 2.5 million, maybe together with *Mischlinge* and all that hangs on, 3.5 million Jews. We can't poison them, but we will be able to take some kind of action which will lead to an annihilation success... The General Government will be just as *judenfrei* [free of Jews] as the Reich."[20]

Frank felt that the Nazis could only free themselves of the "Jewish disease" by extending to *Mischlinge* their tactic of extermination. The policy implemented in Poland and other areas followed this line of thinking. For example, as early as the summer of 1940, the Germans started segregating *Mischlinge* in Poland into ghettos and included them in the plans for deporting Jews to concentration camps.[21] They even included some *Mischlinge* from Greece, Hungary, and Italy for deportation. The German Jewish professor of romance literature Victor Klemperer, of the Technical University in Dresden, had met *Mischlinge* from the Bohemian Protectorate who had to wear the Jewish star under a law decreed after Heydrich's assassination on 4 June 1942. Half-Jewish Danes felt the need to escape from Denmark since the Nazis forced them to identify themselves as Jews, like those in Luxembourg, Holland, northern France, Vichy France, Belgium, Poland, the Baltic states, and Russia.[22] Hundreds of thousands of converts to Christianity and non-German *Mischlinge* ultimately died in the Holocaust.

Today, many historians and most Jews classify as Jews these German Jewish converts and non-German half-Jews, especially from Poland and Russia, who died in the Holocaust, although most of these victims did not call themselves Jews. Even though the majority of the 6 million killed would have labeled themselves as Jewish, a substantial number of them would not have done so. In other words, if one argues that the men documented in this study are not really Jewish, then that same person must also reevaluate his definition of Jewishness when discussing "Jewish" Holocaust victims.

While it may be difficult to accept the fundamental concept expressed in the book title *Hitler's Jewish Soldiers,* there is one key sense in which this phrase is accurate. Hitler's racial laws designated *Mischlinge* as "Jewish" or "part-Jewish." They were *Hitler*'s Jewish soldiers and no one else's, since the majority of the German Jewish population and many *Mischlinge* seemed not to share Hitler's definition.

People often ask, "How could those affected by these laws serve?" Most *Mischlinge* served because they were drafted by the Wehrmacht, which, until 1940, required half-Jews to serve. However, they could not become NCOs or officers without Hitler's personal approval.

In April 1940 Hitler decided to order the discharge of half-Jews from the armed forces because their presence created problems. Many came home after the Poland campaign in 1939 to find that the authorities had severely persecuted their relatives. Hitler did not want to protect Jewish parents and grandparents because of the service of their children and grandchildren, so he discharged the half-Jewish soldiers. Many, however, remained on active duty, with exemptions from Hitler or because they had hidden their Jewish ancestry. Also, several stayed with their units for months after this discharge order, due to the war with Norway in April and the invasion of France in May 1940, which slowed the bureaucratic process of discharging them.

The authorities did not widely enforce this discharge order until late summer 1940, and even then, many officers ignored it. In addition, the search for half-Jews in the service often consisted solely of requiring soldiers to sign ancestry declarations stating they were not Jews. Many *Mischlinge* signed this statement in good faith, since they were not Jews according to their understanding. Others just lied and remained with their units. Known half-Jews who had won combat medals or battlefield promotions could apply for an exemption from the racial laws, enabling them to remain in the Wehrmacht because of their valor. Thousands submitted applications. Even before 1940 several half-Jewish officers had received exemptions from Hitler and obtained high ranks.

The military also drafted quarter-Jews. Unlike the half-Jews, they had to serve throughout the entire war. Yet they, like their half-Jewish counterparts, could not become NCOs or officers without Hitler's approval.

The majority of half-Jews discharged after April 1940 returned home and resumed their studies if they had distinguished military records or found work until 1944. Then Hitler had them, as well as other nonveteran half-Jews, deported to forced labor camps of the Organization Todt (OT).[23] They were joined there by the "Aryan" husbands of Jewish wives, many of whom were fathers of half-Jews at the camps. Fortunately, they were not in the camps long, and their treatment there was less severe than in the concentration camps. Thus, most survived these places of persecution.

The Nazis treated these partial Jews as objects without any self-determination. Hitler probably would have further persecuted and in many cases exterminated them had he won the war.

Historians have so far not closely examined the experiences of *Mischlinge*. These stories will give the reader a sense of what it was like to be a *Mischling* in the Third Reich, exploring many enduring lessons about the human condition.

Jews and *Mischlinge* Hiding Their Identities

Many Jews and *Mischlinge* hid their identities from the authorities while serving in the Wehrmacht. They accomplished this by falsifying their ancestry documents, changing their names and/or lying to authorities, finding someone to protect them, and behaving inconspicuously. Their actions display how intense and creative the will to survive can be. Their stories range from simple situations in which the Wehrmacht drafted half-Jew Arno Spitz after he falsified his documents to the experience of Rabbi Simon Gossel, who survived two years in Auschwitz only to find himself serving in the Wehrmacht in 1945.[1] Stories like these abound, making the history of the Third Reich more complicated.

Half-Jews Helmuth Kopp and Arno Spitz remained in the armed forces by not truthfully answering their ancestry declarations. Both served the entire war without much trouble. They considered the dire consequences if the authorities discovered their lies, but refused to dwell on this possible outcome. Few such men remain alive today, because serving on the Russian front was usually deadly. By war's end, Germany had suffered over 6 million casualties, and Russia lost over 20 million people. Most German casualties of war, including 75 percent of combat deaths (2.3 million), happened in Russia, and many Jews and *Mischlinge* who served there died in battle. One *Landser* (soldier) said Russia was "like a cold iron coffin" with death lurking everywhere.[2] Kopp and Spitz feel lucky they survived. Kopp said, "When I look back, my chances for survival were probably no different than had I ended up in Dachau. Sometimes the units I served with suffered 80 percent casualties."

The stories of full Jews Edgar Jacoby, Karl-Heinz Löwy, and Paul-Ludwig (Pinchas) Hirschfeld show how a few Jews survived in the army. Jacoby's experiences demonstrate how horrible one's situation could become if the Nazis discovered a hidden Jew in the ranks. In 1941, the authorities learned that Jacoby served with falsified documents. He ultimately survived because of his "Aryan" wife's protection. Many Jews survived the war because they had married non-Jews since the Nazis hesitated to deport spouses of "Aryans" to extermination camps.[3] Others used subterfuge, as did Löwy, whose story is amazing in its unpredictability. Raised as a religious Jew, he escaped to France before World War II, changed his name when the Nazis took over, and then entered the Waffen-SS, in which he served until the end of the war. Hirschfeld's story also demonstrates how another religious Jew could survive in the Wehrmacht by forging both his religious and ancestry documents. He served on the murderous battlefields of Russia while remaining a religious Jew.

Others found friends in high places with the courage to protect them. Quarter-Jew Horst von Oppenfeld and half-Jew Günther Scheffler, whose stories appear in this chapter, as well as others, found such people of honor. Oppenfeld's family reputation and military record protected him; the bureaucrats simply left him alone. Scheffler stayed in the army because his commanders valued his skills and person more than the Nazi racial laws. These stories were not uncommon. Often Jews and *Mischlinge* remained in the Wehrmacht because someone valued them more than Nazi ideology.

While survival skills or plain luck enabled certain *Mischlinge* and Jews to serve unnoticed, they continued to struggle with how the regime treated Jews, especially their own Jewish family members. Most understood that their future was bleak under Hitler, but nonetheless fought on day by day like any other soldier. They felt that serving in the Wehrmacht would ensure that German society as a whole would treat them as equals to their "Aryan" fellow citizens. They were mistaken. Knowing how they felt about their service and why they served demonstrates once again their tragic situation.

Half-Jewish Gefreiter Helmuth Kopp

Today, Helmuth Kopp gets around using crutches, but he has remarkable energy for an eighty-year-old. Large muscles bulge through his shirt-sleeves from years of supporting his weight. He has lived alone since his

Half-Jew Helmuth Kopp on 27 September 1994 at his home in Berlin after our interview.

wife died, and when he discusses their relationship, one sees he loved her deeply. He has an infectious laugh and frequently nods his head with a quick cackle when he sees you understanding his point. His clear blue eyes sparkle as he talks about his life. He enjoys telling jokes and often makes fun of himself. Although pessimistic, he feels he must discuss his experiences in order to prevent what he suffered during the Third Reich from happening again.

Kopp was born on 10 May 1922 in Insterburg, East Prussia. He was born to a Jewish mother, Helene (née Kaulbars), and a gentile father, Wilhelm, and had four siblings. His mother remained religiously Jewish, and his father was Christian. "However," Kopp said, "my father was like most Christians today. They really don't believe in their religion and went to church only on Easter and Christmas. It was more culture than faith for him." His father served as a private in World War I and, after the war, became a businessman. Growing up, Kopp found himself confused about his religious beliefs since he went to both church and synagogue.

Helmuth Kopp next to the grave of his Jewish mother, Helene (née Kaulbars).

"As a boy, my Jewish relatives told me I was a Jew and when I was with my Christian relatives, they always told me I was a Christian. I guess I was living closer to Jesus than most! However, as a child, I was perplexed about the whole ordeal."

Helene Kopp died of tuberculosis in 1925. Wilhelm was not a good provider and did not want to take care of the kids. Consequently, Kopp's maternal and paternal relatives fought over which family would raise the children. The Jewish family was furious: their ancestors had lived in Germany for over 300 years, and most family members had remained Orthodox. They felt that by rabbinical law the children were Jewish because of their Jewish mother and therefore should come to them. The Christian family could not believe that these children were going to be raised Jewish and fought to bring them up as Christians. They berated Wilhelm for his decision to marry a Jew. Strangely enough, the court's ruling evenly split the girls up between the Christian and Jewish families. The Christian family took the two girls who looked most "Aryan" (that is, blond and blue-eyed). It remains unknown whether the court made its decision based on their physical characteristics. Kopp and two other sisters were sent to live with his Jewish grandparents.

Although Kopp lived with his Jewish grandparents after his mother's death, he often spent time with his father. When his father remarried in 1927, Kopp, at the age of five, was sent to his Jewish aunt and uncle, Sarah ("Susi") and Heinz Moses, and they enrolled him in the Orthodox Jewish school of Siegmundshof. There, he often got into trouble for bringing sausage and butter sandwiches for his lunch after spending time with his father on weekends, but in general, his teachers treated him well.

One year into his second marriage, Kopp's father broke off all contact with his children. "My father was a weak man. I don't think he wanted to worry about us and when he remarried, the woman wasn't interested in us. At first I was excited because I thought I was getting another mother. But I soon learned that most stepmothers are the worst form of humanity, right up there with the Nazis." Kopp also had little contact with his sisters. "The whole situation was tragic. We're only family by blood ties," Kopp said. During the early 1930s, he corresponded with his sister Judith who then lived in Palestine, but that contact stopped as the Nazis gained power and he went into hiding.

The Jewish family with which Kopp lived did not like him and made him feel, he said, "as a *Goy*, and in their world, *Goys* were horrible people. Since *Goys* weren't part of the chosen, they were thought lower than dirt." Although Kopp's mother was a Jew, his grandfather Louis Kaulbars did not consider him to be a Jew. On several occasions when he saw his grandfather during the 1920s and early 1930s, his grandfather hit him with a horsewhip and called him *Goy*. Once, Kopp said, he could not go to school because of his large, red welts. He believes this vile behavior reflected his grandfather's grief at having lost his daughter to a gentile husband and then to death. Also, Kopp was a hyperactive child, and the grandfather found it difficult to deal with him. One day his grandmother chided her husband: "That's our daughter Helene's child!"

The grandfather replied, "No, that's Wilhelm's *Goy!*"

"My soul was hurt," Kopp said. He later added, "The situation was purely *meshuge* [mad]." Kopp did mention that his Jewish grandmother sympathized with him and would say, "It's not your fault that your mother sinned. You now have an extra burden from Heaven to be an even better Jew than others." Kopp did not want to shoulder this burden and thought that any God who placed him into such a situation was "closer to Satan than a Loving Being."

In the early 1930s Kopp's Jewish grandparents and his guardian and aunt, Sarah Moses, intended to emigrate to Palestine, where her two sons Horst and Werner Moses already lived. Kopp thought he would go, too. "I wanted to go to Israel, but they wouldn't take me," Kopp said. Instead, Sarah planned to leave the boy behind and asked Berlin's Jewish Community Center whether the Ahava orphanage there would accept him. The director of the orphanage, Herr Rothschild, asked Sarah, "Is he Jewish?" His aunt answered yes. "Then the director asked if I was circumcised. When she answered no, he told her that they would only take me if I was circumcised." That was why she had him circumcised at the age of twelve in a traditional but belated *Bris* (Jewish ritual circumcision). "Circumcised penises don't heal as well on twelve year olds as they do on babies," Kopp said gruffly. "With a few days of life, who the Hell remembers the pain," he continued. But "twelve year olds remember, believe me." After the rabbi had cut off his foreskin, stitches were required to close the wound, and Kopp walked with a cane for six weeks thereafter.

He lived at the orphanage from 1934 until 1937 while most of his Jewish relatives emigrated to Palestine. Though his aunt and uncle Moses gave up their plan to emigrate to Palestine and stayed in Germany, they did not want to support him anymore. So Kopp could not leave the orphanage.

In the summer of 1937, he ran away from his school because his Orthodox classmates and teachers treated him badly. He also did so to avoid persecution by the Nazis.

Gefreiter Helmuth Kopp (second from front, left column) marching with his unit during training in 1941. (Military awards: He should have received the Wound Badge, but was afraid to report his wounds because he thought the authorities might discover that he was a half-Jew when they reviewed his army file.)

In 1939, when his father died, Kopp lost hope of protection from a Christian ("Aryan") relative. His father's family did not want to have much to do with him, and most of his Jewish family had emigrated to Palestine. For those few Jewish relatives who remained in Germany, Kopp was not really considered part of the family.

In the fall of 1940, he volunteered for the army, but, as required, had first to serve almost a year in the Reichsarbeitsdienst (National Labor Service), where he built bridges over lakes and swampy areas from December 1940 to October 1941. Right after this service, he entered the Wehrmacht.

As a half-Jew wanting to serve after the war with France ended in 1940, Kopp had to lie about his origins. When asked how he felt about that, Kopp explained that he "didn't want to own up to my Jewish past, especially after how my grandfather had treated me. And besides, I didn't want to end up in a concentration camp. The Wehrmacht was the safest place."

Asked whether his circumcision caused him any problems, he said the army doctors usually lined up the men in a row and simply asked them to pull back their foreskins to check for diseases. Many times, during such procedures, Kopp pretended he had pulled his foreskin back and often no one noticed his deception. When he was questioned about it, though, since his circumcision had left visible scars on his penis, he told examining physicians that it resulted from an infection. Armed with this tale, he never experienced any trouble other than occasional jokes about his "Jewish penis." "If they only knew that it really was," Kopp said, laughing. "I was always worried about what would happen during inspections. I never hesitated to tell doctors that I had lost my foreskin because of an infection caused by the foreskin being too tight around my penis [*Phimose* or *Phimosis*] . . . One day, a doctor said to a colleague, 'Come and see his Jewish tip,' but he was kidding. Later, when I had future inspections, the same doctor did the examination, and said with a laugh, 'Here comes Helmuth with his Jewish prick.'"

He did not encounter much suspicion with his lovers, either. Women, Kopp said, paid little attention to what type of penis a man had, since, as he explained, "Once you're up, there isn't a lot of difference between a Jewish and a gentile penis. And that's what women are most interested in—can you fly the flag or not?" If it was discussed, Kopp simply told the woman the story he gave the doctors.

But one encounter with a woman made Kopp nervous. While he was sleeping with a French prostitute, she commented, "That's strange. With my husband, I can always play with his foreskin. Don't you have any?" "I took a deep breath," Kopp said, "and told her my infection story which I don't think she believed, but it didn't matter. She got her money, and I got to sleep with her. She never reported me . . . We even developed an affection for one another. Our situations were somewhat similar, I mean, we were both social outcasts, and thus, we understood one another."

Even though he enjoyed himself during his off hours, Kopp did not have a lot of time for girls because he was preparing for combat. He entered the tank corps of the army as part of the 257th Tank-Destroyer Brigade and drove a self-propelled gun (turretless tank having a fixed cannon on a moving platform). He was sent to the Russian front near Charchov, and from April to July 1942 his unit was engaged in battle. He drove the self-propelled gun and remembers that he stopped counting after his group of six men had destroyed 24 Russian tanks.

Although his own self-propelled gun was hit by enemy fire several times, none ever penetrated its armor. "We wore radio headsets and often heard the death cries of comrades. Self-propelled guns next to us would get hit and I'd hear the men screaming inside as the flames engulfed them. They were friends and I knew their voices. Many gave their last words to heaven and their mothers," Kopp said. After a battle, Kopp and his buddies found it difficult to go to the burned-out chassis and see their buddies, often mere black skeletons slumped over twisted metal. "When I saw the bones of my comrades, I always thought that this would not happen to me. In my mind, I always thought that this could only happen to the next guy, not me."

Confronting death made many examine the regime and what was going on around them. Kopp said that it made him hate the Nazis. Combat forced *Mischlinge* to think about Hitler, and many grew to resent the fact that they were persecuted and sent to battle at the same time.

After four months on the Russian front, Kopp's brigade had lost over 50 percent of its original 120 tank-destroyers. The Wehrmacht then sent his unit to Brest, France, at the end of July 1942 to recuperate, resupply, and train for a new unit.

In France he spent a lot of time "chasing girls and drinking wine. French women were so easy." When not partying, he and his comrades trained for close combat against tanks. They no longer would assault tanks with self-propelled guns, but would do so by using demolition charges as units attached to the infantry. They learned how to lie in wait for tanks to fasten mines and satchel charges to them. They were told that they were becoming an elite force that would protect the infantry against attacking Soviet tanks.

They practiced digging deep holes and waiting for a tank to roll over them so they could attach their explosives to its bottom. "However, in training, we got a false sense of what a tank could do to us while using this tactic. When the tank rolled over us in training, it would only stop and twist itself a few times and then move on. As a result, we remained safe in our holes. However, in Russia, when the Soviets knew a hole was there, they would roll over the hole, stop, and then rotate the tank back and forth until our comrades in the hole were mashed like pancakes. I still can hear the screams of my friends as they were drilled into the earth," Kopp said.

In November 1942, his new unit, attached to the Sixteenth Infantry Division, was sent to Russia at Tsarskoye Selo outside of Leningrad in the siege of that city, a siege that would claim 1 million lives before the city was liberated in the spring of 1944.[4] Kopp took part in reconnaissance missions. "Whenever the men would see a Russian tank, they would yell 'Where's Kopp, the tank killer,'" Kopp said with a laugh. In March 1943, his company relocated to Schlüsselburg on the southeastern side of Leningrad to prevent the Soviet counteroffensive from breaking up the siege. Kopp distinguished himself there.

In March one of his friends was injured in no-man's-land as he tried to return to the German lines. Obviously in a lot of pain, he screamed for help. Kopp went to his superior and asked if he could rescue his friend. Though the commander told him not to, Kopp jumped out of the trench, ran to his bleeding comrade, and saved him. His superior then immediately promoted him to Gefreiter (private first class). "Not bad for a Jew, huh?" Kopp said, laughing, "And besides, if that'd been me, I hope someone would have saved my ass . . . In war, your love for your fellow comrade was all you had."

The vast majority of *Mischlinge* comment upon how strong the camaraderie was within their units despite their supposed racial differences. It was not only combat that united these men in friendship; they were also brought together by the horrible events they witnessed. While fighting in northern Russia, Kopp witnessed two executions of partisans. One involved the hanging of ten Russians who had helped the Soviet army. "It was a sad day to see those young people dangle from the ropes and kick for life," Kopp said, shaking his head. "I thought as I watched those partisans die that if they knew about me, then I could also be strung up on a lamp post and find myself kicking my way to death."

For Germans, "partisans were not eligible for the consideration due to a man in uniform. The laws of war condemned them to death automatically, without trial."[5] The partisans knew such treatment awaited them if they got caught and thus they fought tenaciously. They also conducted psychological warfare by taking German prisoners, killing them through mutilation, and leaving them in an area where the Germans would find them. A German officer wrote that he discovered some of his comrades "with eyes gouged out and ears and noses cut off."[6] Scenes out of Dante's *Inferno* were common in the area where partisans operated, and the Germans often encountered comrades with their "faces smashed open with axes . . . wounded men tied with their head inside the gaping bellies of dead comrades; amputated genitals . . . [men found] tied up and naked, on a day when the temperature had dropped to thirty degrees below zero, with their feet thrust into a drinking trough which had frozen solid."[7]

Seeing dead comrades, whether from combat or partisan guerilla warfare, affected one greatly. Kopp talked often about how he and his comrades fought on battlefields covered with the dead. The smell was horrible, something between decomposing fish and rotten fruit, and watching the bodies decay before their eyes and noses was traumatic and horrifying. After they walked over the land soaked with death, the men's clothes and boots would smell of rot for weeks thereafter. Often they watched their close friends die and then slowly decompose before their eyes.

So, the combat experience for men like Kopp and many others in this book was one of utter horror. They were confronted with the horrible reality of facing and causing death on a daily basis, which most in "civilized" nations never encounter. One can only imagine the psychological and emotional toll warfare exacted from these men.

After several months in combat, Kopp contracted trench foot, a debilitating condition resulting from overexposure to cold, wet weather. So in June 1943, the army sent him back to the rear to heal, and then to the Tank Killer Reserve Brigade at Saarbrücken.

After a few weeks in Saarbrücken, Kopp was transferred to northern Germany and became a dispatch driver for the army's supreme headquarters driving high-ranking officers around Berlin. "It was a great job and I was able to spend a lot of time committing *Rassenschande*[8] after work," Kopp said. Following five months in Berlin he was transferred to a military prison, where he served as a guard for four months.

Then the army sent him back to Russia, but shortly thereafter he fell ill with an infection and entered a military hospital at Paderborn. After six weeks there, he was transferred back to Saarbrücken to his reserve unit.

In February 1944, the military assigned him as a technical instructor to the Grenadier Regiment Neuhammer 1 and he returned with this regiment to the eastern front, this time to Moldavia, Romania. While stopping at a train station in Hungary, he saw a Jewish forced worker hitting another Jew. He walked up to the man and asked, "Why are you beating him?" After a moment of silence, the man answered, "I'm responsible for having these people here work. If we're caught not working hard, they'll murder us. This one wasn't working." Kopp threatened to kill him if he saw him whip another person. When Kopp returned to his comrades, they wondered why he wanted to help Jews. He explained that no one should mistreat another.

Eventually Kopp's unit moved from Moldavia to fight at Jassy, Romania, in late summer 1944. A few weeks later, the Soviets encircled his regiment, originally about 3,000 men but now seriously reduced by casualties, and after several days of vicious fighting took the survivors prisoner near the Prut River. At this battle, the Soviets trapped fifteen or sixteen German and several Romanian divisions, which eventually resulted in Romania's capitulation.[9] "It was a bloodbath before we finally gave up," Kopp said.

Asked why he continued to fight, he said that though he knew Germany would not win the war, one fought at this stage for one's comrades and to avoid becoming a prisoner. Kopp also fought because he felt scared. As one German wrote, "The idea of death, even when we accepted it, made us howl with powerless rage."[10] Eventually the members of Kopp's unit were taken prisoner, and he accepted his fate, feeling at least happy that the war was over for him. Luckily, he survived. After two years in a Russian POW camp, he returned to Germany in 1946.

When asked if he was aware of the Holocaust at the time, Kopp stated that, yes, he had heard about systematic exterminations during the war.

In 1942 he knew the Nazis had sent Jews to Riga, where they shot them, including his aunt Susi and his uncle Heinz Moses. In Latvia, near the city of Dünaburg, Kopp also learned about Himmler's SS shooting Jews. He even heard the firing of machine guns. This probably occurred on 1 May 1942. After the Nazis murdered several Jews that day, the surviving people in the Dünaburg ghettos numbered only 500, ultimately bringing down the population even more from its original 16,000 one year earlier.[11] Others told Kopp that special German units continued to kill partisans and Jews elsewhere.

When asked if he felt a sense of guilt because of his military service, Kopp stated that he did not. "What were my choices? Stay in the army and try to survive or go to a concentration camp? . . . Had I gone to the camp, I probably wouldn't be here today. I'm happy I'm alive."

When asked if he felt connected to his Jewish roots, Kopp said that he has always felt Jewish, although he does not share Orthodox Judaism's view on what is kosher and what is not. "I'm proud of my Jewish heritage," he said. Even though he does not believe in God, at the beginning of his time in combat, he did say the Shema (an affirmation of faith, considered the holiest of Jewish prayers) a few times and asked the Lord for protection. But after a few days in battle, he stopped believing. He described how several Catholics in his unit prayed and crossed themselves before battle and then died, while he would not cross himself and survived. "When you fight in a war, you really see that God doesn't give a damn about humans or about justice. After my face had been sprayed with the brains of comrades, I realized that God doesn't care about us. When you hear the screams of dying men plead for God's help and then God does nothing, you spit on God."

Kopp wanted to believe in the God of his religious teachers but after his war experiences, he feels that God simply does not exist. As another German wrote after he prayed to God to help his dying friend who had had his face blown off: "God did not answer my appeals. The man [his comrade] struggled with death, and the adolescent [the writer] struggled with despair, which is close to death. And God, who watches everything, did nothing."[12] Many soldiers, like Kopp, believe that events in war prove the nonexistence of God.

After the war Kopp tried to emigrate to South America. To distance himself from the Nazis, he told everybody he met that he was Jewish and recited the Shema to prove it. In Berlin he asked a rabbi who had contacts in Colombia for help. When Kopp entered the rabbi's office, he saw other *Mischlinge* and Jews there. When the rabbi found out about Kopp's army service, the rabbi said that Kopp must have shot Jews if he had served so long. According to Kopp, "This rabbi was a fanatic. I was more *Goy* than Jew for him. All he cared about were full or religious Jews. He couldn't believe that I didn't shoot them. I told him, 'You think because I served in the army, I hated Jews. That's crazy!' Then I left."

For Kopp, turning to Jews for help was often humiliating. He quickly learned that most would never understand his situation and that, regardless of Halakah, many Jews would reject him.

Many of his relatives had emigrated to Palestine during the 1930s. When asked whether he contacted any of them after the war, Kopp shook his head and said, "I tried to establish contact with my Jewish relatives after 1945, but they rejected me because I had fought 'for Hitler' in the Wehrmacht . . . my relatives call me the Jewish Nazi. They don't like to have contact with me at all . . . my aunt actually told me that it would've been better had I died in a concentration camp than serve in the Wehrmacht. So they believed death was better than serving in the army. At least I'm alive today."

Another relative in Israel does not consider Kopp Jewish. His cousin Horst Schulz told him that even as a goy he should never have served in the Wehrmacht. So Kopp quickly learned that establishing contact with his Jewish family was painful and unproductive because they felt only disgust for how he survived the Third Reich. As a result, he tried to forget the war and his Jewish past.

When he returned to Berlin in 1946, Kopp married, had a family, and became a businessman. For years he struggled with traumatic memories of combat and the Gestapo and would often wake up at night in a cold sweat. He now feels it important to talk about his dreadful life during the Nazi years. "If I do so," Kopp said, "I might have some small influence on preventing an asshole like Hitler from coming into power again."

Surprisingly, Kopp discusses his past in a very matter-of-fact manner. His experiences show how critical family support and love are in developing healthy self-esteem, especially when one is young, and that in times of extreme crisis, supportive relatives mean more than anything. Since his family was dysfunctional, Kopp did not have this support and had to rely on himself for survival. He often laughs when recalling the horrible situations he faced and does so not only to alleviate his trauma but also because he does not want to complain. Looking at what Kopp has gone through, it is amazing that he can still smile. He exemplifies the triumph of the human spirit. "The difference between me and most people today," Kopp observed, "is that I am a lucky bastard and I know it. Enjoy the day because tomorrow we die. Luckily, I will die naturally and not on a field of battle or in Hitler's destruction."

Half-Jewish Lieutenant Arno Spitz

Arno Spitz is of medium height and has white hair, clear blue eyes, and a mustache. His stocky frame gives the impression he could have been a powerful wrestler when young. When asked a question, he takes his time to answer. He has a bright mind and continues to believe that what he experienced during the war was unremarkable. Yet, when one listens to his story, it comes across as anything but unremarkable. Perhaps for men of his generation, some of the events he describes seem common, but for the majority of people in the West today his world of combat, death, and Nazi terror present a reality many have a difficult time comprehending.

Spitz, born 24 April 1920 in Berlin, had a Jewish father, Walter, who converted to Christianity to marry his wife, Christine. At that time, Jews in Germany often assimilated and converted. Many Jews who converted did so for social acceptance.[13] Spitz's father did not believe in Christianity and thought religion and God were nonsense. He believed, as does his son Arno, that man created God. He only converted for love. Arno's mother, a Lutheran minister's daughter, remained somewhat religious, but she did not raise her children with a strong belief. She was a decided philo-Semite, and the Spitz family maintained friendly relations with Jews. Nevertheless, once in Arno's presence in mid-1933, she called Jews "cowards" for leaving Germany without "good" reason. This remark motivated the young Spitz to be courageous in everything he did, especially while in the military.

Half-Jew Arno Spitz in his garden in Berlin in 2004.

During World War I, Spitz's father served in the army's chemical department. He later became the director of a pharmaceutical factory. He felt the Versailles Treaty would not provide a lasting peace and looked forward to the day when Germany would regain its respectability internationally. Under the terms of the treaty, the Allies at the end of World War I forced Germany to yield a considerable part of its territory and pay heavy reparations. As a result, Germany fell on hard times economi-

Arno Spitz in 1934.

cally. But Spitz's family prospered due to his father's creative intelligence and good contacts.

Spitz lived on a beautiful estate in a village near Eberswalde outside of Berlin and enjoyed a privileged life. Although anti-Semitism did exist in Germany, the family did not experience problems before 1933. Having a Jewish father concerned Spitz only after the Nazis gained control in Germany and imposed a discriminatory framework of social values. Yet, Spitz's father did not think Hitler's tenure would last very long. He was, of course, unfortunately proven wrong.

The Nuremberg Racial Laws promulgated in 1935 classified Spitz as a half-Jew. He now worried about dating "Aryan" girls. He shied away from several invitations from girls to start a relationship, which gave him a sense of "lost youth."

By 1937, his father, due to the persecution, lost his ability to support the family and had to sell his estate. He tried to make a living producing pharmaceuticals in Austria and the Baltic and Balkan countries, but did not succeed.

In March 1938 Spitz passed his *Abitur* (high school examination) and finished at the top of his class. Since the Nazis had started to bar half-Jews from studying at universities except after military service, Spitz decided to volunteer for the Luftwaffe (German air force). Before entering the Luftwaffe, he had to fulfill the required half-year in the National Labor Service.

On 9–10 November, which came to be called Reichskristallnacht (Reich Crystal Night, which came to be called in English Night of Broken Glass), the Nazis arrested some 30,000 Jews, murdered around 100 Jews, burned hundreds of synagogues, and destroyed countless Jewish-owned businesses.[14]

Following this pogrom, Spitz's father left via Riga for the United States in July 1939. Two of Walter Spitz's brothers had already emigrated to that country in 1933 and felt fortunate since the United States denied entry to most Jews. Yet another brother had gone to Chile.

After his national service and while waiting to enter the military, Spitz worked as a road construction laborer and stayed with his mother in emergency quarters in Falkenberg. His three siblings—brother Peter, a merchant marine officer, and two sisters, Gerda and Miriam—had found acceptable job opportunities in Berlin. In March 1939, the Luftwaffe placed Spitz in a communications unit at Bernau north of Berlin. After finishing basic training there, he was selected to join a marine air force communications unit in Prussia.

In July 1939, with war on the horizon, his group boarded a ship for Pillau in East Prussia. His superiors told him and his comrades to stay belowdecks so that the Allies would not become concerned about troop movements to Prussia. Spitz and his fellow soldiers worried about the coming conflict. When the war started, his superiors attached him to a small motorized naval air force communications unit to set up airport control facilities on newly acquired airfields. They assigned him to take charge of telephone services of an operational airfield at staff headquarters, keeping him out of combat when Germany launched its invasion of Poland.

At this time a friend of his father's, Axel Nehls, who commanded a reporters' unit, advised Spitz not to draw the attention of the authorities. As a result, while in the service, he did not discuss his ancestry. Also, as far as he knows, no reference to his Jewish past existed in his papers. Spitz believes his commander, Lieutenant Erich Berker, who knew about Spitz's background, falsely testified that Spitz was an Aryan, thus protecting him.

While in charge of a telephone switchboard at a provisional navy airport in East Prussia, Spitz made friends with HE 59 sea-biplane pilots. After they complained about difficulties in orientation on high seas far from communications relay stations, Spitz developed an automatic coupler using his high school training in physics, which the Pillau airport engineer sent on to General Ernst Udet, the supply chief of the Luftwaffe. Soon thereafter, Udet sent Spitz a letter commending his efforts. That incident encouraged Spitz to apply later for navigational training.

After Germany invaded Denmark in April 1940, Spitz's unit moved to Aalborg, where it remained during the French campaign in May. One year later, in April 1941, after Germany invaded Greece, the military stationed his unit at the Aegean coast town of Kavalla and later near a shipyard south of Athens. Soon Spitz was promoted to Unteroffizier (corporal) and eventually managed to join the paratroopers, an elite Luftwaffe unit. In spring 1942, he entered jump school near Guetersloh, west of Hanover.

For the first four weeks Spitz and his peers trained in infantry tactics and field survival. One evening, after they retired to bed, their superiors ordered them to gather their gear and get ready to ship out immediately. Without ever having made a jump, his unit traveled directly into the Demyansk battle in northern Russia. They joined a large contingent to relieve 100,000 Wehrmacht and Waffen-SS soldiers who had been encircled there in an area of about 20 by 40 miles during the winter of 1941–1942.[15] On reaching the battlefield, Spitz's unit immediately attacked a Soviet

Arno Spitz (last rank lieutenant) with (from left to right) sister Gerda, mother Christine, and sister Miriam in 1944 at Freienwalde. (Military Awards: Close Combat Badge in Bronze, EKII, Infantry Assault Badge, and Wound Badge)

position heavily defended by bunkers. At daybreak, Spitz's group focused on a specified bunker about 500 meters away.

As Spitz crawled forward on his belly, he lost contact with his men. Small blueberry bushes covered the marshy ground. "Strangely enough," Spitz recalled, "although we were attacking, just like a sheep, I'd randomly pick berries with my lips and eat them as I continued on my elbows and knees." Spitz had to keep his head close to the ground as a continuous flow of German heavy machine-gun fire flowed overhead into the enemy's bunker.

As Spitz's group moved forward, Russian artillery shells rained down on them. Body parts flew in every direction as the shells tore into the Germans. The sounds of war made ears ring and confusion reigned on the battlefield. In the words of another soldier, "The world was seething with death."[16]

Chewing his blueberries, Spitz continued to crawl forward into this chaos. Due to his steady approach, he reached the bunker alone. He then attacked and sprayed two Russian soldiers lying dead next to it with submachine gun fire and waited for reinforcements.

Hardly any others in his unit survived. His battalion had originally numbered around 300, but only a handful remained alive. The artillery barrage had cut down most of his fellow paratroopers. For his bravery and accomplishments on that day, Spitz's superiors awarded him the Close Combat Bar in Bronze—a medal awarded to those who had "seen the whites of the eyes of the enemy," Spitz explained.

One reason for Spitz's brave acts arose from his inferiority complex as a half-Jew. He simply felt he had to do more than others. This was common among half-Jews. Many sought glory on the battlefield as a means of improving their self-esteem as well as protecting themselves and their families.

The few surviving remnants of Spitz's battalion returned to Germany at Bergen-Belsen near Lüneburg for further training and to get reequipped. Spitz had no idea a concentration camp lay nearby and commented, "I never knew about what horrible crimes were going on there at the time." While training at Bergen-Belsen, Spitz found he did not like the new paratroopers. Many were troublemakers and rejects. He therefore began to look for a new outfit.

One day in late summer 1942, he heard that an antitank unit was being formed at his base. "In an uncustomary move on my part, or any *Unteroffizier* for that matter, I approached the battalion commander and asked to be taken," Spitz said. The officer gave Spitz a searching glance and then accepted him.

After training, he returned to Russia to an area north of Demyansk at Staraja Russa near the great Ilmen Lake. In 1943 the front remained largely quiet, but during the winter, the Red Army started its rollback operations in the northern front and things heated up. Spitz's unit engaged not only in several local skirmishes but also in repulsing Russian infantry attacks using antipersonnel shells. Spitz's unit, the Twelfth Luft-waffe Field Division, Antitank Battalion 43, was outfitted with the Pak 97/38 French 75 mm and the German 8.8 cm Flak cannons.

In late 1943, they came under heavy fire. Spitz's unit fought back tena-ciously. Running out of antipersonnel shells, they were in danger of be-ing overrun; they called back for more supplies but did not receive the help they so desperately needed. Spitz volunteered to drive a truck to the supply depot to get ammunition, and his company commander approved the mission. As Spitz and some of his comrades drove away, the whole horizon lit up with the fires and flashes of warfare.

They drove all day through swampy areas and burning villages to reach the Army Corps' headquarters. When they arrived late at night, Spitz told the orderly that he wanted to see the supply officer, a general. "That's impossible now," the man said, "the general is asleep." Spitz felt exasperated. He knew their comrades would not survive much longer at their position without cannon support. Spitz insisted that he see the gen-eral immediately. Seeing Spitz's desperation, the orderly returned to the tent and woke his commander. "The general was actually kind to me. He promised that he would make sure our truck was filled up with the an-tipersonnel ammunition by morning," Spitz said. Personnel there loaded the truck overnight while the driver and Spitz slept a few hours.

After the truck was loaded, Spitz and his comrade returned to a disas-trous situation. On the road outside the village where they had fought the day before, Spitz met his commander, Captain Kupke, and the battal-ion commander, who informed him that the Russians had killed most of Spitz's comrades and had captured their cannon. The trip to acquire am-munition seemed to have been in vain. Not giving up hope, though, Spitz suggested a counterattack. There were only four of them: the two offi-cers with their pistols and Spitz and an orderly with a submachine gun. They decided to try the daring plan and entered the darkening village street with its empty wooden houses. The sun sank below the tree line as they moved forward.

Nearing their old positions, Spitz and the other soldier next to him re-ceived enemy fire. They answered with their submachine guns. Suddenly, the man next to Spitz was hit and dropped to the ground, dead. Now en-raged, the two officers and Spitz yelled "Hurrah!" and charged the Russians, firing as they ran. "I know this sounds romantic. Yelling and charging is stuff of the movies. I lost my mind in that moment, but it worked. Since it was dark, the enemy must have thought there were more of us and their group retreated," Spitz explained.

When they retook their old positions and cannon, they found their comrades dead. Rigor mortis had already set in, making the dead rigid in their death positions. Their eyes were wide open and their mouths were contorted. Not wasting time to bury their fallen comrades, Spitz and the two officers quickly removed their cannon with a truck and placed it behind the shrinking front, leaving their dead comrades behind.

Spitz's commander awarded him the Iron Cross Second Class and promoted him to Fahnenjunker-Feldwebel (officer candidate sergeant) for his actions. "A soldier like you," said his commander, "should become an officer." Spitz did not feel like a great soldier. He just felt lucky; he feels that he survived war because he could sense danger and avoid it. He does not know how to teach someone how to develop this sort of intuition, but he had it, and it saved his life.

Spitz's outfit later joined other units that continued their retreat into Estonia. On 4 April 1944, a shell splinter wounded Spitz during a frontline inspection. "I always believed I was untouchable," Spitz said, "I mean, being in so many near-death experiences, I thought I would never get wounded." Blood ran down his foot and out of the ripped hole in his boot. Because he could no longer walk, his commander carried Spitz on his back to the next medical attendant.

Medics transported him to the rear echelons where other wounded soldiers awaited transportation to a first-aid station. The injured cried out in pain and screamed for their mothers. "The ones who had been shot in the gut were the worst," Spitz said, "they screamed until they'd slump over, dead in a pool of blood." Until observing these wounded soldiers, Spitz had not considered war to be particularly dangerous. Until then, he "had just played in war like a theater production." He knows this sounds strange today, but it was how he felt then.

Spitz was sent to a hospital in Lithuania and later to Schwerin in Mecklenburg. Soon the Soviets entrapped the army he had served with on the Kurland peninsula in the Baltic region, and many comrades disappeared under Russia's rolling advance.

Upon Spitz's recovery, the military attached him to the 139th Mountain Regiment in Klagenfurt, Austria. He attended Officer Candidate School and became a lieutenant. When asked how he got by the ancestry forms for officers, Spitz explained that he did not sign the "Aryan" declaration and left the blanks empty about his family. No one seemed to notice this omission.

"Only the first year did I worry someone would find out I was a half-Jew, but when it never became an issue, I felt protected," Spitz said. While serving, he felt he had a relatively free life. In his opinion, the majority of his comrades were somewhat critical of Nazi ideology. He and others fought for Germany and not for Hitler. "I did my duty, that's all," Spitz said.

When asked about his decorations, Spitz downplayed them. "Yes, I received some medals for bravery, but I was really not a good soldier," he claimed. "I was just lucky that my true ancestry was never known."

His brother, a decorated ship merchant marine captain, also never encountered problems because of his ancestry. Even one of his sisters, Gerda, served in the Wehrmacht and survived in Hamburg serving in an antiaircraft flak unit, and the Nazis seemed to ignore her. All his siblings survived the war.

In the spring of 1945 Spitz became aide-de-camp to Colonel Buckner, commander of a mountain brigade in Bavaria. As the war entered its final weeks, the Americans captured Spitz, but he escaped. He now was on his own. With luck and his English language skills, he soon became a liaison officer between surrendered German units and the American army.

Regarding his awareness of the Holocaust, Spitz claims he knew nothing about it before the war's end. He lost his aunt, Claire Spitz, who had suffered persecution as a Jew while staying in the Jewish Hospital in Berlin. In 1944, the Nazis deported her to the east. Thereafter, Spitz never heard from her again. His mother wrote him about Dr. Tannenbaum, a Jewish friend of the family who was deported. He thought that only *Ostjuden* were repatriated into Poland, but that the Nazis gassed them along with all other Jews was beyond his comprehension. Only after the war did Spitz learn what Germany had done to the Jews. "I couldn't believe what had happened," he said.

He mentioned that during the war he hardly even heard anti-Semitic comments from his comrades. This was simply not something they talked about. "What's written about this after the war," Spitz said, "doesn't correspond with my experiences."

He did recall that while driving through a Russian village, he saw a civilian man hanging from a tree. Was he a partisan? Spitz is horrified that not just a few partisans, but millions, were brutally murdered. He believes that war is nonsense and wishes that countries would resort less to the use of arms. "War's simply hell," Spitz said.

Spitz said he does not feel Jewish but added, "However, when I meet remarkable and congenial Jews, I'm glad that I'm somehow related to them. However, I wouldn't call myself a Jew. I'm a *Mensch* just like everyone else."

After the war, Spitz founded and managed a publishing house in Berlin and did his best to forget those days when he was forced to live as a hidden half-Jew.

Spitz delivers his testimony with utter detachment. Although he discusses remarkable events, the tone in his voice leads one to believe he feels he is just talking about ordinary events. Maybe this is how he copes with his experiences, or maybe he feels that compared with what could have happened, he is lucky to be alive because he did not fall victim to battles like Stalingrad or extermination centers like Auschwitz.

And unlike Kopp, who still struggles with what his Jewishness really means for his life, Spitz chooses not to identify with his Jewish ancestry. He seems to be bored with many definitions people use to describe themselves, including Jew and Christian. Spitz describes himself as a humanist and thinks people need to see their common humanity instead of their differences. He feels people often mix up these differences with religious prejudice that dictates who has the right way to live versus who does not—a prejudice the human race needs to eradicate if it wants to have a war-free world. This is what is important to Spitz—the pursuit of tolerance and no more war.

Jewish Captain Edgar Jacoby

Edgar Jacoby had a flare for the dramatic. Having been a movie director in both Germany and Hollywood in the golden age of film, he knew his

Edgar Jacoby, seen under the umbrella wearing a hat and bow tie and holding a clipboard, was busy in Hollywood from 1924 to 1928 directing films. This photograph was taken at Universal City in May 1927.

way around the high society of power and influence. When photographed, he often struck a pose to make himself look dapper and handsome. His chiseled features made him appear athletic, and his demeanor gave the impression he was extremely confident, almost cocky. Yet, looks were deceiving. He had a weak heart and felt insecure about his place in society due to his racial background.

Edgar Nikolaus Joel Jacoby was born the youngest child of four on 4 May 1892 in Moscow, Russia, to a German family. His father, Albert, was Jewish but had converted to Christianity. His mother, Alma (née Hirschmann), was also Jewish but had been raised a Christian. Edgar and his siblings (Käthe, Gertrude, and Albert) were brought up in the Lutheran Church.

The Jacoby family lived in Moscow because of the family's business.

Edgar Jacoby served during World War I on the western front as an officer. He earned the Iron Cross, both First and Second Class, for his bravery. He not only directed in Hollywood, but also played characters. Here he is playing a German pilot from World War I in a 1926 Universal film that was shot in Texas at Kelly Field.

Albert Jacoby ran factories in Moscow, Tbilisi (now in the Republic of Georgia), and Lugansk (in Ukraine) that processed cotton, camel hair, and other textiles. In 1894, the family returned to Hamburg, where they led a comfortable, middle-class life. After Edgar Jacoby finished high school in 1911, he traveled overseas on an apprenticeship. To learn more about cotton farming, Jacoby traveled to Texas and worked on a plantation. His father felt this opportunity would prepare him to enter the family's business.

When World War I broke out in 1914, Jacoby, caught up in patriotic enthusiasm, returned to Germany to serve. He made it back home in November 1914 and enlisted in the army. He fought as a soldier in the Ninth Army Corps.

During the war, Jacoby's two sisters worked for the Red Cross in Germany as assistants. Yet, his brother, Albert, remained in Astrakhan, Russia, the site of one of the family offices. After the war started, the

Russians confiscated the business and he had to report daily to the police. Later, the Russians allowed him to return to Germany in exchange for Russian prisoners of war.

Edgar Jacoby had his major combat experience near Rheims, France. Toward war's end, Jacoby took command of a company. One superior wrote that Jacoby represented a perfect leader. Another superior wrote of Jacoby that while he fought in the Twelfth Company of Infantry Regiment 84 outside of Rheims, he showed incredible bravery as "a cold-blooded warrior." Although suffering a combat wound to the hand and another to the head, he continued to fight. His superiors decorated him with the Iron Cross Second and First Class. His second wife, Marianne, said that during an attack by the French, Jacoby killed over twenty men. He told her how disturbed he felt "slaughtering" a few of them with a bayonet when his machine gun ran out of ammunition. Their faces still pursued him in his dreams.

After hostilities ceased, Jacoby returned to Hamburg and was reunited with his siblings. Around this time, he married Betty, a gentile. The young couple soon had a daughter, Vera. Jacoby had difficulties finding work in Germany after World War I. But eventually, he became an assistant director in the film industry in Hollywood and moved to the United States in 1924. Although successful, in 1928 he returned to Cologne, Germany, to make films in his homeland.

When Hitler came to power in 1933, Jacoby moved to Berlin hoping to disappear in the large city. Even so, his wife divorced him because of his Jewish background. According to Marianne Jacoby, Edgar said that Betty "became anti-Semitic and called me a dirty Jew." Betty hoped the separation would help her better support their daughter. Although a *Mischling*, his daughter, Vera, had to join the Hitler youth group for girls (Bund Deutscher Mädel—BDM). Tragically, she died in 1937 at the age of sixteen when she fell off a human pyramid and broke her neck during a BDM exercise. Vera's death devastated Jacoby and he fell into a deep depression. Thereafter, he immersed himself in his work.

To escape Nazi persecution, Jacoby's brother, Albert, emigrated to the United States in 1939. Albert's wife followed him in 1940 on one of the last ships leaving from Italy for America. But their two daughters had to remain in Germany for lack of funds.

The family of his sister Gertrude also encountered serious problems at that time. Her husband, Baumbach zu Kaimberg, lost his government job due to his wife's Jewish ancestry and because he refused to divorce her. As a result, the family became penniless. Unable to support his family, he hanged himself.

Now Gertrude, no longer protected by her Aryan husband, emigrated to Argentina. Settling down in Buenos Aires, she barely earned enough to live on. Even so, Jacoby's other sister, Käthe Himmelheber, eventually sent one of her daughters, Erika, age twelve, to Argentina to join Gertrude and help her in building a life there for both of them. Käthe, who in the meantime had divorced her Aryan husband, could not join her daughter because she had been committed to a mental hospital. Käthe's other daughter, Lisa, remained in Germany and served the Wehrmacht as a secretary. She felt embarrassed to have a Jewish mother and, like most *Mischlinge*, hid her origins. Luckily for her, she found people in the Wehrmacht willing to help her conceal her racial background. Käthe's ex-husband did not care for his daughters, whom he called "half-Jewish mongrels," so they could not rely on him for help.

During this time, Jacoby had found work with UFA (Universum Film AG) film company in Berlin, undoubtedly the best of the German studios. While filming on the Baltic Sea, he fell in love with a woman named Marianne Guenther. Tall, energetic, blond, and blue-eyed, she was beautiful and full of life. She eventually joined Jacoby in Berlin and found work at UFA. He worried about their future since the Nazis had prohibited marriages between Jews and Aryans.

Though Marianne knew about Jacoby's background, she continued their relationship and became pregnant in 1937. They feared the repercussions of having violated *Rassenschande* now that proof existed they had had relations. Both worried the Nazis would execute them if they found out, especially since Jacoby did not have the Aryan papers to marry her. Marianne simply told him, "But that doesn't change anything. I still love you." To escape persecution and enable them to get married, Jacoby falsified his papers and married Marianne in 1937. Edgar registered himself as an "Aryan" in his documents and no one noticed his forgery. That year, their son, Klaus-Edgar, was born. Having false documents, though, did not alleviate Jacoby's fear that someone would discover his secret.

Marianne Guenther in
1936 on the Baltic Sea, not
long after she began
dating Edgar Jacoby.

In March 1940, not long after World War II broke out, the Wehrmacht
drafted Jacoby as a reserve officer. Marianne said that no one guessed he
was a Jew. "When in uniform, he looked like ten Aryans, to use the stupid Nazi terminology," she said. Because of his experience in film, he became commander of a propaganda company documenting the German
victories during the French campaign of 1940. He also worked on the
weekly military Wochenschau news reports run by the Propaganda Ministry. Both he and his wife hoped this job would protect them.

The constant fear Jacoby lived in caused him stomach problems. In
one of his military reports, his superior mentioned that Jacoby often reported sick. His stressful job required him to travel throughout Germany and work with demanding people. Between 1937 and 1939, he and

Edgar Jacoby (last rank captain) in his dress whites in June 1941. He was company commander of Propaganda Company 696 in France. (Military awards: EKI, EKII, and Wound Badge)

Marianne had two more children, a daughter, Barbara, and a son, Manfred, who, sadly, died four months after his birth. This added yet more pain to his life, but having already lost comrades in World War I and his daughter Vera, Edgar had learned how to deal with such pain. Moreover, according to his wife, he did not have time to grieve. Edgar worried about his family and their future and, unbeknownst to him, time was running out for him because the authorities would soon discover his lie.

In the summer of 1941, right before Jacoby received the rank of major, his origins were brought to light when his sister Käthe Himmelheber attended a Nazi NSF (National Socialist Women's League—a Nazi Party organization) meeting at Pinneberg. A high-ranking party officer, Alfred

Edgar Jacoby with his children Barbara Jacoby (left) and Klaus-Edgar Jacoby (right), in a photograph taken after a military parade in Berlin in 1941.

Krömer, identified Käthe as Jewish and later contacted her landlady, Johanna Krohn. He then met with Johanna and told her that she needed to evict Käthe because Jews were unwanted in Pinneberg.

To Krohn's credit, she had supported Käthe and known about her ancestry. However, now she had to report the situation and force Käthe to leave her apartment. Thirty minutes after Krohn had met with Krömer, Käthe showed up at Krömer's office, upset. She did not understand how he could just send her out on the street, especially since her brother served in the Wehrmacht. Krömer, shocked by this information, informed the military authorities, describing Käthe's "insolence (*Frechheit*)." That same day, Krömer also made sure that Käthe's boss fired her from her position at Fa. Wuppermann AG. Back at Jacoby's duty station in Fontainebleau, France, his commander informed him about what had happened with his sister. Jacoby stuttered that he found this accusation

"absurd." He then instantly fell into a depression and suffered a heart attack. Later, he told his wife he felt "as though my heart was going to fly
out of my chest. I couldn't breathe and I was scared." His sister's actions
had revealed his true ancestry and his false documents no longer could
hide his identity.

Edgar's unit immediately sent him to a hospital due to his heart attack.
Soon thereafter, Käthe wrote to Jacoby in the hospital that she now had
to live in Jewish housing, though she did not feel or "think" Jewish.
Nonetheless, the documents on her ancestry "proved" her Jewish background. She pleaded for help.

While recuperating from his sickness, he wrote his sister. In a July letter to her, he explained that if he was not so sick, he would have come to
Hamburg and dealt with the "shitty situation" she had created. Furious,
he wrote: "My God! We soldiers have enough problems without having
to take care of the mess you've created." He explained that she had made
his situation unbearable.

From his military experience, Jacoby should have known that the authorities would censor his mail. Consequently, he probably committed
to paper ideas and "facts" he thought would perhaps mitigate his own
situation. He asked her, "Since when and how come have you described
yourself as a full-Jew?" The fact she now had a Jewish identification certificate surprised him. He then requested she explain what she had told
the authorities about their relatives and to send the family papers in her
possession to him. He scolded her, saying that before she tried to become a member of a Nazi organization, she must first have her papers in
order—something, he explained, only he could do. He warned her to
stop making claims about their ancestors that she obviously could not
know and said he would soon travel to Hamburg to put the family's documents in order. In case she failed to understand the situation, he told
her that if the officials should push her for more information, "tell them
they should wait until I'm there to answer them." He pleaded with her
to think about his wife and children and what they might face if she continued to talk about their family the way she had. "It all can come to a
quick end," he warned her.

But the Abwehr (military intelligence service) told Jacoby's commander that his sister was indeed a full Jew. Even so, the commander

allowed him to go to Hamburg to attempt to sort out the situation. Not surprisingly, he failed. One of his old commanders, Colonel von Arnim, heard about Jacoby's problems and exclaimed, "When Edgar earned his Iron Cross in World War I, we didn't ask him to prove his Aryan ancestry. We only asked him to prove himself in battle." Yet this support, although noteworthy, did not help.

In August 1941, the OKW (Armed Forces High Command) wrote the OKH (Army High Command) personnel department that because of his Jewish ancestry, Jacoby could not stay. The army arrested him under the suspicion that he was a spy. Despite the fact that he was a World War I officer decorated with the Iron Cross and in poor health, the army brought Jacoby before a military court and discharged him and then deported him to a forced labor camp. Although he was found not guilty of the charges of espionage, and Field Marshal Wilhelm Keitel, the chief of staff of the Army High Command, refused to sign the verdict that Jacoby had lied about his ancestry, the Nazis still sent Jacoby away for punishment. He now had to wear the Star of David instead of the Iron Cross and to add "Israel" to his name. His sister Käthe was deported to Theresienstadt.

Jacoby's wife, Marianne, feared the future. She did not know how to feed two little mouths with her husband locked up in a forced labor camp and she immediately appealed to the authorities to release him.

Meanwhile, Jacoby's situation was not as deadly as one would think. He considered himself lucky that while he was in the forced labor camp, he always found people to protect him. Most camp authorities could not believe that the government could mistreat a World War I veteran decorated with the Iron Cross. Many felt sympathy for him and tried to help him in small ways. The family believes that was why, after several months of incarceration, the camp authorities returned him to Berlin. Marianne thinks that the camp commander, also a World War I officer, found a way to get Jacoby sent back home because he did not feel right locking up a war veteran. According to Jacoby, since the court had found him innocent of the charges filed against him, it was only right that he could go home. But because the bureaucrats labeled him a Jew, it took more time than usual for the court to honor its findings about him.

Luckily for Jacoby, his brave "Aryan" wife refused to divorce him and this must have had a profound effect on the way bureaucrats handled his case. Those Jews whose "Aryan" spouses divorced them usually found themselves deported to a concentration camp. Nazi authorities often pressured Marianne to leave him, but she refused to do so. One day, a civil servant asked her, "How could you marry a Jew in 1937?" Marianne answered sarcastically, "Well, why do people usually marry?" He then encouraged her to divorce him. She replied that she would not. The bureaucrat coldly answered that she should do this to have a better husband. Everyone in the office looked at her and she suddenly became upset and said, "I'll stay married to my husband as long as I live." She then left.

Remarkably, while being protected by his wife living in a so-called privileged mixed marriage (*privilegierte Mischehe*),[17] Jacoby started to secretly work on films with UFA and Tobis and even helped produce some films for the Wehrmacht. His employers knew about his situation but supported him. This enabled him to feed his family.

Nonetheless, he and his wife continued to live in fear. They would board streetcars through separate doors and not walk together on the streets. However, they continued to live in the same house. Then, in the summer of 1942, things took a turn for the worse. UFA had to fire Edgar for racial reasons. The army's case of treason against him was revisited in June 1942, and the authorities sentenced him to seven months in prison. From September 1942 until March 1943, the Nazis incarcerated him at Plötzensee in Tegel near Berlin. And then a few months after his release, the Gestapo arrested and imprisoned him at their compound in Berlin at Burgstrasse. Soon thereafter, Marianne received a phone call informing her that the Gestapo had put her husband in jail. When she asked for the caller's identity, the caller hung up. Later, they found out someone had denounced him to the SS.

For days, the brave Marianne went from one office to another with two little children in tow to find her husband. The bureaucrats again tried to convince her to file for divorce. They explained how much easier life would be if she did so. Marianne refused. She told them that they should feel ashamed for pressuring her to do this "cowardly act." According to the historical record, Jews who had Aryan spouses were indeed protected for a longer time than those Jews who were single or married to other Jews. As a result, Marianne's resolve to remain married to Jacoby probably saved his life.

From the jail at Burgstrasse, the SS moved him to a basement jail at Alexanderplatz in Berlin. After ten days, he was transferred to the concentration camp Grossbeeren right outside Potsdam. Then after three weeks, he was moved to a camp at Wartenberg in the Sudetenland. Jacoby later reported that once the camp's SS men found out about his combat service, they treated him better than others. After several months at Wartenberg, the SS returned him to a prison in Berlin. Confused by the moving around, Jacoby feared his life would soon end.

At the same time, although Marianne had small children, she was called up to take part in forced labor. When she reported, the bureaucrats there saw the absurdity of forcing her to do such work while taking care of two children and they sent her home.

Marianne's days were fraught with tension. For instance, one day as Marianne made her way through the streets with her children, a woman stopped her to look at her daughter, Barbara, and commented, "That's not a German child." Marianne responded, "What do you mean? I'm a German, my family are German, and her father served in World War I as an officer." "That isn't a German child," the stranger said again and walked away. Shocked, Marianne could not believe her ears. As she walked away, she worried about her daughter. "I guess she felt Barbara was Jewish because of her dark hair and dark eyes, and I was as blond as a poodle," Marianne said. She and her children lived under a shadow of fear chained to a life of discrimination.

On 22–23 November 1943, during one of the heavy Allied attacks on Berlin, several bombs hit Jacoby's prison and destroyed it. In the chaos, his jailer opened his door and freed him. He explained that the bombs had destroyed the files and no one would look for him. Edgar could not believe his luck. He walked through the burning city streets until he reached his home early in the morning. His heart overflowed with joy as he hugged his wife and children. Later, strangely enough, he even received his civilian clothes from the Grossbeeren camp (the personnel probably thought he had died and, thus, returned his personal effects to the family). Amazingly, he survived in hiding until the end of the war.

After the Nazis finally capitulated, Jacoby moved to the town of Nikolassee outside of Berlin and became its mayor. His ability to speak English and communicate in Russian were ideal skills to have in postwar Europe and he wanted to take an active part in rebuilding Germany. He also busied himself with increasing his family, and in 1945, his fifth child, Christian, was born.

After 1945, Jacoby and his family started to hear about the Holocaust and to learn first-hand of the toll it took on Jacoby's relatives. One day, his cousin Alice visited him. She had survived the war, but the SS had murdered her four-year-old Jewish twin daughters at Auschwitz. Jacoby's sister Käthe returned from Theresienstadt in poor health and lived with him and his family. In 1954, his other sister, Gertrude, came back from Argentina, demoralized and decidedly aged beyond her years from her hardships.

In order to prevent Nazism from happening again, Jacoby helped to found and worked for a Christian-Jewish solidarity organization, Die Gesellschaft für Christlich-Jüdische Zusammenarbeit. The members of this group focused on creating more understanding between Jews and Christians and fostering tolerance. The group's founders felt that by creating a dialogue between the two faiths, they could help prevent anti-Semitism.

Although mayor, Jacoby still needed a job to support his family. It proved difficult to receive compensation from the government. Eventually the city employed him in Berlin in film festivals, during the course of which he met the actor Gary Cooper.

To his wife's amazement, Jacoby also attended his veteran reunions because he felt patriotic and connected to his comrades. He believed that when a person's nation calls him to arms, he must fulfill his duty to the state. He felt that one should not feel shame at having served his land. Most soldiers throughout history are proud of their service and feel an attachment to their brothers-in-arms. Surprisingly, this feeling is often expressed by the men in this study, although they served a government controlled by Hitler.

While his immediate family had survived, Jacoby never recovered his health. In 1956 he died of heart failure at sixty-four.

So how did Jacoby view himself? Although he was brought up as a

The author with Marianne Jacoby in November 1996 going over documents related to her late husband, Edgar Jacoby. (Photo credit: Ian Jones)

Christian, he really did not believe in any religion. But when the Nazis came into power, they labeled him a Jew. "Why couldn't people simply view each others as human beings?" he often asked rhetorically.

He claimed he did not know about the Holocaust while it was happening. Had Marianne not remained married to him, the Nazis would have probably sent him to a death camp. The authorities did not know how to handle Jews married to Aryans, and Jacoby was lucky his wife remained loyal to him. Had she divorced him, "then he would've known about the Holocaust," his daughter Barbara said, "right before they shoved him into a gas chamber."

Edgar represents many in this book in that he failed to comprehend what the Nazis meant to do to those they labeled Jewish. Probably due to his honorable service, as well as his patriotic feelings, he sometimes failed to take the actions one would have thought necessary to protect himself and his family. As family members started to leave Germany and the race laws became stricter, one wonders why Jacoby did not use his U.S. contacts to escape. Yet his loyalty to his country, in addition to his belief that he could hide his origins, caused him to remain, which in hindsight was a mistake. Jacoby's attitudes were similar to those of thousands of Germans of Jewish descent, who also never thought their ancestry would lead to their deaths.

Ironically, Jacoby represents a person whom many religious Jews and Nazis would have called a Jew although he would have never called himself as such. Jacoby illustrates so clearly what Martin Gilbert said: "Tens of thousands of German-Jews were not Jews at all in their own eyes."[18] Yet, here again, the Nazis did not care what one thought about oneself. What mattered was what the Nazis thought of a person, and for them, Jacoby was simply a Jew.

Jewish Waffen-SS Rottenführer Karl-Heinz Löwy

Karl-Heinz Löwy was a well-read and worldly man. During our conversation, he often quoted Heinrich Heine and Johann Wolfgang von Goethe and made several references to the wonderful relationships he had with numerous women. When he smiled, he lit up the whole room. He spoke with his hands, and his eyes opened wide when he expressed an important point. Rather tall and of slender build, he was a person who enjoyed being active. He often leaned forward eagerly to discuss his life—he was excited to talk.

Löwy believed his story about his experiences as a full Jew in the Waffen-SS was more dramatic than Shlomo Perel's tale in the movie *Europa, Europa.* "I don't think Perel tells the whole truth," Löwy said, adding, "I'll do my best to be honest."

Löwy was born on 25 December 1920 in Munich into a family that had fled from the Spanish Inquisition to Germany four hundred years earlier. His parents raised him as a religious Jew. Besides being Jewish, they were zealous patriots with a strong military background. This combination may sound strange today, but this was common among Jews in Germany at that time. His maternal grandfather, Schoelein, had been a reserve captain and an honorary member of his regiment and was a distinguished businessman in Ingolstadt, Bavaria. He said that he was a

Karl-Heinz Löwy at his home in Munich, 1992. During World War II, he was a Waffen-SS soldier. (Military awards: EKI, EKII, and Close Combat Badge) (Photo credit: Alfred Haase)

German first and a Jew second. In addition to his military and business activities, he was a passionate family man who deeply loved his wife and four daughters.

When World War I broke out, Löwy's grandfather encouraged his daughters to work as Red Cross nurses. One of his daughters, Löwy's mother, received several decorations for her service. Löwy's grandfather, although advancing in years, served in the army during World War I. He was a "100 percent German patriot and proud of his service to *Kaiser, Volk und Vaterland*," Löwy said, adding, "This sounds tragic today to those who have heard about the Holocaust, but that was the case." Several of Löwy's other relatives also fought in the German and Austro-Hungarian armies.

His grandfather placed much emphasis on education when he visited. He always had Löwy read Proverbs to teach him wisdom. When he tucked him into bed at night, his grandfather read works to him by the Swiss author Gottfried Keller and the German Jewish poet Heinrich Heine. Later, when Löwy served in the Waffen-SS, he carried some of Heine's works in his backpack.

His father, Arnold, was born in Vienna and raised in a traditional Orthodox home. He owned a brush factory in Rosenheim, Upper Bavaria. Löwy remembers his observant paternal grandfather putting on his *Telfilin* (phylacteries) and saying his Hebrew prayers every morning. He opposed his son's marriage to Löwy's mother because she came from Germany ("the land of barbarians") and was not religious.

As a child, Löwy worked hard in school and during his Torah classes learned his prayers and Bible stories. His family celebrated the religious holidays but did not practice strict Orthodox Judaism. The traditions the family observed resembled something like moderate Conservative Judaism in the United States today. Though his family felt proud of being Jewish, they were wary of the *Ostjuden* (Eastern Jews), whom they found primitive.

As the Nazis gained power in the early 1930s, some members of Löwy's family became concerned and his mother's sister Dolch left for Switzerland. However, most of Löwy's relatives did not believe the systematic persecution of Jews would get as bad as it did. They felt the Nazi Party would soon go away like many parties of the Weimar Republic period.

In 1933, when Hitler became chancellor, Löwy's family immediately experienced problems. Several acquaintances who had previously treated them politely now avoided contact. Anti-Semitism was growing in Germany, but Löwy's family still sent him to Hebrew School and celebrated the *Shabbat* (the Sabbath). On 6 December 1934, he had his Bar Mitzvah in the large Munich Temple. Yet, things continued to worsen for the family and they moved away from Munich, seeking a life of anonymity like Arno Spitz and Edgar Jacoby. By now his father's adultery had led to his parents' divorce. "My mother actually caught my father in the closet screwing a maid. That didn't go over well with my mother," Löwy said. As a result, Löwy moved with his mother to Berlin. They believed they could disappear in the large capital.

Löwy excelled at the Jewish Adass High School but could not escape persecution. The children of pro-Nazi parents often attacked him and beat him up. When asked if he had wished back then that he was not Jewish, he said no, that he was proud of his Jewish past. As a young man he was aware that some of the greatest thinkers in history—including Albert Einstein, Sigmund Freud, and Heinrich Heine—were Jewish, and knowing this gave him strength.

During the mid- to late 1930s, Löwy often visited his Aunt Dolch and her family in Basel, Switzerland, where he met the Grenacher family, which had two children, a son and daughter. Löwy would take the daughter out on dates, and he became friendly with the son. He had no way of knowing then that the son, Werner Grenacher, would later save his life.

In 1939, Löwy left Germany with his mother for Lyon, France, to escape persecution. He took odd jobs to support his mother and himself. When the war broke out in 1939, the French police rounded up Löwy and several other Germans and detained them in a soccer stadium. Among the detainees were many Jews from Austria and Germany, and several of them protested that they despised Hitler. Representatives from the French Foreign Legion arrived later and told those who wanted to prove they hated Nazis to join the legion. Löwy did so to support his mother.

After his training, he was sent to Fort Elatters in the Sahara Desert. During the period known as the Phony War—between 1 September 1939 and 9 May 1940, the date when fighting broke out between the Allies and Germany in the west—Löwy did not see any action. After France lost the war, he returned to that country, which was now under the Vichy regime, to be with his mother.

Soon after his return to France, he started to work odd jobs as a milkman and manual laborer to support himself. By this time, his mother had married a Belgian diplomat, and Löwy, adopting his stepfather's surname, falsified his identity from Karl-Heinz Löwy to Henri Boland.

After he lived for years under this assumed name, the authorities discovered he had falsified his documents and imprisoned him at St. Paul for six months. But when he was released, he continued to live under his false identity. After the Allied invasion of North Africa in November 1942, all of France came under German control, and now Löwy had to worry about hoodwinking the German authorities, who were more thorough than the French.

One day in 1943, while Löwy was at work, German military police started sweeping the town. He quickly disposed of his false papers and told the police that he was Werner Grenacher, an ethnic German from Switzerland. He said that his papers and wallet had been stolen on the train, but that he had traveled to the German-occupied sector to enlist in the Wehrmacht for ideological reasons. He gave them Grenacher's birth date, mother's name, and where he was born and was sent to a draft office, which then sent him on to Paris. At one of the military bases in Paris, he joined several hundred men who had also volunteered. An officer asked all *Volksdeutsche* (ethnic Germans) to step forward, which Löwy did. They were then told that they were going to serve in the Waffen-SS. Löwy was shocked. He had not expected to serve in Hitler's elite force and did not know that most often non-German citizens could not serve in the Wehrmacht, but had to serve in the SS military arm. By war's end, of the 940,000 men serving in the Waffen-SS, only 250,000 were actually German. Although the SS preached racial purity, it did not let it get in the way of its recruiting quotas except for those with "Jewish blood." Unlike the Wehrmacht, which then drafted half- and quarter-Jews, the Waffen-SS did not allow anyone in its ranks with any Jewish ancestry.[19] So no *Mischlinge*, much less Löwy, a full Jew, could reveal their true ancestry if they wanted to remain in this organization.

After the authorities registered Löwy, they sent him to the Sixth SS–Mountain Division, based at Hallein near Salzburg. During the medical examination, the doctors told him and his comrades to pull back their foreskins. Löwy acted as if he had foreskin and pretended to pull it back. Nobody noticed his circumcision. "For a few moments," he said, "I felt I was a dead man. However, after I saw how easy it was to hide it and that nobody really stared at my penis, then I stopped worrying. I thought that if someone ever asked me about it, I would just tell them it was removed as a child because of an infection. However, I was worried once I was in battle. I often thought, 'What will happen if I get wounded and they see my circumcision?' That often made me think because it might be hard to explain the situation when you're in pain. I guess my circumcision played more of a role in my fears than I'm willing to admit, but I survived the war and it never became an issue."

Besides Löwy's circumcision, his other physical characteristics would not lead most Nazis to believe he was a Jew. With his blond hair and gray eyes, many Germans thought he looked "Aryan," which helped him conceal his origins. He believes he was the only Jew in the Waffen-SS. It was a horrible situation. Every morning when he awoke, he thought, "Will I survive this day?" Often, after asking this question, he consoled himself with the Shema, the holiest Jewish prayer.

Löwy said there were "thousands of possibilities that could've put someone on my trail." While serving, he did his best not to do too much or too little to draw the attention of his superiors. He wanted to blend in as best he could.

One day, he thought his secret had been discovered when his sergeant ordered him to step forward and yelled, "You're standing there like a Jew. *Junge* [boy], do you know you look just like a Jew the way you're standing?" Löwy shivered, but when he straightened up, the sergeant let him return to his place in line. He was only "screwing around" with him.

For several months, Löwy trained hard with the mountain troops. Although he and his comrades studied Nazi ideology, he does not remember it playing much of a role in their lives compared with learning how to fight. However, he does recollect intensively studying Hitler's life. Their superiors taught them to fight for Hitler and accept his ideals as their own. The Germans had to condition Löwy's comrades to their new leader and his views of a transformed Europe, since they came from Finland, Holland, Switzerland, France, and Denmark. After months of training, his division entered battle in the Karelia forests on the Finland/Russian border. Before they left for war, they pledged allegiance to Hitler, but during that ceremony, Löwy remained silent. No one noticed.

"I wasn't about to give my oath to that maniac," Löwy said. This small protest had a profound effect on Löwy. One can understand why he felt revolted by this oath when looking at the words. It read: "I swear to you, Adolf Hitler, as Fuehrer and Reichs Chancellor of the German Reich, loyalty, and courage. I vow to you, and to the superiors appointed by you, obedience unto death, so help me God."[20]

Knowing the realities of Nazi Germany, one may feel puzzled by the fact that the men in this study who knew about Nazi persecution did not actively oppose the regime. People often shake their heads when they hear about "protests" of the sort Löwy made and ask why these men did not do more. Most who knew about or suspected atrocities declare the authorities would have killed them if they had acted against the Nazis. A realization of helplessness is almost universal among *Mischlinge* and Jews who served in the armed forces under Nazism. One must not forget that Jews and *Mischlinge* caught in the Nazi juggernaut had no freedom to act on their own convictions. They did what they were told to do and in the army that meant following orders.

While fighting the Russians on the border with Finland, Löwy and his comrades often engaged in hand-to-hand combat. "It was like fighting a thousand years ago," Löwy explained, "except we had rifles instead of swords." In fighting this war of position, once they took over an area, they had to hold it at all cost. During one battle, they overran an island in a large lake, using rubber boats to get there. In the ensuing fight, one of Löwy's comrades died and Löwy found himself alone when Russians approached his position. A fire fight broke out and Löwy felt a bullet graze his face. He knew if he continued to fight, he would die. So he played dead. Amazingly, the Soviets thought they had killed him and left him alone. A few minutes later, his comrades rescued him when they counterattacked. Playing possum in this case saved his life. "My survival instinct is strong," Löwy commented.

After the Waffen-SS suffered horrendous defeat at the battle of Salla in 1941, Wehrmacht units incorporated Finnish soldiers into their ranks to help teach the Germans how to fight. So Löwy had constant contact with Finnish personnel and learned their tactics. Ironically, many Jews in the Finnish army found themselves serving with Waffen-SS soldiers, so Löwy might have fought near other Jews also faced with dealing with

Germans ideologically opposed to their racial background. The Germans respected the Finns' combat abilities and valued their alliance and, thus, left Finland alone to deal with its Jews as it saw fit.[21]

Löwy described the Finnish soldiers as brutal. "Both the Russians and ourselves were scared of them," he said, "and that should tell you something." He describes the Finns as guerilla warfare masters. They would sneak into Russian encampments and slice the throats of sleeping enemy soldiers without making a sound. One day he and his fellow soldiers came across Soviet troops the Finns had just massacred by cutting through the soldiers' necks so viciously that the vertebrae at the back of their throats were revealed. They did it in such a way that the victim would not scream because the air exited the sliced windpipe while the Finn shut the mouth and nose of the victim with his free hand.

Löwy disliked the fact that he served on the Russian front because he could not desert to the Soviets. They did not take prisoners often and those they took did not survive long in Soviet POW camps, especially as Waffen-SS veterans. One German soldier wrote that "the war in the east had degenerated to the point that we equated surrender to suicide."[22] Also, as historian Omer Bartov wrote, Wehrmacht personnel "had been taught that both on the personal and on the national level surrender to the Red Army was equivalent to giving oneself up to the devil."[23] So for self-preservation, Löwy decided to stay with his comrades, whom, surprisingly, he liked. He asked for forgiveness from the Jewish people for feeling friendly toward his anti-Semitic brothers in arms. They were the best comrades anyone would want in war, he added.

Because Löwy distinguished himself in battle, his commanding officer awarded him the Close Combat Badge and the Iron Cross Second and First Class. In the fall of 1944, the Finns made a separate peace with Russia. When German forces did not exit the country as quickly as Finland wanted, the Finns attacked the Germans, and Löwy's division protected their retreat. During the fight, one of his superiors "had *Halsschmerzen* [neck pains, in this case referring to where the Knight's Cross, roughly the U.S. equivalent of the Medal of Honor, was hung]" and decided to take a hill that the Finns had secured. He took the thirty-five men who were left in Löwy's company and stormed the position. After the fight only six returned alive. Löwy was one of them.

Löwy emphasized the difference between the Waffen-SS and the Death's Head SS, which ran the extermination camps. "The Waffen-SS soldiers served on the front just like Wehrmacht soldiers. The Death's Head SS were the real criminals who ran the camps. Saying this though . . . had my comrades known about my Jewish past they would have hung me up on the first tree." While historians like Charles Sydnor would disagree with the distinction Löwy makes between the Death's Head and the Waffen-SS, it is interesting that a Jew would hold this opinion about his organization.[24]

When the Allies invaded Normandy, France, in June 1944, Löwy was still fighting in Finland. In December, the military transferred his unit to the western front to confront the Americans. He met green American troops hurriedly thrown into the line to counter the German thrust code-named *Nordwind* (North Wind). "The Americans were nothing like the Russians—in some respects, they were so naïve. We simply slaughtered them," he said. When they attacked, many would scream and yell. Some U.S. troops did not properly camouflage themselves and often their tactics were pathetic, according to Löwy. When asked whether he felt guilty killing U.S. troops, he said in war, you lived according to one principle, "either them or me." He said he sided with himself. Later, the United States would prove successful against Waffen-SS units as they learned how to fight the Germans in defeating the Sixth SS Mountain Division at Reiperstweiler and Wingen in the Vosges Mountains in 1945.[25]

During battle in 1944, Löwy, who was by now a Waffen-SS Rottenführer, was shot through the leg. After spending a few weeks in a hospital, he rejoined his unit at Trier. The men's morale plummeted and many foresaw Germany's end. A few said they would shoot themselves if Germany lost because they did not want to live under Jews. Löwy said they claimed they fought against a Jewish Bolshevik world conspiracy and added, "That's how brainwashed they were." This belief dominated the thoughts of many soldiers. When Löwy heard defeatist talk by his comrades, he always made it a point to say that Hitler would defeat the Allies with his new weapons. He knew he could not say that the war was over although he knew it to be true.

One night at Trier, he sneaked away from his unit and deserted to the

French. He discarded his SS uniform jacket with his medals (abandoning his medals made him sad), intending to tell anyone he met that he had escaped from a camp. He also felt nervous about the tattoo under his left arm with his blood group (all SS soldiers had this "mark of Cain"). But he could speak fluent French and this helped Löwy convince his captors to treat him well.

Löwy said that during the war he knew more about the Holocaust than most but not in the detail given today. When he served in the SS, his comrades often said that it was good to get rid of the Jews, but most, in his opinion, did not know how the Nazis murdered them.

After the war, he found out the Nazis had deported his father with his family from Vienna to Minsk, where they died. Luckily, his mother and her family survived in Switzerland. "I felt horrible about my situation but my family was glad I had stayed alive," he said. "I wasn't ashamed of how I endured and haven't kept it a secret from my family. Yet there are some who didn't understand it and were upset, but not my mother," he continued. "She was a typical Jewish mother and thought I was the best person in the world." One day Löwy met a Jewish man who said it would have been better had Löwy died in the camps rather than having served in the Waffen-SS. Löwy told him he was "talking like Hitler, who said the only good Jew is a dead Jew. I didn't go to the camps and thus I survived." He did not feel guilty for his service in the Waffen-SS because it saved him from dying in Auschwitz. "I wanted to survive," he said, "and nothing else." And Löwy's opinion seems to be grounded in the Talmud: "He who sees a way to live and takes it not is like a man who sows but does not reap, like a woman who gives birth to children and then buries them."[26] Philosopher Immanuel Kant further states that "it is a duty to preserve one's life and moreover everyone has a direct inclination to do so."[27]

Obviously, troubling problems arise with this type of reasoning. In coming to terms with his survival, Löwy rationalized that it was acceptable to kill several people in combat in order to preserve his own life, and during the process he had a small role in defending the Reich and prolonging the Holocaust. However, his response to anyone critical of his Waffen-SS service was "What else could I have done?"

At the time he was interviewed, Löwy participated in the Jewish

Community Center in Munich. He celebrated some Jewish rituals and hoped Kaddish (the Jewish prayer for the dead) would be said for him after he died. Yet he said he did not believe in God. "If there's a God," Löwy asked, "then why does he let so many horrible things happen?" He loved Israel and said that whatever Israel does is correct. "I'm in body and soul an Israeli, but I wouldn't want to live in Israel." He quickly added, "Too much terror and destruction."

After talking about the pandemonium in the Middle East, Löwy said he did not have much hope for humanity. To correct the problems in the Middle East, he believed, fanatical Islam needs to be eradicated from the earth. "Hitler would've done humanity a service had he exterminated all the Islamic fanatics. History books would praise him today for such acts had he only done so," said Löwy.

After 1945, Löwy experienced some anti-Semitism. When he left a girlfriend in Salzburg for another woman in the 1960s, she yelled at him out the window, "You dirty Jew, get away from here." Later, when they talked on the phone and he tried to calm her down, she replied, "I hate you. The world hates all of you." He complained that anti-Semitism in Austria was much stronger than in Germany. "That's why most of the SS–Death's Head officers who ran the extermination camps were Austrian. Hitler was, of course, Austrian. The Holocaust was done by the Austrians. The Holocaust couldn't have happened without Austria. This tiny land of eight million people has given history so much material to work with," Löwy said.

In 2001, Löwy died. Kaddish was not spoken at his graveside.

Löwy's testimony is rich in paradoxes. Löwy's family, like that of Arno Spitz, moved around searching for anonymity but ultimately failed in this. Like Spitz, Löwy adopted the philosophy that he should not do too much or too little in the military although, ironically, both men were highly decorated. Löwy illustrates the lives of many documented here in how they struggle with others in trying to get them to accept their service, which, especially in Löwy's case, seems to have been why they survived Hitler. Furthermore, he never resolved to his satisfaction his battle with his own identity. The German poet Goethe seems to sum up Löwy's life when he has Faust say:

Two souls alas! are dwelling in my breast;
And each is fain to leave its brother.
The one, fast clinging, to the world adheres
With clutching organs, in love's sturdy lust;
The other strongly lifts itself from dust
To yonder high, ancestral spheres.[28]

It indeed seemed that Karl-Heinz Löwy's breast did have "two souls." His ex-wife supports this claim when she says his entire life was a mystery to her and he always lived with two faces and two lives.[29]

Jewish Lieutenant Paul-Ludwig (Pinchas) Hirschfeld

Paul-Ludwig (Pinchas) Hirschfeld would have liked to live a different life. While serving tea at his home, he apologized that he did not have more to offer, but this was all he could afford with his pension. If not for the Nazis, he explained, he would have built up a large fortune and been more successful at whatever job he would have done. During our conversation, he often referred to God and his relationship with Him and how much Judaism means to him today. His deep, soft voice penetrated the room and when he laughed, his large, rather plump frame would shake. Yet, in general, his mood was often sad.

Hirschfeld, one of five children, was born to Jewish parents on 29 December 1914 in Kleinkonitz in the region of Konitz in West Prussia. His family raised him as a religious Jew. In the climate of anti-Semitism at that time, some of his Jewish relatives converted to Christianity. They did so mainly to escape persecution and believed better opportunities awaited them as Christians. But his parents disapproved of "opportunistic" conversion and believed it cowardly. Hirschfeld's father told him never to feel ashamed of being Jewish. "Anti-Semitism," he said, "will always be around."

Hirschfeld had a fairly normal upbringing until his father died in the late 1920s. Thereafter the family struggled financially. Before the last year of high school, one of his teachers advised him to leave Germany. Hitler had taken power and Hirschfeld's future looked bleak. Hirschfeld felt that to have a free life he had to live anonymously.

The author with Paul-Ludwig (Pinchas) Hirschfeld walking in a military cemetery for U.S. veterans outside Hanover in 1996. (Photo credit: Ian Jones)

In 1935, he moved to Allenstein in East Prussia, registered himself as *gottgläubig* (a believer in God without religious affiliation), and severed contact with his family. Then he forged his *Ahnenpass* ("ancestors' passport," a Nazi document proving Aryan ancestry) and entered the infantry. Many Jews used this tactic to protect themselves.

At his medical examination, although he had to stand nude in front of army doctors, his circumcision did not become an issue. Armed with the story of having had an infection as a child, he never had to use it. They passed him and he entered boot camp. He worried that someone from his hometown might recognize him there, but that did not happen.

Questioned as to why he chose to serve, Hirschfeld answered that if he had remained a Jew in Germany, the Nazis would have deported him to a camp. He felt the army provided the best protection. "Inside, though, I remained a Jew. My service was strictly my way to survive," he said.

After completion of boot camp, he entered the reserves and returned to school. In 1936, he received his *Abitur* at the Lessing Gymnasium in Stolp, Pomerania. Thereafter, he looked for work.

When asked what he thought about Hitler, Hirschfeld said, "As a Jew, I hated Hitler, but I have to respect some of the things he did . . . He had a smart mind and accomplished many things for the economy and especially for the new armed forces. People often forget that Hitler had some good characteristics. Do you think the Germans would have followed a completely evil, deranged madman? No, he wasn't all bad." Hirschfeld's opinion of Hitler reflects that of most Jews and *Mischlinge* documented in this study.

From 1937 until 1939, Hirschfeld worked as a graphic designer in Stolp. When war looked like a distinct possibility in 1939, the army recalled him to active duty. He served as a cartographer and draftsman on the staff of Infantry Regiment 374. In 1943, he became an Oberfeldwebel (technical sergeant) and in May 1944, he became an officer, a position he was proud to attain. He then served as the regimental aide with the Ninety-fourth Kalmücken Grenadier Regiment, a unit on the eastern front.

Hirschfeld said he was a good officer. According to him, on several occasions, he maneuvered his company into positions that protected it from Russian attacks. For his performance, he received the War Merit Cross with Swords Second Class. "They called me the 'Wise Jew' because of my ability to second-guess the Soviets. If they'd only known!" Hirschfeld said. He also received the Wound Badge. He is proud of his military accomplishments and believes God placed him in the army to help other Jews.

"Where my unit marched east into Lithuania, Latvia, and Russia, I often secretly gave Jews rounded up by the SS and Military Police *Passierscheine* (special passes) so they could get food and travel home. I did more for those persecuted Jews than Jews who ran away to foreign countries!" Hirschfeld strongly asserted. He said that he also gave food to starving Jewish children in a Russian village. The opportunities to help Jews gave his service added significance. "It was easy for other Jews to leave Germany and not do anything for those not rich enough to buy their way out," Hirschfeld said, echoing an argument that others also

Lieutenant Paul-Ludwig (Pinchas) Hirschfeld. (Military awards: Wound Badge, War Merit Cross Second Class with Swords, and Sharp-Shooter Badge)

used to explain the value of their military service. "I stayed and did what I could from within the Wehrmacht. Jews today don't understand this. One day, when I was at a Jewish conference in Bonn in the 1980s, I met another Orthodox Jew who had been an officer. He agreed with me that we did more for fellow Jews by staying in the Wehrmacht than we could have done had we fled to an Allied country."

When asked if he knew other Jews who served in the military besides the officer at the conference, he said, "Of course." His cousin Heinz Dommack died in the army during the battle of Berlin in 1945. He claims that he knew a few other educated Jews who avoided concentration

Paul-Ludwig (Pinchas) Hirschfeld holding his War Merit Cross Second Class with Swords in a military cemetery outside Hanover, 1996. (Photo credit: Ian Jones)

camps by changing their religion, falsifying their documents, and serving as officers. One was a lieutenant and the other was a major, Georg-Wilhelm Ohm, who worked in the Luftwaffe's research department in Berlin. Hirschfeld believes that Hermann Göring helped protect several *Mischlinge* and Jews serving in the air force. "Back then a person in uniform in Germany was safe. Who could present himself as a Jew at that time? No one! So they carried their Jewish secret around with them and didn't share it with anybody," Hirschfeld said.

On the topic of guilt, Hirschfeld explained, "Wehrmacht service was my salvation. My brother and sister and her children and husband all died in the Holocaust." At this point, Hirschfeld stopped, choked with emotion, tears streaming down his face. He did witness Jews doing forced labor, and that pained his heart, but he was powerless to do anything. He never felt guilty for what he did, but only for what he was not able to do, like help those Jews he witnessed in need.

Paul-Ludwig (Pinchas) Hirschfeld, in his NCO uniform, with Ruth Loeper on their wedding day in 1943.

"What could I have done?" he continued. "Go to the Gestapo and say that I was an officer and they should protect those Jews, and by the way, also my family? I wasn't stupid. That would've been my death. I did what I thought I needed to do to survive. In 1943, I was able to save my Jewish fiancée, Ruth Loeper. We falsified her documents and married. In 1944, we had our first child, Paul Nathan." Hirschfeld then showed pictures of his wedding, at which he wore his dress uniform, and said sarcastically, "It was probably the only Jewish wedding of a Wehrmacht member."

Hirschfeld claimed that while serving, he retained his Jewish faith as best he could by reciting the Shema every day and saying other prayers when he could. On several occasions, he believes, God spoke to him directly and saved his life.

One time, outside of Leningrad, he and twelve comrades looked for shelter from the dreadful cold of −30 degrees Fahrenheit. They found an old shack and entered it to get warm. In the distance, the sound of machine-gun fire echoed among the trees. After some minutes, he heard his name twice. At first, he thought he had imagined it. Then, thinking an officer had called, he ran outside and announced his name and rank in military fashion. But no one was there. He shouted, "Hallo, hallo, is someone there?"

Suddenly he felt God wanted him to go to a nearby hill, and he obeyed. "As I walked away, I heard a loud, piercing scream shoot through the air as an artillery round slammed into the shack. You know you are safe if you can hear the shriek of an incoming shell, because projectiles seem to travel about the speed of sound—that means the one I heard had passed me by. However, my comrades weren't as lucky. The shell killed them in an eruption of flames. I thanked God for saving my life and prayed the Shema," Hirschfeld said.

"Another time," he continued,

> Three officers and I were driving away from some attacking Soviets. Suddenly, God told me to get off the road. I told the driver to stop. He did so. I spotted a road to our right not marked on our map. I directed him to take it. The colleagues argued that this was foolish because they had no idea where that road led. "Our lines lie in the direction we're driving," they said. I told them that I felt strongly about this. If they didn't turn, I would request to leave the car and march back to our lines. Finally, they agreed and we took the alternate route and a few hours later, we arrived safely at our lines. My comrades were angry because they felt I had wasted valuable time by taking this longer route. Later, we heard the Russians killed several Germans on the road we had originally planned to take. The Soviets had outflanked us with tanks and machine guns. We would've died had we not taken the detour. God saved me again.

Reflecting upon how closely death followed him, Hirschfeld said he thought it would have been a tragedy for him as a Jew to have died while wearing a German uniform and then buried according to Christian ritual. He was happy to have survived for many reasons.

He felt glad to have saved his comrades, many of whom were close friends. Even after 1945, he felt warmly toward them. When he met Furst Ausberg on the street after the war, having not seen him for years, they "hugged each other like brothers." This type of relationship with former non-Jewish comrades has proven difficult for many today to understand, but Hirschfeld's experience mirrors others documented in this study.

Hirschfeld finished this story with a sigh. While "serving Hitler," he did his best not to forget "who he was." After the war, he again became an Orthodox Jew. Since he had lost his identification documents during the war, he had to "prove" he was Jewish. He had to take classes and go through a ceremonial "second circumcision," where a doctor drew a small amount of blood from his penis to confirm his identity according to Jewish law. Eventually Rabbi Lehrmann, Jewish authority for the Hanover region, took Hirschfeld and his family through all the ceremonies necessary to be Jewish and then the community accepted him. In his documents, his name is now Pinchas Ben Elasar.

Questioned about his knowledge of the Holocaust, he said, "I knew nothing at the time. I did know that some Jews were being killed or sent to concentration camps, but I never knew the Nazis had decided to systematically murder millions."

Hirschfeld's wife, Ruth, agreed. "No. It was impossible to know. We at home lived a sheltered life. We couldn't have known."

Hirschfeld had many things on his mind during the Third Reich. Besides being uprooted from their homes and traumatized by the Nazis, he and his wife suffered personal tragedies. They lost two babies during the war, one to birth problems and the other to starvation at the end of the hostilities in 1945.

After 1945, Hirschfeld became a businessman. The last time he was interviewed for this study, he described a vision from God that he hoped would come true. While he was standing in a synagogue praying, "A cloud engulfs me. I cannot see anyone. Then in front of me, I see the form of a man. It's God and he says, 'I have blessed you and made you part of the priestly caste.' Then a large angel comes down and says, 'You've heard what God has said. You still have much to do and I'll always be with you.' Then the angel and God disappeared and I once again see the synagogue." Hirschfeld smiled. "God allowed me to survive in the Wehrmacht for a purpose; namely to live for Him."

There are a few Jews who, like Hirschfeld, survived and still believe in God. Orthodox yeshiva student Simon Gossel made his way into the Wehrmacht quite differently from Hirschfeld. After surviving two years in Auschwitz, Gossel was loaded into a boxcar in January 1945 and sent back in the direction of Germany. He was in poor health and it was brutally cold. One day, the train stopped and to his amazement, the guards asked for German prisoners to get out of the boxcars. Since he spoke German, he knew he could pretend to be an ethnic German, and God told him to get out. So he did. Soon thereafter, since Germany "was using every man they could for the war effort," he found himself surviving as a soldier. Although he was circumcised and had the Auschwitz tattoo, he lived. Describing his situation, he quoted from Habakkuk chapter 3: "I heard and my heart pounded, my lips quivered at the sound; decay crept into my bones, and my legs trembled . . . yet I will rejoice in the Lord . . . my Savior." He went on to paraphrase Psalm 23: "I walked through the shadow of death. I knew God was with me. He was right there with me." So Hirschfeld was not alone thinking God was with him during his survival, especially in the military, but Hirschfeld and Gossel both feel they are rare for having made it through the Holocaust with their faith intact.[30]

Hirschfeld wanted to live his last years in Jerusalem but died in Hanover in 1997 before he could realize this dream. He grappled with his survival techniques his whole life. He, like Karl-Heinz Löwy and Arno Spitz, tried to disappear into society by moving from his hometown to other cities. Yet, once again, this tactic, although giving him a certain degree of anonymity, did not shield him indefinitely from the Nazi military machine. Both Löwy and Hirschfeld felt that by going into the armed forces, they could truly disappear from the Nazis.

Hirschfeld, unlike most in this study, who have rejected God, strongly felt the presence of God during his time under Hitler. He believed the Almighty guided his actions and ensured his survival. His belief in God helped him deal with his past. When asked why God saved him and did not help save 6 million other Jews in Europe, Hirschfeld drew a blank face and said that sometimes God's actions cannot be explained.

Quarter-Jewish Captain Horst von Oppenfeld

At the time he was interviewed, Horst von Oppenfeld was a sophisticated, retired businessman. Although over ninety, he moved with great

Quarter-Jewish Captain Horst von Oppenfeld. He was Klaus von Stauffenberg's adjutant in Africa. (Military awards: EKI, EKII, Panzer Assault Badge in Silver, and Wound Badge)

energy. His expressive, clear blue eyes were keenly aware of his surroundings and he took his time answering questions. He enjoyed the company of women and had been quite the player when young. Though he wanted to contribute to this research, he often seemed uncomfortable talking about his life during the Nazi years and how he dealt with his Jewish background.

Oppenfeld was born in Berlin on 16 July 1913. A descendant of the distinguished Jewish Oppenheim family, he was raised on an estate in eastern Germany. His Jewish grandfather, a banker, had changed his name to Oppenfeld when he married an aristocratic, gentile woman. At that time, he decided to give up banking and become a farmer. Oppenfeld's ancestry is complicated. He was at least a quarter-Jew and possibly a half-Jew. He had Jewish ancestry through both parents, but stated that, among his relatives, it was taboo to talk about it. He never discovered how Jewish he was and even late in life did not care to know.

During World War I, Oppenfeld's father, Rittmeister (cavalry captain) Moritz von Oppenfeld, served as the agricultural and food security advisor to Field Marshal Paul von Hindenburg and General Erich Ludendorff. After the war, Oppenfeld's father took part in agricultural politics during the Weimar Republic.

As a boy, Oppenfeld wanted to become a farmer, and his father promised him one of his family's estates north of Stettin, the capital of Pomerania. In preparation for this, when Oppenfeld turned eleven, his parents sent him to a Prussian boarding school from which, after seven years, he received his *Abitur* in 1932. Most of his classmates went on to the university, but Oppenfeld decided to start farming and began a two-year apprenticeship on a homestead near his father's relatives.

Immediately before and soon after the Nazis took power, Oppenfeld felt shocked when local Nazis beat up citizens voting for the opposition. They also threatened people visiting Jewish shops. His family's dentists, a Jewish father-and-son team who were both war veterans, were forced to close their practice. They emigrated. Experienced, highly respected officials in local government were replaced by Nazis. The Nazis jailed church leaders and political opponents. "The Nazis ruined our society," Oppenfeld said. He also felt nervous after 1933 because he did not know how the Nazis would treat him and his family when their Jewish background became known.

To protect himself and family and to serve his country, Oppenfeld started at this time to serve in the Black Reichswehr (military units providing training in violation of the Versailles Treaty). Since the treaty had restricted the official Reichswehr to 100,000 men, having these secret units helped strengthen its ranks. In 1934, a visiting army sergeant asked for volunteers for military training. Oppenfeld joined. Army life had always fascinated him. He also wanted to continue his family's military tradition and felt the army was devoid of Nazi ideology. Following a two-week exercise, Oppenfeld enrolled for eighteen months of training.

In April 1934, he was assigned to a reconnaissance unit outfitted on motorcycles. They learned how to locate the enemy and quickly gather information for trailing troops. Soon, Oppenfeld had to swear an oath of allegiance to Hitler. He did not like this but complied. The powers of conformity were strong.

Although army life was demanding, the discipline and *esprit de corps* were excellent. The army equipped Oppenfeld's unit with BMW motorcycles. "Handling them was a great sport. What young man . . . wouldn't have enjoyed it?" he said.

After boot camp in October 1935, Oppenfeld entered the reserves. He then returned to his farm and every few months the army called him up for a few weeks of training.

Being "young and politically naive," Oppenfeld admitted, he identified with some of Hitler's policies. He respected how Hitler put thousands back to work with his *Autobahn* project. He admired Hitler when, in 1935, he flouted the Versailles Treaty and expanded the Wehrmacht. But Oppenfeld disapproved of the Nazis crushing political opposition, abolishing democratic institutions, and pressuring civilians to join the Nazi Party.

The only time Oppenfeld had to concern himself with his ancestry was in 1938 when someone denounced him. He had to go to a Wehrkreis (military district) officer in Stettin to explain his ancestry. When the official, a World War I veteran, saw that his father and three brothers had served in the war and that two of them had died in action, the official said "*Unsinn*" (nonsense), closed his file, and dismissed him. The subject of Oppenfeld's ancestry never arose again. He probably remained in the army either because he continued to fall under the Hindenburg exemptions to the military racial regulations of the *Arierparagraph* (Aryan Paragraph), which permitted service by non-Aryans who had served in World War I or had close relatives who had served, or because someone was protecting him.[31]

In 1938 his parents, pleased with Oppenfeld's talent, entrusted him with managing the estate he was to inherit. However, he had to give up this life when war started in 1939. In August of that year, he returned to active duty and never worked his farm again.

Oppenfeld returned to his unit and traveled to the Polish border. His parents, having already lost two sons in war, "made dire predictions about . . . Hitler's pending venture." After the outbreak of World War I,

Germans had marched to war to the sound of music, decorated with flowers by an elated population. Now Oppenfeld and his fellow soldiers knew the reality of war, and they and the population looked upon the coming conflict with foreboding. One of Oppenfeld's father's friends, a noted pre-Hitler politician, told Oppenfeld at the outbreak of war, "This is the end of Germany." Joseph Harsch, a *Christian Science Monitor* correspondent, wrote at the same time that the Germans "were nearer to real panic on 1 September 1939 than the people of any other European country . . . the German people exhibited more real fear of [the war] than the others. They faced it in something approaching abject horror."[32] Nonetheless, the Germans went to war and prosecuted it well.

Under the advance of Hitler's Blitzkrieg strategy, the poorly organized and ill-equipped Polish troops disintegrated. Oppenfeld's battalion drove deep into enemy territory and advanced beyond the Polish city of Brest-Litovsk, where Russia had signed a peace treaty with Germany in 1918. The war soon would come to an end.

The success of the Blitzkrieg style of attack on Poland encouraged Hitler soon thereafter to invade France, an enemy that had successfully resisted Germany for four years during World War I. For over eight months after the defeat of Poland in September 1939, during the so-called Phony War, or *Sitzkrieg* (sitting war), Oppenfeld's battalion waited behind Germany's western border along with 2 million other Germans.[33]

After several false alarms and a record cold winter in Europe, Hitler ordered his legions to roll west through the Ardennes into neutral Luxembourg on 10 May 1940. Oppenfeld's Panzer division came under the command of General Heinz Guderian, who, according to Oppenfeld, "had perceived the strategy of deep penetration with armored force." With Luftwaffe support, Guderian broke through north of the French fixed defenses known as the Maginot Line and crossed the Meuse River near Sedan. Oppenfeld was right in the middle of it.

Guderian continued to push his Panzer divisions on to Calais, taking hundreds of thousands of prisoners. Miraculously, as the advance slowed down because Hitler had issued a "halt" order to his armor, the British mobilized a fleet of naval and civilian ships to evacuate most of their forces and many French at the port of Dunkirk. This kept more than 300,000 Allied soldiers from falling into German hands. Meanwhile, although the French had regrouped their forces, they were unable to prevent the fall of Paris. Totally defeated, the French general Alphonse Joseph Georges threw himself in a chair and cried.[34] Only weeks after the invasion had started, France surrendered.

Oppenfeld and his men moved to the new Polish/Russian border, where on 22 June 1941, they, along with 3.5 million other German soldiers, invaded the Soviet Union.[35] His battalion headed straight toward the Russian capital, Moscow. Barbarossa, as Hitler had named the invasion, took Soviet leader Joseph Stalin by surprise. Hundred of thousands of Russians fell into German hands. In the battle around Kiev, for example, over 600,000 Soviet troops surrendered.[36] By the beginning of July, Oppenfeld's unit had advanced 600 miles, just 150 miles short of the capital. "With the experience of hindsight, it's easy to conclude that this was the apex of Hitler's glory," Oppenfeld said.

Oppenfeld described how eager many captured Russians were to fight with Germany against Stalin, as they hated him for his brutality. "Little did they know that Hitler was no better," Oppenfeld commented. Most were not allowed to fight for Germany because, as Oppenfeld believes, Hitler did not want Slavs serving in the Wehrmacht.

Many Russian civilians initially welcomed Oppenfeld and his men. Several hated Stalin and despised his "murderous political institution." In the Ukraine, civilians presented the Germans "with platters of salt and bread as an offering of welcome as we passed through villages."[37] However, once the Nazis treated the population brutally, the partisan movement sprang up. "The more the German army advanced, the more they defeated and captured enemy forces, and the more brutal Germany's efforts were to subdue an enemy that did not recognize defeat, the tougher and more desperate Soviet resistance became . . . The strategy of racist war permeated every aspect of the struggle . . . strengthening the resolve of the Soviet people and . . . [uniting] them under an all-Russian banner."[38]

In September 1941, Oppenfeld and his unit broke through some defenses deep in Russia until the rainy season turned roads into a quagmire. The highway to Moscow had no hard surface and disintegrated into muddy slush under the heavy downpours. Whole divisions ground to a stop. Thousands of horses died of overexertion and guns and vehicles sank deep into the mud. Soldiers went for days without rations and their leather boots either fell to pieces after being soaked so long or were simply "lost in the mire."[39] The never-ending mud inspired "the sardonic joke about the man who is startled to discover a human face in the mud; the face tells him, 'You'll be even more surprised when you learn that I'm sitting on a horse and riding.'"[40]

Oppenfeld and his men had to wait until a hard freeze to start advancing again and this didn't happen until October. After the freeze, they advanced again, penetrated several miles deeper, and eventually reached Moscow's suburbs by December. Now instead of battling the mud, they had to fight the cold.

The exceptionally low temperatures caused problems for the Germans, who still wore their summer uniforms with raincoats rather than winter jackets. The weather also adversely affected their equipment. They kept their tanks running all night because the cooling fluid became useless when the temperatures dropped to −30 degrees Fahrenheit. One soldier described the time he spent in Russia as a "perpetual shivering fit."[41] The Germans often obtained winter clothing by taking it off dead Russians.[42] Oppenfeld joked that "in September it was 'General Mud,' now 'General Winter' was stopping our advance." He felt he would soon die, if not from a Russian bullet, then from the elements.

The Germans also had to contend with Russia's surprise, their new tank, the T-34, which resisted the antitank guns Oppenfeld's men had. The cannons could not penetrate the sloped, thick armor. Moreover, the Russians had 14,000 tanks. This was 4,000 more than what the Germans had expected.[43] Hitler had expressed to General Guderian his regret at not heeding the general's warnings of Soviet production, saying, "Had I known they had as many tanks as that, I would have thought twice before invading."[44]

During the first week of December, the Russians, who were better prepared for the winter, launched a counteroffensive. The attack took Oppenfeld and his men by surprise and they retreated, leaving much of their equipment behind. Like most retreating armies, they suffered heavy casualties as they moved to the rear echelons.

Questioned about atrocities, Oppenfeld recalled how the German army mistreated thousands of half-naked and starved Russian POWs. He saw how German guards executed many who, because of sickness or injuries, could no longer walk. "This was no way to treat POWs, but I could do nothing," Oppenfeld said.

Over 3.3 million of a total 5.7 million Russian POWs died in German camps. The Nazis treated them horribly and the prisoners often were put into concentration camps without food and water. A cynical German soldier described a horrible scene: "When we [threw them a dead dog] there followed a spectacle that could make a man puke. Yelling like mad, the Russians would fall on the animal and tear it to pieces with their bare hands . . . The intestines they'd stuff in their pockets—a sort of iron ration." Often there was no food, so cannibalism became common. A German said that once he witnessed among a brawling group of Russians one man awkwardly waving his arm high in the air. To his horror, the German realized it was just an arm and that the group was fighting over who would eat it. Head of the Luftwaffe Hermann Göring cynically said to the Italian foreign minister Count Galeazzo Ciano about Soviet POWs, "After having eaten everything possible, including the soles of their boots, they have begun to eat each other and, what is more serious . . . a German sentry." The Germans allowed such atrocities because, as historian Omer Bartov wrote, they had come to "believe the murders they were ordered to carry out were an unavoidable existential and moral necessity" against the evil Soviet hordes.[45]

Often in the Nazi-run POW camps for Soviets, the dead would lie in the same place for weeks. The epidemics were so horrible that no German guard would enter the camps without a flamethrower, which, "in the interest of 'hygiene,'" he would use to set alight the dying and dead "on their beds of verminous rags."[46]

In May 1942, after eleven months in Russia, the military sent Oppenfeld's division to France to recuperate. "Leaving Russia was like a gift from God," Oppenfeld said. For his brave acts during the Russian campaign, the army gave Oppenfeld a company command and awarded him the Iron Cross First Class. He received this medal for protecting several wounded men and not allowing them to fall into enemy hands.

While in France, Oppenfeld and his subordinates trained replacements; received new weapons, equipment, and vehicles; and enjoyed their time away from combat. Soon, though, the Wehrmacht sent them to North Africa to support Rommel's Afrika Korps.

The British had already defeated Rommel in Egypt and at El Alamein, Libya, at the time Oppenfeld and his men flew to Tunis in sluggish JU 52 transports. The planes had no guns, so Oppenfeld and his men opened the plane's windows and fired their machine guns at enemy aircraft. "What a ridiculous defense concept against fast, heavily armed British Spitfires!" Oppenfeld remarked.

When Oppenfeld arrived in the desert, a hopeless situation faced him. The Afrika Korps lacked ammunition, gasoline, and food supplies, and Rommel stood on his last leg. Oppenfeld did not think the army would survive long.

In January 1943, Oppenfeld's father died. Granted leave to attend the funeral, Oppenfeld flew from North Africa to Italy and then traveled by train from Naples to Germany. During that time, he heard Field Marshal Friedrich von Paulus had surrendered the Sixth Army at Stalingrad and thought Germany would now lose the war. After this massive defeat, Oppenfeld observed a profoundly depressed population. In February, Oppenfeld returned to his company in Africa.

During the closing months of war in North Africa, Oppenfeld's responsibilities changed drastically. He had to give up his company and became the adjutant of the Tenth Panzer Division's leading staff officer, Lieutenant Colonel Klaus Count von Stauffenberg. Oppenfeld respected Stauffenberg for his professional brilliance and gentlemanly behavior. They set up their headquarters in a captured British bus with their desks next to each other. Although Oppenfeld had no credentials for this job and made mistakes, Stauffenberg treated him respectfully. He served only six weeks under Stauffenberg, a leader of the plot to kill Hitler in 1944. Then events in Oppenfeld's life took yet another turn. During a tense battle, Stauffenberg lost one eye, one arm, and two fingers of the remaining hand. He was given first aid and sent to a hospital by plane. Oppenfeld never saw him again.

Oppenfeld says of Stauffenberg, "I feel privileged to have been the aide to Stauffenberg, the officer, the citizen, the human being, and a role model *par excellence*. Had he survived the coup, he might have become not only a military but also a political leader of postwar Germany."

Soon after Stauffenberg's departure, Oppenfeld fell into enemy hands. At that time, the Afrika Korps had hardly any supplies and the end was in sight. The Tenth Panzer Division commander, General Friedrich (Fritz) Freiherr von Broich, had just attended the last meeting of commanding officers. He told Oppenfeld: "Our Supreme commander, General [Hans-Jürgen] von Arnim, told us, 'Hitler threatened me not to surrender the Afrika Korps. Mind you, he didn't say that to you. So, use your own judgment and keep in mind the welfare of your units.' Let us tie a white shirt to the end of my carbine, Horst, then take a motorbike and drive me to the English." Oppenfeld obeyed. The British accepted the surrender "without the slightest intent to humiliate the Germans," and Oppenfeld became a POW.

Oppenfeld was transported to the United States, where he would remain a POW in the Midwest, a few miles from Concordia, Kansas, until the war's end. As a POW, Oppenfeld said he became so impressed with America that he wanted to live there. He had nothing to return to in Germany because his farm had been expropriated by the Russians and Germany lay in ruins. Later on, he came to the United States, where he studied and worked as a World Bank agricultural economist.

When asked about his awareness of the Holocaust, Oppenfeld took a deep breath and shook his head. "I knew things weren't good for Jews and that I needed to be careful . . . but I never thought they were gassing people." One day, far behind the fighting, Oppenfeld heard machine-gun fire and inquired of some soldiers of a construction battalion, "Are there partisans here?" "No," they answered, "don't you know what's going on here? Last night SS police surrounded this town, identified and segregated all Jews—men, women, and children. Over there they made them dig a deep ditch, shot and buried them." When Oppenfeld expressed his skepticism, one of the soldiers said, "Look at these horse-drawn wagons, loaded with the shoes of the poor killed people." Oppenfeld and his men, who had never heard about such crimes, were horrified. When asked why he did not try to stop it, Oppenfeld claimed that he "lived for the day and didn't pay much attention to all of it." Many, like Oppenfeld, quickly adapted to their surroundings and did what was expected of them.

When asked whether he felt Jewish, Oppenfeld said he did not. "I had no contact with Jews. My ancestors who were Jews had converted."

Asked why he thought Jews have had so many problems, he replied that they, especially Orthodox Jews, do not assimilate. "Their problem," he claimed, "is due to the fact that they want to be different—they think they're better than everyone else." The fact his family did not want to remain different "saved [his] life."

When asked if he ever felt guilty about his service, Oppenfeld said no, and then explained he should not feel guilty for serving his country—"It was my duty."

As a Prussian, Oppenfeld was raised with the ethical norm that one remained loyal to the Fatherland no matter what. His service was something he believed was necessary, and he felt that he did not really have another choice.

Most likely, the Nazi propaganda and the horrible events he learned about in Russia did cause Oppenfeld some trauma. Many *Mischlinge*, as well as full Jews, struggle with the fact that they served a regime that oppressed and killed people like them and their relatives. Yet most respond to this fact by asking, "What were my options?" One must keep in mind the existential and the morally prescriptive elements of their decisions.

Like Arno Spitz, Horst Oppenfeld felt his story was boring. And this is important to note. The lives of many *Mischlinge* were influenced by events beyond their control. They were powerless to shape what was happening and thus they felt insignificant and not responsible for many of the situations they found themselves in.

Half-Jewish Unteroffizier Günther Scheffler

Günther Scheffler is a man of slender build, yet his physique shows that he was an athlete when younger. In fact, he played field hockey for years. He believes his conditioning helped ensure his survival during World War II. Often he explains that he feels amazed that he survived the war. He can give "sixty reasons" why he should have died but has a difficult time finding one why he ultimately survived. He thinks that he has had more luck than anyone else on the planet. During the interview, he sat close to his wife, whom he clearly cherishes. Scheffler feels content with his life.

Born on 4 April 1918 in Kiel, he was the youngest of three sons. His

Half-Jew Günther
Scheffler (last rank
Unteroffizier).
(Military awards: EKI,
EKII, Campaign
Medal, and Wound
Badge)

father, Max, was a gentile from a hard-working family of six children. Scheffler's Jewish mother Helena (née Weiss) came from Königsberg. She worked as a talented pianist, giving lessons before she married. Scheffler's maternal grandfather, Julius, a successful entrepreneur, had converted to Christianity to help his business, and had five children with his wife, Cäsilia, also a gifted pianist. When her daughter Helena married Max Scheffler, Cäsilia converted to Christianity to protect the family from problems.

Many German Jews converted to Christianity starting in the eighteenth century. They frequently did so not out of religious conviction, but to better their lot in a society that was increasingly prejudiced. As with many religious people, they accepted a faith not because they wanted to live it, but because they desired for others to perceive them in a positive light. Most joined the majority to avoid the effort it took to remain part of a minority.

Scheffler's Jewish family also had a strong military tradition. One of his mother's brothers volunteered for service in 1914 and became an officer. The other brother died in battle in World War I. Yet, until Hitler came into power, Scheffler did not know about his Jewish background, and no one bothered his family about it.

Scheffler had a normal childhood, and his parents raised him in the Protestant tradition. They prayed both before and after dinner and often attended church, particularly when his gentile grandmother Ursula visited. But Scheffler and his brothers disliked their paternal grandmother's insistence on religious observance and good manners. They called her "*die Hexe*" (the witch).

When Hitler came to power in 1933, Scheffler learned about his mother's background and his family started to worry. "I felt horrible to discover I was half-Jewish. It embarrassed and confused me," Scheffler said. "You heard how bad the Jews were and I became insecure. I felt that we were second-class people." When Scheffler had to enter the Hitler Youth in 1934, he discussed his application with his father. He encouraged Scheffler to insert "Stein" instead of "Goldstein" for his grandmother Cäsilia. He did so and nobody asked him about it. "My family tree then looked quite Aryan," Scheffler said, smiling. He enjoyed the Hitler Youth with its camping activities and war games.

In 1935, the Nazis issued the Nuremberg Laws, which prohibited Scheffler and his brothers from marrying Aryans and pursuing certain jobs. His family discussed leaving Germany, but they had neither the money for such a move nor relatives abroad for support. Yet other relatives did move. A Jewish cousin emigrated to Israel with her family.

In school, Scheffler lived in fear that someone knew about his Jewish past. One day, his teacher asked if anyone had Jewish ancestors. Since his mother and Jewish grandparents had converted, Scheffler felt they were technically not Jewish and remained quiet. The issue was not discussed again.

In 1936, Scheffler noted that before and after the Olympics, the Nazis dramatically toned down their persecution of Jews. "Store signs discouraging Jews from entering were taken down. I felt life might return to normal," he said. Hitler had actually ordered that such anti-Semitic posters be removed. "Hitler could afford to bide his time in dealing with the Jews."[47] However, several months after the Olympics, the signs returned and the persecution increased.

In 1937, Scheffler finished high school and started working for Siemens. Also in that year his parents divorced. His father became a Nazi and distanced himself from his "Jewish family." He worried that, because of his Jewish wife, he might lose the business he had inherited from his Jewish father-in-law. He even complained in front of his wife and children that his greatest mistake was marrying a Jew and acquiring three "Jewish" sons to support. Scheffler's mother felt so distraught by her husband's mistreatment that she tried to commit suicide by drowning herself.

Even though Scheffler's father held on to his business, he seems to have had problems keeping it solvent. Eventually he had to find other work. Ironically, Max had been a World War I comrade of the half-Jew Erhard Milch, who helped him get a job. In 1944, the Luftwaffe needed people, so Milch, now a field marshal, reactivated Max as a major, and he served at Luftwaffe headquarters in Berlin.

When asked how he knew Milch was a "half-Jew," Scheffler said, "We all knew back then. I continually heard jokes about it and everyone knew that Hitler had declared him an honorary 'Aryan.' Hitler could decide who was Jewish and who wasn't."

Scheffler remained at Siemens until drafted into an artillery battery in Potsdam in December 1939. He hid his ancestry and remained in the army although he had mixed feelings about his service. On the one hand, he wanted to serve because it allowed him to be like everyone else and possibly protect his family. On the other hand, he hoped Hitler would lose the war because this would give him a life free of discrimination. He knew that only a German defeat could rid him of Hitler. "I felt torn in many ways back then. Not only were we half-castes split by the Nazi racial laws, but also the whole situation split our souls," Scheffler said. Many *Mischlinge* felt divided between loyalty to their nation and hatred toward the government in control of their country that persecuted them. Consequently, the Nazis actually forced them to come to terms with their Jewishness. Many developed an attachment to the origins of a loved one—in Scheffler's case, it was his mother. They had to struggle with questions of identity.

Scheffler did his best to perform his duty as a soldier and hoped thereby to protect his mother. In 1940, he became a member of the 193rd Artillery Regiment in the Saarland. After Hitler's decree of April 1940 ousting half-Jews from the Wehrmacht, someone wrote to Scheffler's unit about his ancestry. But his commander ignored this complaint and Scheffler remained in the battery during its attack on France. "It really wasn't a war. The French didn't fight back. We continued to follow retreating troops," he said. When the French war was over, his battery returned to Potsdam.

In summer 1940, the army discharged both of his brothers, Hubertus and Karl-Heinz, because they were half-Jews. At this time, Scheffler's *Spiess* (nickname for first sergeant) asked the battery whether any half-Jews served among them. Scheffler remained quiet. He reasoned that if it became a topic of discussion later, he would simply explain that his Jewish grandparents had converted to Christianity. "I convinced myself that my grandparents weren't Jewish because they converted. I didn't want to admit they were Jewish though I knew it," Scheffler said. His subterfuge kept him in the army. Though his captain eventually found out about his past, he respected Scheffler and retained him, valuing him as a person more than he did the racial laws.

When asked why he thinks his brothers were discharged but he was not, he explained, "They were asked whether they were *Mischlinge*. I was just asked about Jewish grandparents and could honestly rationalize that they were Christians—a small difference—but one I could defend." Yet his Jewish ancestry continued to oppress him like "a large rock on my back." "Today I probably wouldn't have lied," Scheffler continued, "but back then I didn't want to leave, and I really felt it protected my mother."

On leave, he always visited his Jewish mother in uniform. He wanted people to see that she had a soldier son. This was common among *Mischlinge*.

In the invasion of Russia in 1941, Scheffler's battery fought around Leningrad. "I cried during this conflict," Scheffler said. The chilly, wet, and muddy landscape took its toll on his nerves and one night, as he tried to sleep in a pit of mud and icy water, he wept, bemoaning his fate. "Didn't one of America's famous generals say 'War is Hell'? Well, my war was a very cold Hell," Scheffler said.

When Hitler declared war on the United States in December 1941, Scheffler and his comrades knew they would not win. He thought, "How will I be able to get out of this shit alive? I actually continued to fight to survive. I couldn't say, 'I want to go home.' That would have meant my death. The military police would have surely killed me had I tried to desert. We were shot at from the front and from the back." He did admit that he thought about desertion, but said this was not an option on the Russian front. The Soviets did not take prisoners.

By 1942 the Germans had encircled Leningrad. Scheffler was stationed at Kronstadt west of Leningrad, where they bombarded the Russian lines. The Soviets, using outdated tactics, sent waves of soldiers in the attack but the Germans just mowed them down with heavy machine guns. Scheffler remembered men getting their heads blown off and their brains splattered over the ground and the horrible smell coming from unburied bodies. Often, he could see the skin of the dead bubble as the maggots feasted on the flesh in the hot sun. The stench affected soldiers so much in one sector that Russian soldiers sometimes fought with their gas masks on.[48]

In the summer of 1942, while on leave, Scheffler traveled to Munich with his brother Karl-Heinz. During this trip, Scheffler's secret was almost revealed. As military police conducted a document inspection on the train, Scheffler and his brother showed their papers. Scheffler was wearing his uniform but his brother wore civilian clothes. As the official looked through their military passports, he expressed confusion as to why only one of them served. "I worried what would happen if the policeman asked what 'n.z.v.' written in my brother's passport actually meant," Scheffler said. (Standing for nicht zu verwenden [not to be used], "n.z.v." was usually a dead giveaway that one was a half-Jew.) "After we explained it meant that the army had placed him in the reserves, the policeman just smiled and handed our papers back. I had the feeling that he knew but didn't care." Had the policeman wanted to, he could have reported Scheffler for falsifying documents.

Though the Leningrad front remained stable, Scheffler believed the loss at Stalingrad in 1943 proved Hitler would lose the war. In 1943, the Russians pushed the Germans back west and Scheffler's battery started a full retreat. While fighting around Ilmen Lake in 1943, Scheffler was wounded and was sent to Estonia to recuperate. There, he heard that the SS took Jews to large ditches and executed them. However, he thought neither he nor his mother was in danger. "In that climate, you just thought of your survival and did not understand the horror around you. You lived one day to the next," Scheffler said.

But it was also in 1943 that his mother told him the Nazis had deported his eighty-three-year-old Jewish grandmother to Theresienstadt. Ironically, she had earlier received the Nazi "Mother's Cross" for having so many children. "I was sad and angry and didn't understand it. Unfortunately I couldn't help her," Scheffler said.

After two weeks of recuperation, he returned to his unit. By 1944, his company was in Riga. He knew the war would soon end and hoped he would survive. "Yet, I never thought I would really survive. I just asked God to allow me to live one more day after the sun went down," Scheffler said. When asked whether he felt strange serving as a half-Jew, he said he did not think much about it. He knew that this sounds odd today. "I also, in a strange way, took pleasure in proving, secretly of course, that Jewish men were brave warriors." According to Scheffler, he and others felt more concerned about receiving mail, sleeping with girls, and surviving than about philosophizing about the war.

During this time, his commander realized that he could not promote Scheffler to officer because of his Jewish background. Scheffler found this frustrating, but he knew if he tried to become an officer, the Nazis would discover his lie because of the extensive background check the proposed promotion would trigger. Since the officer valued Scheffler and wanted to keep him, he kept him at his current rank. So Scheffler, who had received the Iron Cross Second and First Class, the Eastern Campaign Medal, and the Wound Badge, had to resign himself to remaining the "eternal" Unteroffizier (corporal).

Scheffler had received one of his Iron Crosses during the battle for Stalingrad. His battery, along with several infantry divisions, moved forward between Moscow and Leningrad to draw away enemy units from the southern front. In the deep snow, they fought crack Soviet troops.

Their actions allowed several infantry units to maintain the integrity of the forward lines.

During one battle, the Soviets attacked with a great "Hurrah." "We only had pistols and a few grenades," Scheffler said, "and right before the Russians attacked, our infantry came with their MG 42's [machine guns] and we fired into the lines and killed most of the Russians. The Soviets thought they were going to take over an undefended artillery battery. That day I was a warrior." He described himself not as a hero, but as a person who knew how to get out of the danger and fight effectively.

The Russians often used mass formations to overwhelm the Germans by sheer numbers. Frequently, they had to get drunk on vodka to conduct these operations.[49] Although these tactics were suicidal for the first few waves, most Germans facing such attacks admired the "blind heroism and boldness" of these soldiers "that even a mountain of dead compatriots wouldn't stop. We knew that under such circumstances combat often favors simple numerical superiority . . . we would throw ourselves back into battle to try to drive off the red monster about to devour us."[50]

The sight of the dead troubled Scheffler. He described the pain of seeing comrades sprawled out on a battlefield covered in blood, intestines, bone, and brain matter.

As the war wound down, Scheffler found himself fighting outside the East Prussian port city of Königsberg in 1945. While the Russians overran it, he managed to leave on one of the last ships. The Soviets conquered several port towns in eastern Germany, causing much panic. Mingled in with the fleeing soldiers were civilians and in the commotion, many families became separated. One soldier wrote: "The children were the most heart-wringing. Many were lost. When they tired of calling for their mothers, they collapsed into floods of tears . . . These were the smallest ones, too young to grasp any explanations. Their faces, dabbed with tears which instantly froze, remain one of the most pathetic images of that time."[51] Russian planes would often unmercifully strafe the crowds waiting on the landing docks, killing many.

German soldiers remaining in Königsberg and other Prussian port towns died or spent several years in Soviet POW camps. Scheffler's ship luckily made it to western Germany in May 1945 and soon thereafter, he became a British POW. Six months later the English released him. "I had incredible luck," Scheffler said. "Most of my comrades entered Soviet captivity and did not return." For example, out of around 100,000 Germans sent into Soviet POW camps after Stalingrad, only a few thousand came home after the war.[52]

When asked about his knowledge of the Holocaust, Scheffler said that he did not know about it. He knew that the Nazis persecuted Jews, but that they systematically murdered them lay beyond his awareness. He did know that the Nazis deported people, but nobody spoke about it. However, the details about the Final Solution, according to Scheffler, remained unknown. "People just didn't know that most Jews were being killed," he added. He does not feel guilty for his service and explains that he tried to protect himself and his mother during the war. He was saddened by what happened but did not feel responsible.

Did Scheffler believe he was the only half-Jew in the Wehrmacht? After talking about his two brothers who served, he said that he knew of three other partial Jews who served besides that "famous asshole Field Marshal Milch. Everyone knew he was a half-Jew and he denied his ancestry his whole life." "I had a good friend, Wolfgang Kröncke, who was a quarter-Jew. His grandmother was Jewish and his mother was half-Jewish," Scheffler continued, "and he even became a first lieutenant. He had relatives who were high-ranking officers who protected him. Oh, I also knew about another half-Jew who served—Schwarz. He died in battle in Russia. Another quarter-Jew whom my wife knew was taken prisoner after Stalingrad. His name was Klaus Fichte and her best friend was his sister. But since he was a doctor, he survived his five years in POW camp in Russia due to the better treatment he received." Fichte was a direct descendant of the famous anti-Semitic philosopher Johann Gottlieb Fichte. Of course, Klaus's Jewish ancestry came through his mother's side.

When asked during the interview if he felt Jewish, Scheffler said he did not. His wife added at this point that when they were traveling in Israel, several Orthodox women asked her why they had come. She explained that they had always wanted to see Israel and added that her husband was a half-Jew. "That's interesting," one of the women said, "was his father or mother Jewish?" When Frau Scheffler answered that it was his

Günther and Ursula Scheffler, 1996.

mother, the woman responded that Scheffler was a Jew by Halakah. "That was the first time I ever heard about Jewish Law," Scheffler said. He believed that Jews are the smartest people in the world and was proud of this aspect of his Jewishness, but he did not feel Jewish, "regardless of what some Orthodox Jews believe," he added.

After the defeat of the Nazis, Scheffler felt as if he was born again and had a new life. Once Hitler killed himself, he could live as a free man again. "Hitler misused the nationalism of the Germans. We were taken advantage of," Scheffler said. After 1945, he returned to Siemens and retired in the 1980s.

Many of Scheffler's relatives were not so lucky during the wars. His gentile uncles Georg Scheffler and Willy Scheffler both died in World War I. One "Aryan" cousin, Jobst Scheffler, died in Russia in 1941, and another cousin, Eberhardt Reinecke, died in 1942 as a U-boat officer. One half-Jewish cousin, Annegret Dankwardt, died during an air raid in Berlin. Scheffler ended our conversation saying, "The war taught me never to give up. It also showed me how to survive."

Scheffler's life illustrates how random survival in war can be. He was luckily always in the right place at the right time. Although fifty years had gone by, Scheffler felt a sense of awe at how he made it through it all. His brother Karl-Heinz commented: "After fighting four years in the bloody fields of Russia and escaping the Soviets, who were no better than the Nazis, and then surviving the Fascist pigs we had, I can say a man cannot have more luck than my brother."

Scheffler's story exemplifies how many *Mischlinge* were fighting two wars—one on the battlefields against Germany's enemies and the other at home against the Nazi persecutors of their families and themselves. They experienced incredible burdens of trauma with the "physical hardships, the psychological burden, and the often crushing anxieties of death and killing that constitute the everyday life"[53] of combat while also worrying about their families' and their own persecution at the hands of their countrymen. Jewish and *Mischling* soldiers not only served in the armed forces controlled by a government hostile to them as "racially" inferior beings, but many also witnessed the disappearance and occasionally the death of their relatives. Tragically, the *Mischlinge* had to remain loyal to a regime that was never loyal to them.

Conclusion

The stories of the soldiers in this chapter, whose racial origins remained unknown to the Nazis, illustrate the diverse experiences one could have in the Wehrmacht. Although all except Jacoby experienced combat in World War II, their motivations to fight and their feelings about their participation ranged from service being a grim choice made solely to survive the Nazis, like Löwy, to serving proudly, like Oppenfeld. More importantly, these men demonstrate that the main activity of Wehrmacht personnel was fighting and not killing Jews, a misconception that often is voiced by those with a superficial knowledge of the war and Holocaust. In other words, when people ask, "How could these men serve and kill their relatives?" they display how ignorant they are of the time and people.

When these men discussed the Holocaust, most claimed they did not truly understand what was going on. This is hard to believe because many lost relatives in the *Shoah*. They do admit they should have known more, but ultimately they either repressed what they heard and saw or failed to understand the systematic murder common under Hitler. Many did not want to believe that their fellow citizens did what Hitler had always promised he would do—eradicate the Jewish people. This is a sad testimony to people's inability to understand man's inhumanity to man until it is too late. The majority documented in this chapter learned later how horrible Nazism was, but this knowledge after the fact did those victims little good back then. Yet, their acknowledgment of this and their willingness to discuss their past and pain will help some make a difference in the future. At least, this is their hope.

Looking at their religious convictions, one finds it interesting that six out of the seven finished the war with no belief in God. Most had exposure to religion, both Jewish and Christian, as youths, but World War II and the Holocaust offered them enough proof that God did not exist. As Kopp said, "Plato said only the dead have seen the end of war. Well, I say further that also the dead discover there's no God. Most humans believe in God because they want to live forever. War shows us what a myth this is." Most of the men in this section saw how religion was abused during the Third Reich. Most Christian leaders they knew were moral failures and most Christians around them failed to live according to the creeds of love and kindness. Moreover, some witnessed how their families used religion, both Christian and Jewish, to discriminate against one another, as seen so clearly in Kopp's story. This damning commentary on religion will also be shown later with Friedrich Schlesinger's and Dieter Fischer's biographies. Thus, most in this study had nothing to do with religion after the war.

These men's experiences show how fragile the human condition is. Most of us are swept along by events beyond our power to control. Consequently, most of these men did their best to survive a situation that had turned unforgiving and cruel.

Given the circumstances, these men were lucky not only to survive the war, but also to escape the Holocaust. In one sense, their survival physically and emotionally is more complicated than that of those who survived Auschwitz and other extermination camps. In such a situation, it is difficult to draw the line between the "bad" and "good guys." With Jews and *Mischlinge* serving in the Wehrmacht and even in the Waffen-

SS, knowing where to draw that line remains difficult. Although the men in this chapter did not know about the horrors of the *Shoah* then, today they have had to cope with losing relatives while they served in an armed force controlled by Hitler that helped create an environment for the death machinery. Had the Nazis known about many of these men, they would have "exterminated" them, especially Kopp, Löwy, and Hirsch-feld, who were technically "full Jews" under the Nazis. Although not heavily analyzed during this study, the weight of such issues must have had a strong impact on their lives.

The lessons of these men demonstrate how difficult it is to look at the Third Reich in extremes of black and white. Not every German soldier was a Nazi and not everybody of Jewish descent died in Auschwitz. They also demonstrate that the Wehrmacht had some honorable men among its ranks, especially those who knew about the Jewish backgrounds of their men and still helped them by not divulging this knowledge, as seen with the superiors of Scheffler, Oppenfeld, Jacoby, and Spitz.

These men's stories illustrate that, provided they did not die in combat, the Wehrmacht offered a good hiding place. As a result, the men claim they can live with the fact that they served in this organization even after the facts about the Holocaust became known. Ultimately, these stories show that the survival instinct is strong. These men did the best with the options presented them, which in most cases were few and usually clear-cut if one wanted to continue living.

2

Half-Jews, the Wehrmacht, and OT
Forced Labor Camps

The plight of thousands of half-Jewish men during the Third Reich began for most with military service and ended with forced labor. Although the Third Reich required half-Jews to serve in the Wehrmacht, it still treated them like second-class citizens and persecuted their families. Often while serving, these men would receive news that a father had lost his job, a parent had been put in prison, or a grandparent had committed suicide.

One wonders what many thought when their loved ones were taken away from them either due to suicide or deportation. Many were able to delay and even sometimes prevent the persecution of some relatives because of their military service, but countless other family members did not benefit at all. Ultimately, most relatives were caught in the Nazi net of genocide.

Some men discussed in this chapter would never have survived World War II had they been allowed to serve throughout the deadly Russian campaign. The Nazis had issued discharge orders for men known to the authorities as half-Jews on 8 April 1940, but these men often served throughout late 1940 and into 1941. The cases of Helmuth Kopp and Günther Scheffler (chapter 1); Karl-Arnd Techel and Friedrich Wilhelm Schlesinger, presented in this chapter; and Horst Geitner (chapter 4) illustrate that some half-Jews served well into the war in Russia and even for its entire duration. A small minority—such as the half-Jews Field Marshal Erhard Milch, General Helmut Wilberg, Captain Ernst Prager, and Lance Corporal Dieter Fischer—received official exemptions from Hitler to remain in uniform because of their commendable abilities and service; thus many served throughout the war.

When the army discharged a half-Jew, he returned home and usually found work or continued his studies if he had a distinguished military career. But in 1944, the Nazis imprisoned most discharged half-Jews in Organization Todt (OT) forced labor camps. Some avoided this by going underground or having bosses who retained them as "employees essential to the war effort." Although many had a chance to escape, the majority reported to the deportation centers designated by the Gestapo or local employment offices.

The half-Jews discussed in this chapter display diverse experiences with family dynamics, comrades, superiors, the racial laws, and Jewish identity. Many of the decisions they made reveal not the flexibility of their choices, but their constraints. Had the war been prolonged or had Hitler won it, these men would have shared the fate of the Jews in the death camps.

Half-Jewish Gefreiter Karl-Heinz Scheffler

Karl-Heinz Scheffler is a bitter and sarcastic man. Unlike his brother Günther (discussed in chapter 1), who rarely talks about their dysfunctional family, Scheffler often mentions how it affected him from 1933 to 1945. He is angry about his youth and about how Hitler and his father stole his innocence. Scheffler would love to have had a chance to relive his life in a different time and place, a wish shared by many half-Jews. He often makes a point of discussing it; he expresses his opinions openly about how and why his life has turned out the way it has.

Born on 13 August 1916 in Berlin, he was one of three brothers; an older brother, Hubertus, was born on 23 December 1914 in Kiel, and younger brother Günther was born on 4 April 1918, also in Kiel.

The marriage of Scheffler's Jewish mother, Helena Weiss, and gentile father, Max, was not a happy one. Members of the Weiss family often married non-Jews. Helena's three brothers had also converted and married non-Jews. As a boy, Scheffler did not know about his Jewish past, and no one bothered his family about it. Only in 1934, when the new German government implemented its campaign against the Jews with laws like the Aryan Paragraph, did Scheffler and his brothers find out about their Jewish background.

When Scheffler learned of his ancestry, he said he "felt horrible to

Karl-Heinz Scheffler at
dinner in Frankfurt,
circa 1994.

know I was part of the subhumans the Nazis hated. I was young, nervous, and I didn't even know what it meant to be Jewish. I mean, who is
a Jew?" During that time, Scheffler read Hitler's *Mein Kampf,* something
few Germans had done. He found Hitler's ideology horrendous and says
that "everything that pig wrote about he did. His whole blueprint of destruction was there—the destruction of France and Russia and the systematic killing of Jews . . . everything was there. I should've taken it
more seriously."

His father, feeling pressure from the Nazis, started to distance himself
from his family in the 1930s. He worried that if he remained married to a
Jew, he would lose his business, which he had inherited from his Jewish
father-in-law. He said his greatest mistake in life was marrying a Jew,
which left him three "Jewish" sons to support. In 1937, he divorced his
wife, who fell into a depression and tried to drown herself in Krumme-
lanke Lake outside Berlin.

Max became a Nazi and ignored his sons throughout the Third Reich. Scheffler said: "He always was putting us down. 'You guys are losers,' or 'Your mother is a disgrace,' or 'I wish you never had been born.' Simply horrible." Their sports club provided the only place where Scheffler and his brothers felt free from persecution. They played tennis, soccer, and especially field hockey well, and their skills seemed to matter more than their family tree. The other "Aryan" kids in the club treated them as equals, even though they knew about the Scheffler Jewish background.

The brothers thought about emigrating but had no money. "Where would we go and who would have taken us?" Scheffler said. "Besides, Germany was our home."

After their father left the family, the sons did everything they could to protect their mother. They felt military service would do the most to help. They also came from a strong military tradition and did not see anything wrong with serving. Three of Scheffler's Jewish uncles, all brothers of his mother, had served in World War I. One died in battle and two became officers.

In March 1937, Scheffler started his seven-month service in the Reichs-arbeitsdienst (National Labor Service). While there, he noticed another man, Rudolf Sachs, who also had a Jewish mother. They then discovered a third half-Jew, Hannes Bergius, in their platoon of twenty-two men. He said, "There must have been numerous half-Jews in the Wehrmacht if our platoon is an example."

On 15 November 1938, the Wehrmacht drafted Scheffler into the Twenty-third Antitank Regiment along with Sachs and Bergius. He had a difficult time adjusting to army discipline, and one of his superiors considered him physically and intellectually inferior to most soldiers. One day when an NCO ordered Scheffler to do some "stupid job," Scheffler refused and told the man to "shove it up your ass." He was punished with three days in the brig. He simply did not like the Wehrmacht.

Prior to the campaign against Poland, Scheffler served in the 176th Panzer Abwehr Regiment on Germany's western border between the Moselle and the Saar. He remembers the excitement of his fellow soldiers later, in France, over their victories. "It was really sad to see the French attack our positions with bad tanks. It was almost embarrassing and I actually laughed at those poor bastards. We took care of their tanks with-

Panzer Abwehr Regiment 23 at Potsdam Sans Souci Palace for the taking of the oath to Hitler, circa summer 1939. Here is the *Nachrichten* (Communications) Platoon. Out of the twenty-two soldiers here, three are half-Jews: Karl-Heinz Scheffler (middle row, fourth from right); Rudolf Sachs (front row, third from right); and Hannes Bergius (front row, far right).

out any problems," Scheffler said. This must have been a rare occurrence, because in fact, the French had relatively good armor, superior to what the Germans had, and plenty of it. They just didn't use it as well as the Germans did.

Scheffler participated only in a few engagements throughout Luxembourg and along the Maginot Line. In June his unit took part in the battle of Verdun, where he witnessed several atrocities. He saw German soldiers take black colonial French prisoners out into the fields and execute them. It made him wonder what they would do to him, another "racially inferior person." Soon thereafter, Germany defeated France.

Karl-Heinz Scheffler (last rank Obergefreiter) riding a BMW Wehrmacht
motorcycle with side carriage, 1940.

After three months of occupying France, the army transferred his unit
to East Prussia. By now, Scheffler had adjusted to the army lifestyle and
had become a good soldier. While working in his regiment's office, he
read the order ousting half-Jews from service and reported his status to
his commander. Although his superior did not want to see Scheffler go,
he complied with the decree. In July 1940, Scheffler, having just been
promoted to Obergefreiter (private first class), was discharged. "It felt
strange, but I am sure glad it happened," he said. "My whole company
disappeared at the battle of Stalingrad. No one returned." After his discharge, Scheffler returned to Berlin and wrote to both of his brothers
about the regulation.

At home, after some intense arguments, his father finally agreed to
hire him in the family's company. Scheffler said it was hard for him to
hear his father yell "Heil Hitler" and play the part of a Nazi. "My father

was the biggest coward ever. I was surprised that he hired me. I would not stay there long."

When Hubertus received news from Scheffler about Hitler's discharge order, he immediately reported this to his commander. Since his ancestry documents were not filed, it took his unit three weeks to get the paperwork to prove that he was a half-Jew, disqualifying him from service.

As discussed in chapter 1, Scheffler's brother Günther reacted differently to the news that half-Jews could not serve. He, unlike his brothers, felt safe in his unit. Günther went to his officer when he found out about the laws and requested to stay. Without hesitation, his captain told him that he could. Günther did not want to return to civilian life, where he had experienced problems related to his Jewish status. He felt that he lived among equals in the army. A few of his comrades and superiors knew about his ancestry, but they protected him.

Besides his good experience with his commanders and comrades, Günther hoped that as long as one of his family members served, the Gestapo would leave his mother alone. Service to the Fatherland seemed to protect them against persecution. This was a common belief among several families.

In 1942, Karl-Heinz Scheffler left his father's company for a job in a consulting firm. During this time, he bought a pistol on the black market. He told himself that if anyone tried to deport his mother, he would shoot him. Earlier the same year, the Nazis had deported his old, sick Jewish grandmother to Theresienstadt and this troubled him greatly. Later, someone who had accompanied his grandmother to the station reported that when she boarded, she smiled, waved goodbye, and said she would soon return home. Scheffler never saw her again. "Luckily, my Jewish grandfather died in 1932 and did not have to experience all the shit under the Nazis," Scheffler said.

In October 1944, the Nazis deported him, along with other half-Jews, to an OT forced labor camp near Sitzendorf in Thuringia. He had thought he could avoid deportation, but someone, probably in his workplace, denounced him as a half-Jew. Soon thereafter, he and other half-Jews boarded a train to an unknown destination. When they arrived at the camp with towers behind barbed wire, Scheffler knew his future looked bleak. He worked in a plant that produced synthetic gasoline from coal and as a member of a construction crew building roads. Working conditions were horrible. They did not have much to eat and the sparse food they received was of poor quality.

Scheffler had bad eyesight and needed glasses to work. He learned that if he broke his glasses, he would have to go into town to get new ones. This would give him a whole day. He broke his glasses several times when he worked there and amazingly was given daily passes every time to get them repaired. "This was one way I got out of work and I'm surprised that they did not punish me for it," Scheffler said. One morning in March 1945, he woke up to discover the guards had abandoned their posts. Along with a few others, he returned to Berlin.

When he reached his home in Zehlendorf, a suburb of Berlin, he happily found his mother alive and well. "I took my mother in my arms and told her how glad I was to see her," Scheffler said with emotion. Yet, life was still dangerous. As he walked around the streets of Berlin in April, he saw bodies strung up on lamp posts with signs around their necks accusing them of desertion. Scheffler worried about what the Nazis would do to him.

Yet, both he and his two brothers survived the war.

Scheffler said that by 1943 he knew about the extermination of the Jews. The Nazis had already deported his grandmother, and his brother Günther wrote how he had heard that the SS had driven Jews to a ditch and executed them. "I never understood why my brother remained a soldier. What he saw was horrible. That was the first time I heard anything about this," Scheffler said. However, strangely enough, he was never scared for his own life. "I was only scared for my mother. I did not think they would harm half-Jews like they did Jews," Scheffler claimed. Knowing what he does about the Third Reich today, he felt lucky to have been spared the trauma and the pain many had experienced. "I'm so happy that I came through this history with so few problems," he said.

Scheffler said that while he did not feel Jewish, he never felt embarrassed about his Jewish mother and he now takes a special interest in Israel's current events. When asked what he thinks about the fact that Halakah considers him Jewish, he said he believes Halakah is just another racial theory placing people into "in and out groups." "Sometimes you just have no control over what laws are out there. The Nazis called me a half-Jew with their laws, and religious Jews call me a Jew according to their laws. Whatever happened to people deciding for themselves who they are?" Scheffler asked, shaking his head. He claimed he has no contact with Jews and cannot understand any racial theories. He believes most people are weak and change with the society in which they live.

A case in point occurred after the war when Scheffler's father suddenly saw the advantage of having a Jewish wife again. Remarkably, Helena took him back and they remarried. "It was sad. My mother always loved my father. He didn't deserve her love," Scheffler said. Their three sons were the groomsmen—"this just doesn't happen," Scheffler says. The second marriage of his parents did not last. His father had an affair with the maid a year after the remarriage and left his wife for a second time. "What a load of shit," Scheffler said. "We humans sometimes never learn from our mistakes."

Scheffler's story is dramatically different from that of his brother Günther. Quite often research for this book revealed that brothers could have extremely different experiences under Hitler. Sometimes within a family, one brother stayed in the military while others left. Hitler gave some special exemptions while rejecting others.

Scheffler's pain and suffering mirrors that of many *Mischlinge*. Scheffler's father was an opportunist who knew no loyalty to his wife or children and destroyed the family's unity. Indeed, Nazi racial ideology helped destroy families even more by giving some spouses, like Max Scheffler, an added incentive to discard those they deemed unworthy of their time or care.

Unlike a few others in this study, Karl-Heinz Scheffler did not enjoy the military. Since Germany had a universal draft, the Wehrmacht conscripted everyone. The Third Reich banned half-Jews from the military only in mid to late 1940. Nonetheless, many in the army had no business serving. Scheffler was a poor soldier both from a psychological and a "racial" point of view. He shows that many soldiers were not the hardcore Prussian types or pure "Aryans" that many think the Third Reich had at this time.

In his straightforward way, Scheffler ended his interview by pointing out again that Halakah is nonsense, that the Jewish laws of citizenship are ridiculous, and that they are doing more to divide people than to unite them, concluding rhetorically, "You would think the Jews would have learned that racial laws do not work."

Half-Jewish Gefreiter Helmut Krüger

Helmut Krüger enjoys life. He is witty, full of passion, and not afraid to call a spade a spade. People usually take pleasure in getting to know him. Saddened that people throughout Germany have not recognized the plight of *Mischlinge*, he quickly blames Jewish organizations for failing to give adequate attention to the many groups in addition to full Jews who were persecuted by Hitler during the Holocaust. He wants people to learn from the past but fears they rarely listen unless they are directly affected.

Krüger was born 20 January 1913 in Mannheim to a Jewish mother, the former Camilla Davidson, and an "Aryan" father, Max Krüger. He had a brother, Answald, born in Heidelberg in 1918, and a sister, Brigitte, born in Münster in 1923.

As a young child, Krüger knew about his mother's background. He also knew that his Jewish grandfather, the lithographer Ezekiel Davidson, came from Holland and that his Jewish grandmother, Rebeka (née Stern), from Hungary. Krüger pointed out that he represents a *Mischling* of many different "races." He never knew his Jewish grandfather because he died when Krüger's mother was a child. However, he did know his Jewish grandmother, who lived with them. She died in their house in Freiburg on Christmas Eve in 1924, and the family buried her in the local Jewish cemetery. Krüger did not have much experience with Jewish traditions and heard about Jews and Judaism only from his mother when she talked about growing up in Vienna.

Krüger's paternal grandfather, Johann Krüger, born in the German village of Deutsch Evern outside Lüneburg, served in the army as a reserve soldier and worked as a municipal secretary. His paternal grandmother was Mathilde (née Leidenroth), from Halle. The son she bore in 1884 was Helmut's father, Max.

Max's family did not know any Jews or know about Jewish culture. They felt apprehensive about Max's marrying a Jew, but Camilla's personality quickly won them over, and the families grew to accept one another. In 1923, Max began a prestigious position managing the Freiburg Theater.

Helmut Krüger in 1994 at his home in Berlin.

In 1930, amid the political chaos of Weimar, Helmut Krüger, then only seventeen years old, decided to join the Communist Party because he felt it would fight the Nazis. A year later, due to growing anti-Semitism, his mother left the Jewish community. She felt this act would protect the family if the Nazis gained power.

When Nazi persecution spread, Krüger did not understand why some labeled him a "dirty Jew." Even today, he feels strange being associated with Jews because this concept is foreign to him. His family brought him up Christian and he had little understanding of what it meant to be Jewish. He says in Berlin's Jewish Community Center Library, he feels like a stranger doing research there and complains when Jews try to claim him as a Jew. He has no Jewish friends today since "Hitler wiped most of them out." Though he struggled for twelve years to convince the Nazis he was a loyal German, he never succeeded. Today, when he meets religious Jews, they try to convince him that he is Jewish. "It's so confusing," Krüger said.

Although according to Halakah, Krüger is Jewish because of his Jewish mother, he points out that he had nothing to do with his mother's Jewishness. Halakah means nothing to him: "Should I then also be called a Nazi because my uncle, Hermann Krüger, was a local Nazi Party leader? The answer is no just as much as it's no that I'm a Jew." He was born a German and raised as a Christian. Krüger dislikes being called a Jew, not because he is anti-Semitic, but because he does not feel Jewish.

Some rabbis claim that people like Krüger demonstrate Jewish self-hatred, renouncing their Jewishness because they feel afraid to admit who they are. Krüger believes he is a German born by chance to a German Jewish mother who, like many Jews, shed her Jewishness to integrate fully into the dominant, Christian society.

His attitude represents that of many *Mischlinge.* The vast majority do not know much about their own Jewish heritage and feel puzzled when observant Jews tell them they are Jewish. Others, however, feel Jewish not so much because they have Jewish mothers, but because the Nazis persecuted them for their Jewishness. Their Jewish identity was born of persecution rather than of religious or cultural heritage. Until 1933 Krüger's Jewish ancestry rarely became a topic. But after 1933, it dominated his life.

Krüger excelled at mathematics and enjoyed engineering, but after Hitler came to power, the Nazis limited his studies. In March 1933, life for his family changed dramatically. The police searched their home because of Krüger's earlier Communist Party activities, although he had left the Communists a few years before. The police found an antique pistol and arrested Krüger and his father. Through family contacts with the police, they were released after twenty-four hours. But local Nazis later threw bricks through their windows and made threatening phone calls.

In October 1933, Krüger's mother took another step toward protective assimilation and converted to Protestantism. Yet, by late 1933, his father had to leave his job in Freiburg for a smaller and less prestigious theater because of his Jewish wife. His career was ruined.

After his arrest, Krüger fled to Dresden and worked as a bricklayer. In October 1933, his parents and two siblings also left Freiburg and moved to Berlin hoping to escape the authorities and hide their Jewish connection in the big city. Krüger soon followed his family to Berlin to help support them. He worked in a construction company and was able to continue his studies.

In 1935, a cousin of Krüger's father in America offered to help Krüger emigrate. He almost accepted, but decided to stay in Germany because he wanted to finish his studies and lacked the courage to start a new life abroad. Also, he did not feel right leaving his mother, brother, and sister behind to face an uncertain future while he lived free in America.

His family struggled to protect their livelihoods and dignity and came up with few solutions for coping with a seemingly impossible predicament. Krüger's mother tortured herself with blame for jeopardizing her entire family with her ancestry.

Fortunately, Krüger's friends were not bothered by his racial background. "The strange thing then," he said, "was that most people I knew were not racists in spite of being consistently bombarded with Nazi propaganda." He spent most of his free time with young people who were passionate athletes. "They just cared how well you played and whether you were a good pal or not," he said.

Also, in hindsight, Krüger feels fortunate to have had a Jewish mother during the Hitler years. Had she been Aryan, he claims, he might have joined the Nazi Party or the SS. He knew many who succumbed to the seductive power of Nazism.

In 1935, Krüger volunteered for service as a way of protecting his family. He felt that appearing home on leave in uniform might help improve his family's image. "People would see that our family had a soldier amongst their members," he explained, "and leave us alone." In April 1936, he joined the Wehrmacht. After he completed boot camp, he felt ill at ease swearing an oath of allegiance to Hitler. From July to September 1936, he served with Reserve Battalion 15 in Berlin. Many comrades and superiors felt sorry for him for having a Jewish mother and, because he was such a good comrade, treated him with respect.

Krüger's father's problems continued and in 1936, he lost his job again because of his Jewish wife. To help support the family, Krüger found additional work at a gas station. All the while, Krüger pursued his university education even though he carried the yellow ID card for Jews and *Mischlinge.*

His brother did not have such luck. In 1937, Answald had to leave high school a year before completion because his parents had fallen on such hard times. He then worked in an export company to help the family make ends meet.

Unable to take the stress and believing her husband could earn a better living without the "dead weight of a Jewish wife," Krüger's mother requested a divorce in 1937. She thought she could then resume her Dutch citizenship and circumvent the German laws. Though divorced, Max continued to support his ex-wife and children as best he could and a friend of the family, Wolfgang Koepke, helped Krüger finance his studies. "Not everyone back then was a Nazi," Krüger said.

Early in the morning of Reichskristallnacht, 9 November 1938, Krüger, looking out of his bedroom window, saw SA[1] men vandalizing Jewish stores with clubs and axes during the infamous pogrom. His future turned black.

Although prohibited from dating "Aryans," Krüger did so anyway and was quite a hit with the ladies. In late 1938, he became serious about one special woman named Hertha Eckhardt and they became engaged. She knew about his background but did not care, and her parents accepted him. Her brother did not seem bothered by his sister's fiancé either, even though he served as an SS man and a personal guard of Robert Ley, head of the German Labor Front. In 1939, Krüger applied to the government to marry Hertha but received no response.

In August, the army called him up for service in the Seventh Infantry Regiment. He and his comrades were accompanied by their girlfriends, fiancées, and wives to the train station to report for duty. Unbeknownst to them, they were headed to war.

In the Polish campaign, Krüger's unit saw no action as they marched to Radom and Sielce on the River Burg, the demarcation line agreed

Half-Jewish Gefreiter
Helmut Krüger
pictured in 1940
wearing the Iron Cross
Second Class. (Military
awards: EKII and
Wound Badge)

upon by Stalin and Hitler in August 1939. Throughout the fighting, his
unit marched through bombed-out villages and along roads lined with
the remains of dead horses, Polish civilians, and soldiers caught up in the
maelstrom of battle. Sometimes his unit would march 20 miles a day
with full packs weighing over 70 pounds.

During Krüger's time in Poland, he did not witness much persecution
of Jews. He saw a soldier attacking a Jew, but this was rare. One day,
when soldiers vandalized a synagogue, he reminded them that they stood
in a sacred house. Surprisingly, the men stopped and left. Krüger's intervention was unusual. Most *Mischling* soldiers seemed to worry little
about the mistreatment of the eastern Jews around them. They cele-

brated the victories with their comrades and hoped that their service would alleviate their discrimination back home.

After the Poland campaign, Krüger was promoted to Gefreiter (private first class). He jokingly says that he had reached the rank the "great warrior" of the "German Reich, Adolf Hitler, had during World War I." He also became the squad leader of eleven men although according to law, half-Jews were not supposed to occupy leadership positions in case they "started acting like Jews."[2]

His unit was then sent to Germany's western border and in January 1940 had its first casualty during the "Phony War." Alfred Palm, a good friend of Krüger, died. A few days before his death, on hearing that Krüger was a half-Jew, he had confided in Krüger that he was dating a Jewish girl. They agreed that Hitler and his racial laws were absurd.

While his unit readied itself to invade France in spring of 1940, Krüger volunteered for reconnaissance missions. As a soldier, he always had Nazi expressions ringing in his ears, such as Jews are "flat-footed cowards." "By some dumb logic, I felt I had to prove them wrong." So Krüger volunteered for dangerous missions. When Krüger's officers awarded him the Iron Cross Second Class for his bravery, he hoped the medal would secure protection for his family.

Yet Krüger increasingly came to dread the future and thought about ways to escape. Often, while staring off into no-man's-land, Krüger contemplated deserting to the French, but he did not want to endanger his siblings and mother. One man in his unit actually did run to the French. After Germany defeated France, the Nazis found and executed him.

While in France, his unit marched an average 35 miles a day and hardly saw any action. Krüger felt excited by Germany's victory over France in only a few weeks.

After the cessation of hostilities in the summer of 1940, Krüger was hospitalized with a severe case of the flu. His officer, Lieutenant Oesterwitz, visited him and during their conversation asked if Krüger had heard the rumor about a half-Jew serving in their ranks. Krüger lied and said he had no idea. He did not think his superiors would check the personnel files for possible non-Aryans.

Krüger did not know that Hitler had ordered the discharge of half-

Jews in April 1940. He did not want to leave his fellow soldiers, whom he described as a wonderful group of guys and a surrogate family. This affection was apparently mutual. For example, for his birthday in 1940, his comrades threw him a party where they all got drunk.

In late 1940, Günther, one of his comrades, suddenly left the unit for a job back home. At least this was what he shared with Krüger. Later Krüger learned that Günther was a half-Jew and that the army had forced him to leave. Krüger felt bad for the soldier who shared his own situation but now became even more convinced that he should hide his ancestry. He did not want to leave a place where he felt he could protect his family and himself. On several occasions, his mother sidetracked the Gestapo by showing them pictures of her soldier sons. They would leave claiming they could not deport a mother with children in the army.

In April 1941, the army finally discovered Krüger's secret and discharged him. Another soldier, hearing about Krüger's upcoming dismissal, said he envied Krüger for going home. His commander, Lieutenant Teuke, a Nazi Party member and SA man, tried without success to retain him. He could not believe that the Wehrmacht would dismiss a man with the Iron Cross.

Many comrades envied his dismissal. Ironically, several half-Jews were worried about leaving because they faced an uncertain future, but their comrades only saw that they could go home and escape combat.

So Krüger felt disappointed having to leave, but when looking back felt lucky the army discharged him because the Soviets decimated his company during the battle for Moscow in the winter of 1941–1942 and his comrades now "fertilize Russian soil." In the first month of the invasion of Russia, German losses had already exceeded those they had incurred in the west and by November 1941, infantry "formations had lost half of their personnel." By March 1942, the casualties would rise to over a million, with 250,000 being either killed or missing in action.[3] These numbers reflect only the first eight months of the war in Russia, which would go on for several more years. In the face of such statistics, the envy of Krüger's fellow soldiers is easily understood.

Krüger's brother, Answald, had a different relationship with the army. He also received the Iron Cross Second Class and served in the elite special operations force of Brandenburg Regiment 800 as a Gefreiter. Answald, unlike his brother, admired Hitler's successes, although he had a difficult time justifying his political views when the very political system he supported persecuted him. In March 1942, the military also discharged him for racial reasons. "He was an excellent soldier and thrived in battle . . . His discharge was one of his greatest disappointments," Krüger said.

Krüger admits that people like himself and his brother were lucky. He thinks of the thousands of half-Jews who remained in service and probably met their deaths in Russia. "Eighty percent of Germany's killed-in-action occurred on the eastern front," Krüger claims. His estimate is not off by much: Germany suffered 3,250,000 combat deaths during World War II, of which some 70 percent—2,300,000—occurred in Russia.[4]

When asked if he knew other half-Jews in the army, Krüger said that everyone knew that Field Marshal Erhard Milch was a half-Jew. Following his discharge, he also met a few other half-Jewish veterans who were part of his circle of friends or who had served in his unit. And in 1944, he heard from a major in the Armed Forces High Command (OKW) that 80,000 half-Jews and men married to Jews had been discharged by the Wehrmacht. His sister, Brigitte, heard a similar rumor from professors at her university.

Once discharged, Krüger continued his studies in Berlin and later worked for a construction company in Brest, France, building U-boat bunkers. Paradoxically, the Nazis placed a group of Jewish forced laborers under his control, most of whom the authorities later deported to an unknown destination.

In February 1942, he reapplied for permission to marry Hertha, with whom he was now living, attaching a supporting letter from his former commander, now a company commander and bearer of the Ritterkreuz (Knight's Cross). Nonetheless, his application was denied and he continued to live with Hertha in a *wilde Ehe,* or "wild marriage." In November, their first child, Gabriele, came into the world. "It was such a happy moment in my life because everything else had been so shitty," Krüger said. But Hertha could not claim Krüger as the father because she feared the Nazis would charge her with *Rassenschande* (racial defilement). After the birth, she denied knowing the father and "admitted" that her baby was born out of wedlock. It was difficult for Krüger to walk away from the hospital unable to claim his own daughter. Soon after the birth Krüger took his fiancée and child to the village of Deutsch Evern where his gentile relatives lived. There, a cousin of his father and the town's local Nazi Party leader, Hermann Krüger, made sure that Hertha received papers allowing the family to house her and the baby.

Also in 1942, Krüger and his brother moved their mother, Camilla, and sister, Brigitte, out of their apartment in Berlin to one in Wannsee (suburban Berlin) without telling the authorities about it. However, in February 1944, the SS found out where Camilla lived and picked her up in a furniture wagon for deportation. Brigitte witnessed the horrible event and called Krüger who, in turn, quickly called up his brother. They all then traveled to where they knew the Nazis were holding Jews for deportation at Grosse Hamburger Strasse. There, they saw their mother through a window with tears in her eyes. Helmut yelled at his brother Answald, "Where is your shitty Brandenburg Division now?" While the authorities held Camilla for several hours, Brigitte brought her some clothes. Soon thereafter, the Nazis deported her to Theresienstadt, where she remained until war's end.

After their mother's deportation, Krüger and his brother visited SS headquarters in Berlin to ask for her release. There, they met Adolf Eichmann's deputy, SS major Rolf Günther, at the entrance. When they explained their situation, asked for the return of their mother, and added that they were willing to serve again, Günther looked at them hatefully and said, "Every criminal is courageous," and left. Krüger and his brother also tried to reenter the army at different Wehrmacht offices to help their mother but were rejected. "We both were traumatized that our military service didn't protect her. We felt alone. We just wanted to survive with our family intact," Krüger said.

In the fall of 1944, the Brandenburg Division became an SS division. Even so, Answald Krüger still had contact with his comrades. One of them, an SS sergeant, felt horrified by what happened to Answald's mother and offered his sympathy. The Krüger brothers even went to Brandenburg's base outside of Berlin near the Sachsenhausen concentration camp to visit this comrade. Helmut Krüger was stunned to see the camp inmates working nearby in their blue striped clothes under horrendous conditions.

In the fall of 1944, things took another turn for the worse for Krüger. One of his Nazi relatives forced Hertha to leave the village of Deutsch Evern and take her child with her. He did not like harboring Krüger's wife and quarter-Jewish child. She and the baby returned to Berlin where they were secretly married in the Swedish Lutheran church.

On 10 January 1945, the Nazis deported Krüger and his brother to an OT forced labor camp. In normal passenger trains they traveled to the encampment at Miltitz-Roitschen near Meissen/Saxony. A large fence enclosed the camp and Ukrainian guards roamed the area with menacing German shepherd dogs. The Nazis immediately put them on work details constructing buildings for processing synthetic gasoline.

Men other than half-Jews worked there, including many husbands of Jewish wives. Krüger later found out these wives had been deported to Theresienstadt like his mother. Many inmates were highly decorated World War I veterans. One wore the German Pilot Badge and his Iron Cross First Class from the Great War and explained that his half-Jewish son was serving in the Luftwaffe under Göring's protection. Another half-Jew had lost an arm in combat and worked in the office as a clerk.

In February 1945, the camp authorities transferred Krüger and his fellow inmates to Coswig, near Dresden, where they worked alongside Russian and Polish POWs. In the middle of February Krüger witnessed the horrible Allied firebombing of Dresden, which probably killed around 35,000 civilians. After the bombing, he and his fellow workers had to clean up the streets and bury the dead. He hated the fact that the Allies bombed German cities, but accepted it knowing this strategy would help end the war sooner.

Laboring away in the OT camp, Krüger realized what could eventually happen to him unless he escaped. Consequently, he, along with others, planned to break out, and in March they successfully did so. Krüger and some comrades were sent to pick up some machine parts, and on the way to Hamburg, Krüger went AWOL in Berlin. Later, an anti-Nazi military doctor helped Krüger obtain papers documenting him as an injured soldier in case he met military police. These documents proved invaluable since the military police executed numerous men on the spot as deserters (going AWOL) if the men could not provide the authorities with proper papers. For instance, on a street in Danzig in 1945, the Nazis had hanged several German soldiers from the streetlights with placards around their chests labeled "Coward."[5] Krüger wanted to avoid such a fate.

For added safety's sake, the preacher at the Swedish church in Berlin helped Krüger obtain another document stating he was a half-Jew and a persecuted person of the Third Reich in case he fell into Allied hands.

Krüger eventually made it back to the village of Deutsch Evern, where his wife and child had returned. Since it was apparent the Nazis would soon lose the war, some of Krüger's relatives suddenly had a change of heart. When the Allies entered the town, Krüger removed the sign that read "Jews not allowed" at the village outskirts, and he and his wife felt the heavy burden of many years of persecution fall from their shoulders. They now could start their lives as husband and wife in freedom.

When asked about the Holocaust, Krüger stated that he lost about nine relatives in the death camps, including his mother's brothers Nati and Julius Davidson, who perished along with their entire families. He also knew about two Jewish sisters who lived in his apartment complex who committed suicide because of Nazi persecution. However, he did not know about the systematic extermination of Jews under Hitler. "That information was kept secret and besides we had other worries. I think even if I'd heard anything about it I wouldn't have believed it," Krüger said. He now thinks that half-Jews would have been killed had the war continued.

After the war, Krüger continued to have problems because of his half-Jewish status and military past. When he met up with an American Jewish soldier, the soldier told him, "You're still alive so you must've been a Nazi." Krüger had problems at his interrogation when he explained that half-Jews had to serve. Although this confused the Allied interrogators, they eventually cleared him and labeled him a civilian. After 1945, Krüger simply tried to forget his *Mischling* past.

Several months after the war ended, Krüger found out that Russian troops had liberated his mother and that she had returned to Berlin. His reunion with her in late 1945 was one of the happiest days of his life. However, she was a broken woman. The Nazi era had aged her terribly and she died only nine years later. Although she had converted to Christianity, the Jewish community allowed Krüger and his siblings to bury her urn with that of her mother in the Jewish cemetery in Freiburg.

After 1945, Krüger quickly finished his education and started to work as an engineer helping to rebuild Germany. In 1955, he applied for compensation from the government for his persecution. The authorities denied his claim. The officials did not know how he could have served in the Wehrmacht as a half-Jew. Smiling, Krüger commented that "people have little knowledge about half-Jews and their plight during the Third Reich. They don't care about us half-breeds. We're outcasts and will always be stuck between two chairs." Krüger's frustration is common among half-Jews. They feel that history has excluded them from its books and created no place for them.

Although unfounded, Krüger's mother's feeling of guilt for having brought this horrible situation on the family was experienced by many Jewish parents of half-Jewish children. In particular, Jewish mothers often seemed to have felt things more deeply and felt more responsible for their children than did Jewish fathers.

Moreover, Krüger's family's situation mirrored that of many families in this research in other respects. Like the families of Arno Spitz, Helmuth Kopp, and Pinchas Hirschfeld, to name just a few, Helmut's family moved around in order to find an adequate hiding place in Nazi Germany. Krüger's life represents those of many *Mischlinge* in that they felt army service ensured their own and their families' survival. Yet, this tactic proved largely unsuccessful.

However, as Krüger's experience shows, army service did at least delay the persecution of Jewish relatives. This provided a false sense of security because ultimately no half-Jew, much less a full Jew, was safe in Nazi Germany.

As Helmut Krüger and Karl-Heinz Scheffler both state, their discharge probably saved their lives. Many *Mischlinge* like Krüger and Scheffler would have died in Russia had Hitler not made it law in 1940 that half-Jews could not serve. This was the greatest irony of all—percentage-wise, more Aryans than half-Jews died in combat because they were deemed worthy to serve the Reich. The era of the Third Reich is full of paradoxes.

Half-Jewish Oberschütze Klaus-Peter Scholz

Klaus-Peter Scholz lives life with passion and he often uses animated gestures to express himself. As a gay man, he experienced the Third Reich from the perspective of not just one but two persecuted groups. He feels that life has been unfair and his emotions often border on the extreme. Yet, he is kind and feels for others who are in pain. He often mentions his troubled relationships with women and it becomes apparent that he suffered under an overbearing mother.

Scholz was born in Hamburg on 2 April 1918 to a Jewish mother, Olga (Olli) Gertrud (née Samuel), and an "Aryan" father, Julius Scholz. His parents divorced in the 1920s because of his father's wife-beating and extramarital affairs. It was a bitter breakup and Julius refused to pay alimony. As a result, Olga took him to court. She won and he had to pay, but with his knowledge as a lawyer, he made sure that she received the bare minimum. Several family members felt upset that she had married a *Goy* and many scolded her, saying, "We told you that you shouldn't have married him."

Scholz learned about his Jewish background as a child when he told his mother he and some schoolmates had poked fun at Jews on the street. She told him not to do that because she herself was Jewish, then added he should keep their ancestry quiet because if that knowledge got out it could only harm them.

When the Nazis came into power Scholz thought about his future. As long as Hitler controlled the government, he knew he would not fare well. Also, after the political climate changed, his father succeeded in further reducing the alimony from 1,500 RM to a mere 110 RM per month because his ex-wife was Jewish, hurting Scholz since he depended on her income as well. "That was the pig my father was," Scholz said.

In 1933, Scholz's mother sent him to the Hermann Lietz boarding school in Erfurt, but he hated it. So in 1934, he returned to his mother in Hamburg, where he attended public school. After finishing his secondary education, he worked for an import/export company run by Oscar Friedlaender, a Jew.

At that time, he attended a reform temple in Hamburg on Oberstrasse and felt warmly accepted there. "My mother was upset about it," he said,

Klaus-Peter Scholz in the mountains of Tirol at Alplach, Austria, circa 1989.

"but I told her that we cannot hide from who we are. I wanted to be around Jews. She told me that I was taking a step backward."

In 1937, Friedlaender offered to take Scholz with him to Brazil. Friedlaender and his wife knew they needed to get out of Germany and told him they had a business there where he could work. Scholz wanted to leave, but his mother dissuaded him, "You have to serve in the army. And besides, who'll take care of me? You cannot go." He did have to serve, but if he left the country for good, then his mandatory service could have been ignored. Scholz's mother did not make his decision whether to escape easy and after many arguments, he decided to stay. "She told me that nothing would happen to us. Her brother had served four years as an officer during World War I and the Germans would not harm a family with such a brave relative." She was sorely mistaken, but it would take several more years of Nazi rule to prove just how wrong she was.

Sometime in 1937, Scholz's father pleaded with him to get baptized a

Protestant. Scholz expressed surprise that his father suddenly concerned himself about his religion because his father had shown little interest in Scholz at all. The father insisted he do this because it would help the family and his practice. Scholz told him he felt Jewish and did not like Christianity. His father yelled at him that all his troubles in life were due to "that woman—your mother" and to his Jewish son.

The father then suddenly changed his tactics and offered Scholz a gold watch if he converted. Scholz asked, "Are you bribing me with gold?" However, he needed money and decided to do the ceremony. His mother approved of Scholz's baptism and came to the confirmation. However, his father did not allow her to sit with the family, relegating her to the balcony. "That was the type of asshole I had to call father," Scholz said.

In 1938, Scholz volunteered for the army. He thought the sooner he finished his required duty, the faster he could leave the country.

In April 1938, he started his National Labor Service. In his first week there his barracks leader, Obertruppführer (NCO) Krause, called Scholz a typical half-Jew with dark hair and blue eyes. Scholz immediately went to the camp commander and requested to be sent home. When asked why, Scholz reported what had happened. After hearing about the situation, the commander marched back to the barracks with Scholz and yelled at Krause in front of the others that this was no way to treat a man. "Thereafter, I never had any problems," Scholz said.

Scholz completed his labor service and joined the Wehrmacht in November. His mother felt proud and thought his service proved their Germanness. When they walked around town, she told everyone her son had joined the army. Scholz thought his service was simply a necessary evil.

He served as an artillery loader in the Seventy-sixth Infantry Regiment in Hamburg, a motorized tank-destroyer unit. "THAT'S WHY I CAN'T HEAR SO WELL TODAY," Scholz said loudly, with a laugh. He found he enjoyed the camaraderie of military life: "It felt good to serve and that my comrades accepted me after so many years of feeling like an outsider." Many *Mischlinge* felt this way. They wanted society around them to acknowledge them as German citizens with equal rights. Service

Klaus-Peter Scholz as an Arbeitsman in the National Labor Service in 1938, with his mother, Olga (Olli) Gertrud (née Samuel).

restored some of their dignity, but this feeling of equality often stopped when they were passed over for promotions or discharged.

After training, Scholz's company traveled to Berlin to take the oath of allegiance in Hitler's presence on 20 April 1939, the Führer's birthday. "I was in the first row of the company and Hitler stood right in front of me in a Mercedes convertible. I could see his bright blue eyes and they stared right through me." Scholz was armed that day with his pistol, the customary weapon carried by artillery loaders. When asked why he did not shoot Hitler, he said, "I wasn't allowed any ammunition—it would've been difficult to have hidden the bullets. And anyway, I wanted to continue living. I didn't want to die. If I had killed Hitler what would that

Klaus-Peter Scholz (last rank Oberschütze) in his Wehrmacht uniform getting ready for a parade in honor of Hitler's birthday on 20 April 1939. On this day, he and his comrades took their oath of allegiance to Hitler and Fatherland.

have done for me? Death! I would've been a criminal killing the highest authority in the land. Remember, at that time, everyone loved Hitler. He hadn't yet murdered millions of Jews or led Germany into another horrible military defeat in a world war."

On 1 September 1939, Scholz's unit entered Poland. When asked if he felt scared, he said, "Sure, when soldiers go to war, they're always scared. Any soldier who tells you differently is lying. However, we knew we fought against an inferior enemy, and this was proven when we were in battle. After we discovered we were up against poor troops, we lost our fear and the thrill of victory took over." The few times his unit entered combat, it attacked and easily destroyed outdated Polish tanks. Approaching Brest-Litovsk, they overcame the defenders and entered the city. For his meritorious service, Scholz's officer promoted him to Oberschütze (private first class).

After the campaign's end, the Wehrmacht transferred his unit to Germany's western border in preparation for invading France. On 10 May 1940, the unit crossed the Dutch border, continued through Belgium, and entered France. "The French were poor fighters and gave up their country easily. We had few casualties and hardly ever saw the enemy." They reached the northern coast of France in a few weeks and the hostilities quickly ceased. Scholz thought the war was "horrible." However, when asked if he ever felt guilty about serving, he said, "No, why should I feel guilty for something that was required of all Germans? My commander and comrades liked me and I did my duty."

When asked if he felt shy with his comrades because of his sexual orientation, Scholz said no. The quarter-Jew Florian Stahmer, on the other hand, explained that due to his racial status and homosexuality, he "retreated more or less into his Ivory Tower," meaning that he did not associate with many and mistrusted most.[6]

Homosexual *Mischlinge* suffered as both Jewish and "sexual degenerates," two of several groups the Nazis persecuted. Most *Mischling* homosexuals and bisexuals documented successfully hid their sexual orientation, but not their ancestry. For example, the army almost discharged Fritz Bayerlein, the later famous general and Rommel's chief of staff in Africa, in 1934 when the *Arierparagraph* came out. However, because of his abilities, Hitler probably awarded him an exemption. Although he could not hide his quarter-Jewish status, he surprisingly could escape persecution for his bisexuality. Although police files existed about his homosexual activities prior to 1933 and even though some of his subordinates knew about his behavior, Bayerlein prevented that information about his life from reaching the authorities. He became one of the most successful German generals, adding the Oak Leaves with Swords to his Knight's Cross and commanding the Panzer Lehr Division.[7]

Since the Third Reich prohibited homosexuality, when the Nazis found a *Mischling* guilty of this crime, they judged him harshly. For example, half-Jew Herbert Lefèvre had received Hitler's *Genehmigung* (special permission) and served in the navy (see chapter 4 for more about the *Genehmigung*). He was also a member of the Nazi Party and SA. In 1944, a court found him guilty of homosexuality and sentenced him to death. He had misused his position as a cook by giving extra food to fellow sailors in return for sexual favors. Naval judge August Berges ruled that as a half-Jew, Lefèvre should have taken advantage of the chance to prove himself a worthy member of the Wehrmacht. Instead of seizing this opportunity, he had revealed the true "criminal instincts of his Jewish heritage." His party membership and *Genehmigung* did not excuse his dastardly behavior as a sailor. The court, reasoning that Lefèvre should have been extra conscientious in fulfilling his obligations because of his privileged status, showed no mercy. The Nazis hanged him on 6 July 1944; it took him seven minutes to die.[8] In light of this case, Scholz was lucky his sexual status remained unknown.

In the fall of 1940, when Scholz reported to headquarters, his commander explained that they would have to discharge him. A few days later, in Hamburg, the authorities gave him papers stating "that the military no longer wanted me because I was a half-Jew." Scholz said his discharge rescued him from dying in the east. All his comrades died in Russia during 1941 and 1942. "They were slaughtered on the fields of Russia. I'm here today because of Hitler. Hitler allowed me to live. Strange paradox, isn't it?"

After his discharge, Scholz looked for work. When people asked why he was not in the army, he answered honestly, saying, "I'm a half-Jew and I'm not allowed to serve." Hearing this, potential employers rejected him. Since he had no place to turn, Scholz went to his father for help in December 1940.

His father was a successful lawyer with the motto *"Scholz entscheidet schnell"* (Scholz decides quickly). Although his father was a miser and anti-Semite, Scholz knew this was his best chance for employment. His father gave him some money for the first month to pay bills, but no job. In this time period, Scholz failed to find work and returned to his father for further support. Instead of receiving more assistance, Scholz got into a dispute with his father when he refused to help.

During the argument, Scholz mentioned his veteran status and called his father a coward for not serving in World War I. (He knew that before his father visited his draft board in 1914, he had drunk a lot of coffee to make his heart beat quickly. The ruse worked and the board rejected his father, thinking he had a heart condition.) Enraged, his father screamed, "Get out, you Jew! Out, you dirty Jew. And I don't want to have anything to do with you until your Jewish mother is six feet under."

When Scholz returned home, his mother panicked and told him, "I'd hoped your military service would help me. Oh, no, life's over. What am I going to do? I didn't choose to be a Jew. Why's this happening?" Scholz felt irritated and asked, "Mother, what about me? What am I going to do to support us?"

Eventually, he found work in Hamburg at the Peltzer & Sussmann plant. Run by the Wittenburg family, the plant produced air conditioners and heating utilities. Since the owner's wife was Jewish, they made an effort to help half-Jews.

Scholz's mother continued to have problems. Several Gestapo agents threatened her with deportation, and sometime in 1942, the Nazis ordered her to show up for a train headed to Theresienstadt. On her deportation day, 20 July 1942, Scholz accompanied her to the station. She was hysterical. Noticing the panic-stricken woman, an SS man asked what was going on. When Scholz explained, the SS man said that, if he wanted, Scholz could accompany his mother. Scholz declined, saying he could do more for her by staying in Hamburg. "I'm glad I didn't get on that train," he said. "I might not be here today had I done so." On 6 December 1942, his mother wrote from Theresienstadt to wish Scholz a "Merry Christmas," claiming in jittery handwriting that she was all right and healthy.

In July 1943, things took a turn for the worse when a Gestapo agent denounced Scholz for anti-Nazi activities. He was arrested. "The agent had even claimed that I smelled like a Jew," Scholz said, shaking his head. The Nazis then deported him to Fuhlsbüttel concentration camp in a suburb of Hamburg.

Before leaving, he said goodbye to his sister Eva Maria. Later, she explained her brother's problem to her Aryan lover, who had a friend from law school working in the Hamburg Gestapo office. Amazingly, this friend obtained Scholz's release from the camp after only a week there. His arrest may have saved Scholz's life, because his incarceration took place during the ghastly bombing of Hamburg in late July, which killed more than 30,000 inhabitants.[9] "The place where I had been staying," Scholz said, "was burned to the ground."

After his release, Scholz worked gathering steel beams in the destroyed areas of Hamburg, where he came across the charred remains of human beings. "That was horrible to see these burned bodies," he said, waving his hands.

He continued to receive letters from his mother and did his best to always answer her. On 8 August 1943, he wrote her that he felt "happy to hear good news from you" and reported he had survived the last bomb attack. He told her he would send her a food package soon. Many of his letters never reached her. For example, on 23 August, the Organization for Jews in Germany returned to Scholz a card to his mother from 8 August, telling him that letters with news about bombings "aren't allowed to be sent to Theresienstadt."

Scholz's mother wrote a friend on 25 April 1944 that she worried about her children, from whom she had not heard in a while. She felt sad her son had "forgotten her." This was not true. Scholz wrote his mother continually. Very likely the bombings, the breakdown of the postal system, and the Nazis at Theresienstadt prevented delivery of his letters. Ironically, Scholz's mother's outgoing mail always seemed to reach its destination.

In February 1945 Scholz's boss fired him. At the same time, Scholz heard that the Nazis were deporting half-Jews and he felt the walls closing in. He decided to flee to Trendelburg in central Germany, where his sister was hiding. His Aryan girlfriend Ilse Leopold and her family helped him escape.

Remarkably, both he and his mother survived the war. "However, though my mother may have survived physically, she became crazy. The Nazi persecution made her insane," he said. They also lost many family members. Scholz's uncle and his wife and two daughters died in the Holocaust. The Nazis also killed his cousin Alice Rosenbaum (née Kallmes) and her daughter Josefine Rosenbaum (née Elbe) in Riga on 4 December 1941. Right before her deportation, Scholz saw his cousin Alice, who told him, "Don't worry about me, Klaus-Peter. You know I'll not let them do away with me!" The Nazis shot his cousin and great-aunt along with another relative, Liesel Abrahamsohn, after they arrived in Riga. After the authorities sent his uncle Hermann Samuel to the ghetto at Lodz, he was never heard from again. His uncle Heinemann David and aunt Dora David (née Rosenbaum) died in Theresienstadt. When the Germans deported Heinemann, he was nearly ninety years old and was taken away on a stretcher. "Talk about the Nazis having a small penis complex when they send 90-year-old decrepit men off to their deaths for fear of what they might do to the 'Movement,'" Scholz said.

When asked about his awareness of the Holocaust, Scholz said he knew about deportations and the general persecution but not about the systematic gassing of millions. "Who could've thought of it?" he said and added that most Germans probably did not know either, "but had they known, they would've been happy about it. Anti-Semitism is big in Germany."

Scholz went on to explain he is pleased with modern Germany because it has done so much to admit its guilt and has helped support the study of the Holocaust by preserving historical sites and funding archives and museums. He feels the country has done a lot to make restitution to its victims, although he admits more could be done. "I'm proud of the Germans," he said. "They've done a better job than the Japanese, who have been a disgrace with the way they have dealt with their genocidal campaign against China and other nations. Aren't the Japanese about honor and respect? Well, I find them cowards for not admitting what they did during the war. Many of their leaders still visit the shrine where notorious war criminals like Tojo are buried—this is like German politicians visiting Himmler's or Eichmann's grave. The Rape of Nanking is evidence enough that the Japanese were every bit as evil as the Nazis were."

Scholz's statements are true. Japan has a poor record when it comes to admitting its crimes against humanity during World War II, even though these crimes are well documented. At least 15 million Chinese died under Japanese rule alone, and the majority died due to extermination policies.[10] As the *Encyclopedia of Genocide* notes, the 15 million who died did so from "bombing, starvation, and disease that resulted from the Japanese terror campaign."[11]

Japanese officials and historians have "systematically kept all mention of their atrocities out of the nation's history textbooks."[12] Journalist Honda Katsuichi wrote, "Unlike the Germans and Italians, the Japanese have not made their own full accounting of their prewar actions."[13] In the end, Scholz's observation about the Japanese is true, and it is sad that Japan has problems dealing with its wartime past.

After the war, Scholz tried to live in Germany but felt he could no longer remain in a land that had given birth to Nazism. In 1957, he emigrated to Canada, worked for a company that dealt with kitchen appliances, and retired as a director.

In 1958, he decided to reaffirm his Jewish beliefs. "I told my mother, 'We're who we are, Jews. I'm tired of living in denial of this, Mother. I want to be a Jew.'" He went to Rabbi Stern at Temple Emanuel in Montreal and said, "I want to be a Jew and I want to make it official. I've always felt Jewish." Scholz underwent circumcision and became a temple member. He was quick to explain that he converted not because he believed in God, but because he wanted to affirm his cultural and ethnic identity. Scholz does not believe in God and thinks people who do believe in God are misled and weak.

Scholz is exceptional for his passion about his history. He remains traumatized by his persecution and evidently by his relationship with his mother. His story illustrates how difficult it can be to step out of the shadow of pain experienced when young.

Scholz always "felt" Jewish and came to treasure his Jewishness, as reflected by the formal steps he took in 1958 to "make official" his identity as a Jew. He felt that by doing so, he could claim a part of himself that had been denied him. This has helped him deal with the pain of the past and started him on a road of remaining true to himself. Yet during the interview, he admitted, "I struggle with who I am. But isn't that the way all humans live their lives?"

Half-Jewish Unteroffizier Karl-Arnd Techel

With his white beard and handlebar mustache, Karl-Arnd Techel, at the time he was interviewed, looked as if he had stepped out of a nineteenth-century portrait standing next to philosopher Friedrich Nietzsche or Chancellor Otto von Bismarck. He radiated energy and intelligence. As

Pastor Karl-Arnd
Techel in Berlin
before giving a
sermon, circa 1980.

he discussed his past, he explained that God drives everything in life. His belief in God gave him peace and comfort. Consequently, he learned to take life as it comes, because worrying accomplishes nothing and God does everything for a reason.

Techel, born 19 November 1920 in Wilhelmshaven, had a gentile father, Arnold, who served as a career naval officer, and a Jewish mother, Paula (née Pick), who worked as their homemaker. On marrying Arnold, Paula converted to Christianity. She did so for love and because she believed in Christ's message. As a result, she raised her children in a strong

Protestant tradition. Techel had one sibling, a younger brother, Hanns-Dieter, born on 22 December 1921.

When young, Techel did not know his mother was Jewish. In 1933, when Hitler became chancellor, Techel's parents worried about their sons' future and wondered whether they should talk with them about their mother's Jewish background. They decided to keep it quiet, reasoning that "what the boys don't know won't hurt them." Yet they still allowed their sons to spend time with their Jewish relatives, and their Jewish grandmother lived with the family. "Even when she died in 1935 and was buried in a Jewish cemetery, I still didn't think I was Jewish . . . I knew she was Jewish but as a small child I didn't understand that this affected me. So much for being aware of your surroundings as a teenager," Techel commented.

One day, as Techel left for school, his father gave him a letter for his teacher explaining their situation in case his son needed assistance. He gave strict directions that his son should not read it, and Techel obeyed. His father trusted the teacher with this delicate information. Many *Mischlinge* experienced problems in school because, as historian James Tent wrote, "A pattern of social exclusion for *Mischlinge* was emerging all over Germany as National Socialism permeated the educational system."[14]

Techel remembered strange things happening in his home during this time, which, as a young person, he was unable to understand. For example, his father was prohibited from displaying the Nazi flag outside their window, as the neighbors did, because a Jew lived there. Techel's father, a war veteran, found this shameful. Despite such problems and the departure of Jewish relatives from Germany, Techel's family stayed. They did not think life would turn dangerous, especially since Admiral Erich Raeder had offered his help to Arnold.

In school, Techel enjoyed studying the "Aryan" racial theories. Since he was blond and blue-eyed, his teachers often told him that he came from the Aryan "master race." "Little did those people know that my mother was a Jew. That would've shocked them," Techel said with a laugh.

During his boyhood, Techel participated in a Protestant youth group that sponsored camping trips, cookouts, and tours of Europe. The group also conducted Bible studies and community projects. Techel loved his comrades and admired his youth minister, Helmut Siegelerschmidt, who also happened to be half-Jewish.

In 1936, the Nazis disbanded the group and transferred its Aryan members to the Hitler Youth. As a half-Jew, Techel was not allowed to join. Only then did he learn of his Jewish ancestry, and he felt dismayed to belong to an unpopular minority. But the thought that Jesus, "the son of God," was a Jew gave him strength.

Yet, he still felt like an outcast. "It was strange to be in school on days when all Hitler Youth members were required to wear their uniform. It was obvious that those who didn't were *Mischlinge*," Techel said. After the Nazis disbanded his youth group, Techel joined the Confessional Church under Martin Niemoeller, the famous theologian and World War I U-boat captain.

Though everyone knew he was a half-Jew, most of Techel's schoolmates treated him well. However, a bully in his class often harassed him, and one day, when the "punk" pushed him too far, Techel lost his self-control and beat him into a "bloody pulp." "Afterwards," Techel said, "the bully never bothered me again. I'm glad I beat him up. Other than this guy, I didn't have any problems. My other classmates treated me well and I even had a few girlfriends."

But he felt nervous about having girlfriends, fearing the Nazis would punish him for committing *Rassenschande*. In those times, he wished his mother was not Jewish.

Techel finished high school in 1939 and entered the National Labor Service in preparation for the Wehrmacht. Ironically, the Nazis had kicked Techel's father out of the navy because he refused to divorce his Jewish wife. His mother felt guilty at having brought this misfortune upon her family. She considered divorce—a step taken by Helmut Krüger's mother, who believed it would improve her family's situation, as discussed earlier. However, Arnold refused to separate from his wife, whom he loved deeply.

Techel's extended family was suffering. The Gestapo had arrested and then beaten up his aunt Johanna Pick, and one of his cousins, Johanna Sussmann (née Pottlitzer), committed suicide because of Nazi persecution. Her children Irma and Ruth emigrated. Irma traveled to Shanghai, and Ruth to London. He never heard from them again.

Half-Jewish
Unteroffizier Karl-
Arnd Techel in dress
uniform. (Military
awards: EKI, EKII,
Paratroop Assault
Badge, and Wound
Badge)

After Techel finished his National Labor Service in 1940, he entered the paratroopers, the elite branch of the Luftwaffe, right at a time when half-Jews were banned from military service. "They were a crazy group, these paratroopers," Techel said, "and I was proud to be a member." He trained as a field medic and felt excited by this job because it allowed him to help others. Soon after Techel's enlistment, his brother Hanns-Dieter was drafted.

Techel's first action took place on the island of Crete in the middle of the Mediterranean in May 1941. Now an Unteroffizier (corporal), he took care of the medical needs of his company. When he and his com-

Karl-Arnd Techel in camouflage dress with helmet ready for his jump on Crete in 1941.

rades got the news they were headed for combat, they felt excited. He wrote in his diary, "It's finally here. The time that we've waited for so long. The deployment! The 'jump' against the enemy!"

Göring attacked Crete, hoping to regain some of the prestige the Luftwaffe had lost for failing to win the Battle of Britain. Hitler approved the attack and gave the operation the code name Mercury. In total, 600 Junkers-Ju52 planes carried thousands of paratroopers and hauled 80 gliders full of light tanks and personnel. An additional 280 bombers, 150 Stuka dive bombers, and 200 fighters flew air cover and provided ground support. Altogether 22,000 men invaded the island, one of whom was Techel.[15]

As they flew to the drop zone on 20 May, Techel looked at the godforsaken brown rock they were about to assault surrounded by a dark blue ocean. As he jumped with the others, Techel yelled "attack" and then waited for his chute to fill with air.

On the way down, he saw the flashes of gunfire and heard the whiz of enemy bullets fly by his head. He saw men shot in the air and watched their bodies go limp with death. He hoped to hit the ground alive and prayed to God. "Later I found out that the British had been reading our radio messages and knew our drop locations. It was a turkey shoot," Techel said.

When Techel and his comrades landed, they discovered they had missed their target area by several miles. Also, since German paratroopers dropped weapon canisters separately, they had to first scramble around to locate their rifles and machine guns. Unfortunately, the canisters had drifted off course a mile away from their drop zone.

While gathering their weapons, Australian troops attacked them. Only the officers and NCOs with their pistols returned fire. Techel shot back with his sidearm, but "pistols are no match for machine guns they used against us," he explained.

Techel and his comrades set up a defensive perimeter and fought for hours, taking heavy casualties. As Techel tended the wounded, the explosion of an artillery shell lifted him off the ground. As he regained his bearings, he felt the warm ooze of what he thought was blood on his neck. He put his hand to his neck and then brought it before his face. Grayish white gunk stuck to his fingers, and he recognized it as brain matter. Over to his left lay a fellow soldier with eyes wide open. Shrapnel had taken off the top of his skull as cleanly as if a large can opener had done it. His brains lay everywhere, especially all over Techel. He pulled himself together and continued to help the wounded.

The German casualties were appalling. One company of the Third Battalion, First Assault Regiment, lost 112 out of 126 men. By the end of the first day, 400 of the original 600 men of this battalion were dead.[16] Meanwhile, Techel stayed extremely busy saving the wounded. Besides worrying about the Allies, the Germans concerned themselves with the civilian population. Since many Germans did not have their weapons, the Cretans attacked them, "including women and children," using flintlock rifles, axes, and spades.[17] The fight for Crete was a bloody affair.

For twenty-four hours, Techel's group fought a losing battle until a nearby company came to their rescue and defeated the Australians. After several days, the Germans took the island. For his brave actions, Techel received the Iron Cross Second Class, a rare award for a medic.

After Crete, Techel returned to Germany and his unit prepared for the attack on Russia. Germany's invasion of Russia started in June 1941, and a few months later, Techel and his comrades flew to the outskirts of Leningrad near the great Ladoga Lake. During heavy fighting one day, Techel performed what would be his bravest act by pulling a man off the battlefield and saving him from certain death. Wounded in the process, Techel received the Wound Badge.

When asked if any comrade knew about his ancestry, he said none did. He added, "Remember, I also didn't wear it on my sleeve. I was a German with Germans. I didn't find it strange to serve as a half-Jew in the Luftwaffe. I was raised as a patriotic German. I felt like the others. My unit became my home and in order to keep it that way, I knew that I couldn't discuss my ancestry."

In spring of 1942, the military granted Techel leave to study medicine in Germany. While he was attending medical school, the Luftwaffe informed him in October of his dismissal from the Wehrmacht because he had reported his ancestry incorrectly. He was not disappointed, because he had seen too much suffering and was tired of war.

Yet Techel felt mixed emotions about leaving, explaining, "It was a great camaraderie. I felt honored to be a paratrooper and serve Germany, but I hated the fact I had to serve Hitler to do so. When I was discharged I no longer had to struggle with this dilemma. My brother was dismissed later in 1943, and he also expressed relief at not having to serve that madman anymore." Today, Techel feels his discharge saved his life. Most of his comrades died and the longer one served against the Soviets, the worse his odds for surviving became.

Techel was lucky that he was only discharged. Sometimes not revealing one's ancestry got one into severe trouble. According to Holocaust survivor Moshe Mantelmacher, while he worked at Buna-Auschwitz in the work station there, three half-Jewish soldiers arrived who had recently fought on the Russian front. The *Mischlinge* told Mantelmacher that while serving on the front, the Nazis had discovered their lie and deported them.[18]

In 1943, after finishing two semesters at medical school, the authorities forced Techel to leave the university because of his racial background. Dr. Cropp in the Reich Ministry of the Interior wrote Minister of Education Bernhard Rust that he did not think Techel had a good character because he had lied about his ancestry to remain in the military. Rust agreed, and Techel was expelled.

After his expulsion from medical school, Techel worked in a laboratory in Berlin. Living as a civilian, he felt uncomfortable on the street, in the underground, and at work when people asked why he was not in uniform. He made up stories about war injuries for strangers, but could not lie to those with whom he worked, and it quickly became known on his jobsite why he could not serve. Many coworkers shunned him.

In 1943, he fell in love with Irmgard Wendlandt. Her father, Friedrich, wanted to stop the relationship. Although an anti-Nazi and deeply religious, Friedrich worried about the problems that Techel's half-Jewish status could create for his daughter and asked Techel to leave her alone. This hurt Techel deeply, but luckily for him, Irmgard refused to break off with him. Soon thereafter, they became engaged.

As a half-Jew, Techel was ordered in November 1944 to perform forced labor for the Organization Todt—Action B. Such laborers were then called "OT-men" or "B-men."[19] "B-men" is based on *Bewährungsmänner* (men on probation, although Historian James Tent writes that the "B" actually stood for "bastards," which meant "mixed race" in Nazi bureaucratic jargon).[20] About 700 other half-Jews, most of them young, were at Techel's deportation center. After a few hours of waiting, the Nazis sent them to Spandau, a suburb of Berlin. Techel did not know why the Nazis had called up the half-Jews or where the authorities were sending them. He did not even know about Auschwitz until after the war and surprisingly did not fear for his life.

He quickly learned that half-Jews were being sent to OT camps throughout Europe. The Germans deported some to work on defensive works in the west, others to synthetic gas refineries in central Germany, and still others to work camps in France and Italy. This gave him an idea he thought would make his life easier.

He went to the OT office at the deportation center and talked to the OT secretary, Olga Pankraz (née Kornrumpft), who surprisingly was also a half-Jew. He told her that he was a medic and wondered if he could find a camp where he could use his skills. She was helpful and put his name on a different list and he, along with hundreds of other half-

Jews, boarded a train headed for southern Tyrol for an OT camp in Italy. Before they left, they received normal train tickets—"such was Germany's efficiency," Techel said, shaking his head. At his camp, the inmates produced canned foods and built roads, and when needed, Techel tended the sick and injured. The OT commanders treated the inmates respectfully and made special brown uniforms for them since *Mischlinge* could not wear the standard gray OT uniform.

In this camp, he was allowed to write his loved ones and his fiancée, Irmgard. While he labored away in the camp, she was drafted to a flak unit. Confused about how to direct fire on Allied planes, Irmgard asked Techel for advice and he found himself in the strange position of writing to her how best to shoot down attacking bombers.

At war's end in the spring of 1945, Techel woke up one day to find his guards gone and to hear the rumble of approaching Soviet tanks. Freedom was close at hand. When the Russians liberated his camp, he told them that the inmates were half-Jews. The Russian interpreter was skeptical, believing Hitler had murdered the half-Jews. It took several hours of explaining until the Soviets understood that most German half-Jews were still alive. Techel was lucky. Some half-Jews elsewhere were not so fortunate. When half-Jew Karl Helmut Kaiser tried to explain his situation to impatient Russian soldiers, they shot him in cold blood.[21]

Although Techel had served in Russia, he still did not know that Hitler had systematically murdered the Jews. The atrocities dumbfounded him, and he discovered after 1945 that at least eight relatives had disappeared in the east. He also learned that had Germany won the war, he himself would have also been executed.

Many half-Jews did not think their lives were in danger. Even after his deportation, Techel did not believe this marked the beginning of his own end.

When asked if he feels Jewish, Techel said he does not. He knows that by Jewish law, religious Jews consider him Jewish, but "this sounds like the Nazis to me, splitting up people between those who are accepted and those who are not. My Jewishness is just as important to me as it was for the musician Felix Mendelssohn—in other words, it's not. I'm just a human being," Techel said. He continued, "I also have a hard time saying that I'm partially Jewish. I think most half-Jews have a problem with admitting they have a Jewish parent. We are always scared of discrimination."

After the war, Techel married Irmgard, had children, studied theology, and became a Protestant preacher. He enjoyed living his "life for God" and had no regrets. One month after my interview in 1997, he passed away.

Techel was deeply religious, an uncommon quality among the men documented in this research. Many had had some belief in God as boys, but as they experienced war and the Third Reich, they felt the absence of God. Men like Karl-Arnd Techel and Pinchas Hirschfeld are rare in that they were able to survive Hitler's evil with their faith intact.

Techel was also a different kind of soldier because he served as a medic. This helped him in war since he spent his combat hours saving lives, not taking them. Although he provided healthcare to Hitler's armies, he felt he was doing good among the host of bad options presented him.

Half-Jewish Schütze Hans Meissinger

Hans Meissinger approaches history and its lessons as he does everything else—scientifically. He was a NASA scientist and one of the world's leading space engineers. His speech rarely shows emotion, but it is full of content. He comes across as a kindly "grandpa" type who has enjoyed his life and family. He often smiles and his good humor about life would never betray the pain and trauma he experienced under the Nazis. He survived Hitler and has learned that a positive attitude brings out the full richness of life. He said that his experience under the Third Reich was a nightmare and "the sooner you forget, the better." But then he added that you can never truly forget but only repress something unpleasant in the past and that memory is always there.

Meissinger was born on 25 November 1918 in Villingen, a small town on the eastern side of the Black Forest at the source of the Danube River. His family had its roots in Hesse near Frankfurt am Main, and Meissinger considers himself a "Frankfurtonian." His mother, Rosa (née Oppenheimer), was Jewish and his father, Karl August, was a gentile. He had three siblings: a brother, Ernst, born in 1910, and sisters Lilli, born in 1915, and Marlies, born in 1920.

Hans Meissinger in
the mid-1980s.

Meissinger's mother alienated her parents and her entire Orthodox
Jewish family by marrying a *Goy*. She was rebellious and tired of living
in a narrow-minded, strict Orthodox Jewish world and wanted to break
free from it.

After World War I, when Meissinger was an infant, the family moved
back to Frankfurt. Meissinger enjoyed school, excelled in his studies, and
had a normal childhood until 1933, when Hitler came to power. In his
spare time, Meissinger hiked or biked in the mountains with his siblings
or friends. He also enjoyed exploring the ancient Roman ruins scattered
around the Frankfurt region. Living conditions for Meissinger and his
family grew steadily more difficult and threatening under the Nazis' re-

lentless persecution of non-Aryans. At that time over 600,000 Jews lived in Germany and, according to a number of sources, probably well over 1 million *Mischlinge*.[22] Many German Jewish people emigrated during the 1930s, but not all escaped Nazism. Many perished during the Holocaust because they sought refuge relatively nearby in France, Belgium, the Netherlands, and Poland in the 1930s, countries that Germany later would conquer.

Because both Meissinger's Orthodox Jewish grandparents, Seligmann and Fanny Oppenheimer, disapproved of their daughter Rosa's marriage to Karl August, they had little or no contact with her and her children. However, Rosa's two brothers and two sisters and their families maintained normal family relations and often helped her in times of need, especially after her husband left her and the family in 1930. Consequently, Meissinger became familiar with Jewish religious traditions. Some of his relatives, primarily his uncle Joseph Oppenheimer, often invited him to observe Shabbat (Sabbath) and share meals marking religious holidays.

At the time of Meissinger's parents' marriage in 1909, his paternal grandparents had already died. Had they been alive, they would have strongly opposed the union. Most of his father's relatives objected to the marriage, including the majority of his twelve siblings, and some tried to deter him. They did not think it wise to marry a person of such "tainted" ancestry.

By 1930 the marriage of Karl August and Rosa Meissinger was on the rocks. Karl August became unfaithful and left Rosa in 1930 to live with another woman, who soon bore him a son. Meissinger's father wanted a divorce, but his mother refused it since she and their four children depended on his financial support. In 1934, the Nazis dismissed Karl August from the school where he taught not only because of his Jewish wife, but also because he had written articles against Hitler. In 1935, after the enactment of the race laws, it was easy for a non-Jewish German to get a divorce from a Jew and Meissinger's father finally succeeded. The Nazi court understood that he did not want to remain married to what it termed a "racially inferior person."

Although Meissinger's father got rid of his Jewish wife, he still had problems since the authorities had marked him as an anti-Nazi and, thus, barred him from teaching high school. Remaining unemployed, he was able to support himself by writing historical novels that were widely published in Germany.

After 1933, Meissinger's high school years in Frankfurt's prestigious Lessing Gymnasium were adversely affected by his racial status. Nonetheless, only a few of his teachers and classmates treated him poorly. Yet while his friendship with some Aryan classmates remained intact, he associated more with the Jewish and half-Jewish children in class. The Jewish ones ultimately left the school, lucky to emigrate in the mid-1930s. He quickly learned which classmates were half-Jewish, and when asked how, he said, "I don't know anymore. I just knew." Of a class of twenty-five students, he recalls only about five being Nazis. Nevertheless, he suffered discrimination. One day during band practice, the teacher ordered Meissinger out because he was a half-Jew. Also, because of his ancestry, the school did not allow him to compete in athletic events. This depressed him because while the teachers recognized everybody else for their physical feats, he had to stand on the sidelines. The school also excluded Meissinger from field trips, though some of his teachers protested this. In those years, every day, his family felt oppressed, and "it was sad," he said, "to see the circle of 'friends' shrink."

Starting in 1935, when the Nazis issued the Nuremberg Laws, Meissinger had to refer to himself as a "half-Jew" or "non-Aryan" in official documents. These laws made "things worse than one thought possible." Meissinger said that at this point, Germany ceased being a nation of law and decency.

In 1937, Meissinger graduated from high school at the top of his class, with honors. He feels grateful to the principal, who had to fight teachers to let this happen. As was the case for Karl-Arnd Techel's brother, Hanns-Dieter, some half-Jews were not allowed to finish their secondary education.

Meissinger then entered the National Labor Service to complete his mandatory seven months of duty before beginning academic studies at the Technical University of Berlin, the only university that would take him regardless of his background. Later, when at the university, one of his professors, Dr. Kucharski, wrote Meissinger a recommendation in case he emigrated and continued his studies abroad. When Kucharski handed him the recommendation, he asked, "Do you think you can get out of this prison?" Meissinger told him that he indeed hoped to do so, but unfortunately, his efforts to leave failed.

Meissinger and his family unsuccessfully tried to emigrate in 1938 and 1939, but few people in the foreign consulates wanted to help and the family simply did not have the necessary funds. The U.S. Consulate in Berlin even told Meissinger that his family was not sufficiently threatened to warrant immigration visas. Of course, after the war started in 1939, all chances to escape disappeared.

During these years, Meissinger hesitated to date Aryan girls because the laws prohibited such relationships. So he dated half-Jewish girls. "There were ways to find each other," he said. A half-Jewish subculture in Berlin did exist. They jokingly called themselves *Mampes,* after the popular cocktail Mampe Halb & Halb (Mampe Half-and-Half), based on a half-sweet, half-bitter brandy made by the Berlin beverage company Mampe.

Meissinger lived in a part of town where the Nazis destroyed stores and synagogues and arrested and murdered Jews during the pogrom of the Reichskristallnacht, 9–10 November 1938. His family, living in apartments belonging to Jewish landlords, was gripped by the horror of that night. "I felt unwelcome in my own country," Meissinger said.

After three academic semesters, the army drafted Meissinger in 1939. One week before World War II broke out on 25 August 1939, he started his basic training at the Küstrin infantry base, 50 miles east of Berlin. Meissinger felt ill at ease in "Hitler's army," but believed it might help him regain a more normal life as a citizen. Having suffered under the discrimination, he hoped the army would help him regain his self-respect. "I made my peace with being drafted," Meissinger said, "and after all, it was the law, and I had no other choice than to serve." Meanwhile, his older brother, Ernst, barred from teaching at a public school, had taught for five years at some Jewish high schools, first in Frankfurt and later in Berlin. He recalls part of a long conversation with Ernst, who came to visit him at the base soon after war started.

"Is there any way of getting out of serving?" Ernst asked.

"No," Meissinger answered, "though we're half-Jews, we have to serve. They'll kill us if we refuse. And what about Mom?"

Many half-Jews, especially those living in Berlin, called themselves *Mampe*. The term is derived from Mampe Half-and-Half, the name of a popular cocktail in Berlin at the time, which was made with a half-sweet, half-bitter brandy produced by the Mampe company.

"Yes, you're right about Mom. This may help her. I guess I'll have to serve just like you," Ernst replied.

This was the next to last time Meissinger saw his brother before Ernst was killed in action during the 1940 French campaign.

Meissinger and his brother did not find serving strange since they came from a family with a military tradition. Their father had served as an officer in World War I and was decorated with the Iron Cross. Their grandfather, Friedrich Meissinger, had volunteered in the Franco-Prussian war of 1870 as a seventeen-year-old and became a decorated sergeant at the battles of Metz, Gravelotte, and Noisseville. Two of their Jewish uncles, brothers of their mother, also served with distinction in World War I.

Hans Meissinger (last rank Schütze) in spring 1940.

When Meissinger and his brother left for the army, their mother cried. Rosa did not want her sons to go to war but knew they had to. She hoped that the army would dismiss Meissinger from service for a lung ailment he had contracted as a child. But a special medical examination of his condition did not change his status.

After boot camp, Meissinger became accustomed to soldiering and started to feel like a "normal German." During this time, Germany defeated Poland and his fellow soldiers celebrated the victory. But after Poland, Meissinger thought that the Wehrmacht's success actually increased the threat to his family. More power gained by Hitler meant more persecution for them. However, his insecurity did not interfere with his sense of duty.

Meissinger became a good marksman and tried to excel at whatever he did. He found that being a soldier "gave me a sense of not being an 'outcast,' which is what I'd experienced in civilian life." In early 1940, after the army transferred his infantry regiment to the western front near Trier, he started working as a scout and messenger. He reconnoitered and drew up maps of the surrounding region. His engineering background aided him greatly in this assignment. As a messenger, he kept the line of communication open between his company and battalion headquarters. Field telephones were not as widely available as one might have expected.

In April 1940, several weeks before the French campaign, Meissinger's company commander ordered half-Jews to report to headquarters. Their personnel files were pulled and the company sergeant questioned the men about their ancestry and noted their answers. The sergeant informed them that a change of regulations required their dismissal, although they were not immediately sent home. Meissinger volunteered the information about his Jewish mother; he simply felt he had no other choice.

Soon thereafter, in May 1940, Meissinger's company, part of the 230th Infantry Regiment, started to invade France. Along with other units, they attacked through Luxembourg and Belgium to bypass the Maginot Line, the principal fortification the French had built against invasions. When Meissinger's unit entered Belgium and then France, they did encounter considerable resistance and took some casualties through artillery and machine-gun fire. In his company of 120, they had around 10 casualties. Meissinger's company took part in the battles for Sedan, Verdun, and Toul.

On 11 June 1940, a shell blast almost killed Meissinger while he was digging a trench. Fortunately, the soil he had dug up shielded him from the shrapnel. "I was lucky to be alive," he said. "I could've just as easily stood above the trench and been torn to bits." The way Meissinger described his luck could have come from Erich Remarque's novel *All Quiet on the Western Front,* in which one of the soldiers says, "It is just as much a matter of chance that I am still alive as that I might have been hit. In a bomb-proof dug-out I may be smashed to atoms and in the open may survive ten hours' bombardment unscratched. No soldier outlives a thousand chances. But every soldier believes in Chance and trusts his luck."[23]

Meissinger's brother, Ernst, was not so fortunate, and chance was not on his side. On the same day that Meissinger experienced the shell blast, near the city of Rheims, about 50 miles north of Meissinger's unit, the French killed Ernst while he was crossing the Aisne River at Bouilly. The day before he died he wrote Meissinger, "If I have one more day like today, I won't make it." That was the last Meissinger ever heard from him. The loss of one's brother is devastating by itself, but "the fact that he had to die for Hitler was horrible for me and my family. I was shocked, embittered, and saddened beyond words," Meissinger said.

Ernst knew of the impending dismissal of half-Jews at the time of his death, but he never told his commanding officers about his background. His superior, Lieutenant Rudolf Herzog, wrote Meissinger's mother a kind letter of condolence describing how her son had died in battle. He stated how much his comrades and superiors liked Ernst. Hans Metzger, one of Ernst's comrades and friends, also wrote the family after Ernst's death, saying he had been standing nearby when the enemy shot Ernst through the head and that Ernst "died not only for Germany, but for all of you." His comrades buried Ernst in a graveyard in France.

A few months later, Meissinger and the other half-Jews in his company were sent home. Before Meissinger's commander dismissed him, he asked if he wanted to remain in the unit since he was a good soldier, but Meissinger declined, explaining he wanted to follow the law. He also wanted to return home to help his mother, who had already lost one son in the war and lived alone. The officer agreed with Meissinger's decision.

Actually, Meissinger did not want to serve anymore, but he could not then put it in those words. He claims that "being a soldier in the army of the Third Reich naturally gave me a bad feeling. The conflicting emotions are hard to reconstruct today. Of course, I had some confidence that doing what other Germans had to do provided some protection for my mother from the ever-present threat facing her. After I was dismissed from the army, that shield was gone." At regimental headquarters in Brandenburg, Meissinger was officially dismissed. "I was handed my papers and declared *wehrunwürdig* [unworthy of service] and a civilian." Meissinger thought being declared *wehrunwürdig* was absurd in view of his combat record. Ironically, some comrades told him "they wished that they were in the same spot! They didn't want to stay in the army."

After Meissinger's dismissal, he and his mother heard from a comrade of Ernst who wanted to pay his respects to the family. This "friend," Sergeant Plorin, met them at a café in Berlin. Plorin praised Ernst for his camaraderie and described how he had bravely died in battle. During the conversation Frau Meissinger told Plorin the particular agony she felt at having lost her son in "Hitler's army" because she was Jewish. Plorin had not known this about Ernst. Shocked, he cursed the Jews as the cause of all the ills that had befallen Germany. Frau Meissinger tried to contradict this by describing her two brothers, Rudolf and Leopold Oppenheimer, who had served honorably in World War I. In hindsight, Meissinger wished he had "said to that monster, 'For heaven's sake, have you no shame?'" but instead he grabbed his mother and quickly left "the scene of that terrible encounter." Frau Meissinger broke down and cried.

Later, Plorin's wife called Frau Meissinger to add her own insults and threatened her, saying she would soon be deported. With each passing day any illusion that "half-Jews" may have had before April 1940 that their military service would help them was slowly extinguished by ever-increasing anti-Jewish measures.

Soon after his discharge, Meissinger applied for federal financial assistance for his college studies. A civil servant replied that as a "non-German," Meissinger was disqualified from federal aid. Enraged, Meissinger wrote back that since he had served in the military and since his brother had died for Germany, his family had indeed proven they were German. He received no reply.

Nonetheless, Meissinger managed to resume his studies in Berlin, received his engineering degree in 1942 and, with the help of Professor Karl Klotter, found work as an aeronautical engineer at the aviation research institute in Berlin. There he did research on the guidance and control of aircraft and air-to-ground missiles until war's end. He later learned that this institution also had allowed other half-Jews to work there and that his supervisors took repeated steps to protect him from the Nazis. After the end of the war, he sent letters of gratitude to these people for their protection.

Meissinger's sisters, and particularly the younger one, Marlies, had to endure more persecution than he since the Nazis had prevented the women from entering the university and restricted the type of work they could do. To escape threatening Gestapo action, both girls, together with their mother, fled from Berlin in early 1945, escaping to southern Germany.

Meissinger's father, who had largely neglected the family by having his ex-wife and their four children fend for themselves, was greatly shocked by Ernst's death. After 1940, he showed more interest in his ex-wife's survival and protected her by finding places in Munich and Stuttgart to hide her during a period of threatened deportation in 1943 and 1944. Fortunately, Meissinger's mother survived the Nazis.

His father also stood up to family members who were against her. One of his brothers even threatened her with deportation. That brother, Hermann Meissinger, a passionate Nazi, hated that his brother had married a Jew and prevented any contact between his "Aryan" family and "those Jewish people." He expressed his horrendous anti-Semitic hatred in a comment he made after he learned of Ernst's death. When asked to offer his condolence to the family, he just said, "If they want my condolence, they can come and pick it up here." Meissinger's father never forgave his brother. Meissinger gratefully remembers his father's hospitality in allowing him to stay with his new family when Meissinger was stranded in Munich on a trip at the end of the war. His father was learning to be more tolerant and kinder.

Questioned about the Holocaust, Meissinger said he did not know the Nazis systematically murdered the Jews. After the war, he found out that one of his aunts, Bertha Elias, had been sent to a camp in the east and died there. Her husband, Markus Elias, had left her behind in Germany when he emigrated to the United States and eventually became a rabbi in Chicago. Meissinger said, "I hope he made his peace with his cowardly act of abandoning his wife to the Nazis." Meissinger's other aunt and uncle, Joseph and Josephine Oppenheimer, and their daughter Fanny were taken from Holland, where they had emigrated before World War II, to the Bergen-Belsen concentration camp. Fanny and her baby died there, but her parents luckily made it to Palestine in exchange for the release of German prisoners by the British. Their son, Erich, also survived the war, having lived in hiding in Amsterdam with the help of courageous Dutch people.

When talking further about the "Final Solution," Meissinger said,

"Neither Hannah [his wife, who was also half-Jewish] nor I knew much about the Holocaust during the war, nor did any of our friends, but we had terrible fears for the Jewish relatives who were deported. We didn't even hear of Auschwitz! No one could imagine the monstrous genocide that was under way . . . poor ignorant sheep that we were." They could not fathom that "Germany could do a thing like that." However, Meissinger heard a rumor in early 1940 that the Nazis had gassed Polish Jewish prisoners in buses. But he did not fully comprehend what he heard. Only after the war did he and Hannah learn about the Holocaust. He lost four relatives and Hannah two in Bergen-Belsen and Auschwitz.

Meissinger's statements about the Holocaust reiterate what many in this study have said. Both their actions and their testimonies show that most half-Jews truly did not know what was going on. As in Meissinger's case, he did not know what happened to his deported relatives, and not surprisingly, he did not know what was going to happen to him.

Not only did most *Mischlinge* like Meissinger not know about the systematic extermination, but also a large majority of Jews did not understand what was happening. Historian Jonathan Steinberg wrote, "Holocaust records show that Jews themselves often refused to believe what was happening in spite of the evidence of their own eyes."[24] Historian Marion Kaplan also wrote: "But a far more effective barrier to their comprehension was the sheer inconceivability of the genocide. Even those who received information frequently reacted with disbelief or repressed it."[25] So Meissinger was not alone in his ignorance.

When asked if he felt Jewish, Meissinger said he had never felt that way but that he did understand some things about the Jewish faith. Although his mother had broken away from her Orthodox roots, she did not convert to the Lutheran faith of her husband. "She retained many Jewish ideas," Meissinger said, "and often prayed Hebrew prayers with us children." At that point in the interview, Meissinger started to quote the familiar blessing "May the Lord bless you and keep you" in its original Hebrew version. He knew that according to Halakah, because his mother was Jewish, he is considered Jewish, but Halakah means nothing to him.

Meissinger, his mother, and his two sisters emigrated to the United States in 1947. The expertise gained in his job in Germany involving the performance and control of aircraft and missiles helped him find a job in New York. In 1949, he and Hannah, who had been one of his sister's schoolmates, married and in 1955 they moved to Los Angeles, where Meissinger worked on aircraft and spacecraft programs sponsored by the air force and NASA. Hughes Aircraft employed him first, and then TRW Space and Electronics, where he worked for almost thirty years. Meissinger became a successful aeronautical and astronautical engineer and worked in this field as a research scientist and project manager. He published more than fifty technical papers in the United States and abroad, as well as chapters in several textbooks on computers, aeronautics, and astronautics. He is widely known for his contributions and holds five U.S. patents in the fields of computer and spacecraft design.

The story of Meissinger's family is full of tragic events common to many families of mixed descent. That Meissinger's Jewish grandparents rejected his parents' marriage is not unusual. Countless people in this research have talked about the painful acts of rejection their parents, most often their Jewish parent, experienced from their family. As mentioned in chapter 1, Helmuth Kopp's horrible experience with his Jewish grandparents made him hate them for their prejudice and cruelty. Unfortunately, he was not alone.

Yet the rejection could work both ways, as in Meissinger's family. Unfortunately, Meissinger was not alone. We see this also in the despicable behavior of the fathers of Klaus-Peter Scholz and Karl-Heinz and Günther Scheffler and in Helmut Krüger's uncle. The anti-Semitism that Herr Scholz and Herr Scheffler in particular showed their ex-wives and sons illustrates the painful situations that interracial families often experienced in the Third Reich. Meissinger's father, to his credit, helped save his Jewish ex-wife. Sadly, it took the death of his son Ernst to awaken in him the moral integrity necessary to save lives. The Meissinger family's experience with assimilation was typical for the families of many of the men documented in this book. The men themselves were caught in the middle in more ways than one.

Meissinger felt lucky to have survived and still mourned his brother's death. He believed war is wasteful and in most cases unnecessary. This aspect of war is often overlooked. "The unquantifiable cost" of war "is in emotional suffering, by which the pain of one death is often multiplied many times, through the network of family relationships, and in long-term, indeed lifelong, deprivation." Emotional loss can never be made good.[26] Due to such pain, Meissinger questioned why humans go to war at all. He wished people would see how horrible hatred and killing are, but he did not have much hope for humanity. His experience taught him how much harm happens when humans fail to see the beautiful bridges that connect us and instead focus on the tiny little streams of ideology, religion, and culture that divide us. As the German writer Gotthold Ephraim Lessing wrote:

> We must be friends!—Disdain my folk, as much
> As ever you will. For neither one has chosen
> His folk. Are we our folk? What is a folk?
> Are Jew and Christian sooner Jew and Christian
> Than man? How good, if I have found in you
> One more who is content to bear the name
> Of man![27]

Meissinger echoes Lessing's sentiment that we are all *Mischlinge* in one form or fashion.

Half-Jewish Gefreiter Friedrich Wilhelm Schlesinger

Friedrich Wilhelm Schlesinger is a physical wonder. In his eighties at the time of our interview, he still enjoyed mountain climbing and snow skiing. Only his deeply wrinkled face with its weathered skin indicated his age. Otherwise, his energy and activities created the illusion that he is a middle-aged man. Dressed as a refined gentleman, he wore a silk scarf with his starched white dress shirt. He prided himself on his family's business success and plainly enjoyed life's material pleasures.

Schlesinger, born on 27 July 1915 in Werdohl, Germany, was raised as a Christian, as was his Jewish father, Paul, and his gentile mother, Luise (née Stromberg). Luise came from a prominent family of Lutheran preachers and lived a deeply religious life. One of her grandfathers was the distinguished Protestant Erckenschweig minister for South Westphalia, Germany.

Friedrich Wilhelm Schlesinger (far left) at his ninetieth birthday celebration on 27 July 2005, surrounded by his family.

Schlesinger's father's family was wealthy and owned several businesses. His grandfather, Adolf Schlesinger, a successful entrepreneur, had lived in Milwaukee, Wisconsin, and London. He owned hotels, restaurants, mines, and factories in Europe and America. Although born Jewish, he and his wife had converted to Christianity early in life and raised their seven children as Christians.

Schlesinger grew up in a mansion and enjoyed an excellent education. As a child, he did not know about his background. "My Jewish past," Schlesinger said, "was pushed away. We never talked about it." The way Schlesinger found out about this past shocked him.

After Hitler's ascent to power in 1933, the SA absorbed the ultra-nationalistic Stahlhelm youth group, to which Schlesinger belonged. As a proud member of the Stahlhelm, Schlesinger had participated in street fights with Communists. During the ceremony to mark the SA's takeover of his Stahlhelm unit, someone stepped forward and shouted that they could not accept "that Jew Schlesinger." "I was stunned," Schlesinger said. "I couldn't believe they were talking about me because I had not ever thought of myself as being Jewish." He left the meeting humiliated. He immediately called his father, who sent a car for him.

When home, he discussed with his family their ancestry and what to do about it. They asked whether anyone knew any Nazi Party "big shots." No one did. Next, they discussed problems Schlesinger would face in school and thought about moving him to another high school. "I worried about my future," he said. And sure enough, a few classmates mistreated him, and many teachers told him he was unwelcome. Often he felt the poor grades he suddenly started to receive were due to his racial background. A few classmates and even some teachers seemed to watch for him to fail. As a result, he lost his self-confidence.

His mother's brothers, Hermann and Franz Stromberg, as SS members, promised to protect him. They remained close to the family throughout the war and helped Schlesinger and his father where they could.

After finishing his *Abitur* in 1936, Schlesinger started working in the family business in Cologne. For the next few years, he had few problems.

Several universities rejected Schlesinger because of his Jewish past, but Karlsruhe University accepted his application to study mechanical engineering in 1937, probably due to the connections the family had at the college. However, the persecution of his family increased.

Schlesinger's Jewish uncle, Wilhelm Schlesinger, ran a manufacturing plant until the Nazis removed him in 1938. During that year, Schlesinger's uncle and father lost a lot of their clients. One man told his father, "We're really sorry that we cannot do business with you any longer because of your situation. I regret that we must take our business elsewhere." Shortly before Reichskristallnacht in November 1938, his family had to sell their home because the local authorities were making their lives miserable. On 1 September 1939, when Germany invaded Poland, Schlesinger and his family believed the war would quickly end, reuniting East Prussia with the mainland. They did not believe it would continue for five years.

On 6 September 1939, Schlesinger started his service in horse-drawn

Friedrich Wilhelm Schlesinger (last rank Gefreiter), circa 1942. (Military awards: EKII, Wound Badge, Assault Badge in Silver, and Eastern Campaign Medal 1941–1942)

Artillery Regiment 213 at the Priesterwald barracks in Heilbronn. He had a difficult time because he had to clean out stalls for the horses "and shovel their shit day and night." Since he loved mechanical engineering, he desired to serve in a Panzer unit. So he felt upset to serve in a horse unit. After a few weeks, though, he started to like his regiment and believed he was part of an elite unit. He assumed no one there knew about his Jewish background and he did everything he could to bury it.

Schlesinger's parents also felt relief. They told him, "Since you can now become a soldier nothing worse can happen to our family," but they were mistaken.

After boot camp, the army sent Schlesinger's company to the Ruhr region in northern Germany. While stationed there, his depressed father came to visit him. "It was a strange situation to have your Jewish father visit you while you served in an army loyal to Hitler. Back then, I hoped my service would help protect him," Schlesinger said.

At the beginning of 1940, the Wehrmacht transferred his battery to Lower Silesia at Kotzenau (now the Polish town Chocianow) near Lubin, where it continued training. In that town, he dated a young woman and told her his situation. She did not care.

During this time Schlesinger's father became sick. While on leave in the spring of 1940, Schlesinger visited his father in the Jewish hospital in Cologne where he had to stay. It gave him back his self-confidence to have his son, dressed in uniform, come and see him. He also hoped that his son's service would force the Nazis to treat his son as a full German.

The conditions in the hospital were horrible. There was not much to eat and no medication for him. Schlesinger's mother had to bring him his food from home. Schlesinger cried as he left his father at the hospital. That day would mark the last time he saw his father alive. A few months later, his father died there.

The army granted Schlesinger leave to attend his father's funeral. After the burial, he had to take the death certificate to the courthouse. When an official, seeing that his father had died in a Jewish hospital, asked, "Is your father Jewish?" Schlesinger answered yes. Visibly dumbfounded, the official nervously filled out the paperwork.

In the summer of 1940, Schlesinger's unit traveled to Lublin in eastern Poland, a region the Nazis called the General Government. While there, he witnessed how the Nazis mistreated the *Ostjuden* (eastern Jews). He felt appalled to think that some of his ancestors may have looked like the "strange" Hasidic (Orthodox) Jews dressed in their traditional garments. Even children and old people wore the Star of David, and Schlesinger heard that the SS had deported young people from the Jewish sections of town. Schlesinger did not discover where the Nazis sent them. "We didn't want to believe the rumors we heard," Schlesinger said. "How could one believe that people were being sent away to be killed? This was impossible to think."

In the winter of 1940–1941, his unit returned to the German state of

Silesia. Schlesinger and his comrades drank, chased women, and enjoyed life when not training. Then, in March 1941, they moved to East Prussia. There, they repeatedly practiced moving their horse-drawn cannons over difficult terrain, setting them up, and placing ordnance on a prescribed target.

One night in June 1941, Schlesinger stood watch at the radio hut. Suddenly he heard Hitler announcing war against the Jewish-Bolshevistic enemy. Soon the roar of hundreds of planes and the screams of diving Stuka sirens pierced the morning air as they rained bombs on enemy positions. It was 22 June 1941 and the invasion of Russia had begun.

The next day after the attack, Schlesinger's unit followed on the infantry's heels through Lithuania into heavy forestlands. Attached to the 403rd Security Division, his regiment moved deep into Russia, witnessing the destruction done by the advance units: dead enemy soldiers, burned-out tanks, mangled civilians, and killed horses lay along the roads. The smell of death filled the air. During those early summer months the German army labored away in the heat to conquer Russia. The dust kicked up on the dirt roads got into everything, and the metal helmets of the men were magnets for the sun's heat. The uniforms of most showed streaks of salt from heavy sweating. War had become a hot and dirty business.

One day, Schlesinger noticed Germans loading hundreds of Jews onto a freight train. He and his comrades thought they were traveling to forced labor camps. They did not know about *Einsatzgruppen* (mobile killing squads), and death camps were unimaginable. "I didn't know what I could do—should I try to help? Where should I go if I tried to escape? It was a strange situation to be in and I hated being half-Jewish. However, I don't know what would have been better—to have been totally Aryan and oblivious to the danger or totally Jewish and go to the camps. Today, we know that had I been a Jew I would not be here anymore," Schlesinger said. Though he had a chance to ask what was going to happen to those Jews, he kept his mouth shut. "I didn't want to know," Schlesinger said, "and I feared what they might suspect if I showed interest."

By September, Schlesinger and his unit reached Vilna, the ancient capital of Lithuania. Many wrongly think that the Wehrmacht was all mechanized, but 625,000 horses joined the 3.5 million soldiers invading Russia.[28] Their advance continued at a furious pace until heavy fall rains slowed them to a few miles a day.

His commander wanted to promote Schlesinger to corporal since he had performed well. However, Schlesinger remained at his current rank since his commander did not want to risk losing him by having to disclose his racial background. Schlesinger had become his battery's forward observer, a dangerous duty that required him to move with the infantry and radio-target locations. The life expectancy of forward observers was short, usually only a few weeks. Sometimes, he had to run across open fields to his observation position under hostile fire. "The first time I knew they were really firing at me, I became scared. However, in war, you start to get used to the most absurd situations," Schlesinger said.

With falling snow, the situation started to turn worse for Schlesinger and his comrades. They had entered Russia in their summer uniforms because Hitler had expected the war to last only a few weeks. However, he had miscalculated once again and thousands of soldiers froze to death in Russia's heartland. That winter turned out to be one of the coldest on record. General Guderian noted that temperatures fell to −63 degrees Fahrenheit and "it was death to squat in the open and many men died while performing their natural functions as a result of a congelation [freezing] of the anus."[29]

"And the cold wasn't the only thing that was bad," Schlesinger said. "We were also not camouflaged for this environment. Running around in the snow in gray uniforms provided easy targets for snipers, and they were everywhere. We had to cover ourselves with stolen bedsheets from homes to prevent the Russians from seeing us." Schlesinger said that those who were not careful would get their brains blown out.

Still, they continued to move gradually forward and by late November, Schlesinger's regiment was attached to the 255th Infantry Division near Smolensk. His unit made its way slowly to the south of Moscow. In December, they took up positions at Sukhinichi, and by Christmas, after the Soviet counteroffensive, they, along with two divisions, found themselves encircled. The Germans now had to supply them by air.

After several weeks of constant attacks, a Panzer division freed them, and in the bitter cold they marched several miles back to the rear eche-lons. Often their cannons would not fire because traversing mechanisms (moving parts of the gun) had frozen. Throughout the day, temperatures sometimes dropped to −30 to −40 degrees Fahrenheit and at night, it could get even colder. Sometimes the cold would immobilize all weapons except grenades, and so the battle turned into one where it came down to those who could throw the most grenades quickly and accurately.[30]

For the living, the harsh weather damaged exposed skin and men of-ten urinated on their "numbed hands to warm them, and hopefully, to cauterize the gaping cracks in our fingers."[31] It was so cold, Schlesinger said, that urine would freeze before it hit the ground. And in order to use the restroom and not experience frostbite on this part of the body, men had to wrap their penises in thick cloth.[32] Often people would wake up to find others, especially the wounded, frozen to death. The cold took such a toll on men's nerves that many had nervous breakdowns. Some even committed suicide.[33] The elements often proved more difficult to deal with than the enemy.

In February 1942, while attached to the 216th Infantry Division, Schlesinger's unit found itself retreating through a village under artillery fire. He remembers a shell slicing a horse literally in two and a separate blast knocking him to the ground and spraying his leg and arm with shrapnel. Deep red, his blood soaked into the snow. He yelled for help. When he reached an aid station, a medic cleaned his wounds and ex-plained he would recover. However, after a few days, he came down with a fever and his leg wounds started to ooze pus. They operated on his leg and extracted a piece of his pants and some metal. The swelling soon went down and the fever disappeared.

Instead of staying in the hospital, Schlesinger insisted on returning to his comrades. Also, he had seen how the wounded were treated and felt he had a better chance of surviving with his battery than in a field hospi-tal. When he arrived at his unit, the army had transferred it again to an-other division, this time the Eighteenth Panzer Division. One month later the unit moved yet again, to the 208th Infantry Division. "It was typical for a battery to be switched around a lot," Schlesinger explained.

During one battle, he and his fellow soldiers spotted an approaching

Im Namen des führers und Obersten Befehlshabers der Wehrmacht

verleihe ich

dem

Gefreiten
Friedrich Schlesinger
9./A.R.213

das

Eiserne Kreuz 2.Klasse

Korpsgefechtsstand......,den...16.3.........19.42.
Der Kommandierende General
XXIV.Pz.Korps
m.d.F.b.

Generalleutnant
(Dienstgrad und Dienststellung)

Friedrich Wilhelm Schlesinger's document of award for his Iron Cross Second Class.

Russian tank. They immediately engaged it while coming under heavy fire. They hit the tank between the body and the cannon, sending the turret flying into the air. As the men rejoiced, they started to take fire from a nearby house. They tried to connect their cannon to an armored car to get the "hell out of that place," but the snipers killed everyone except Schlesinger, who received only a shrapnel wound. He eventually connected the cannon to the Panzer by himself. "I don't know why I was not hit. Bullets were flying everywhere. However, I got the cannon out of there. I mean, as an artillery man you're not much worth to the infantry without your cannon," Schlesinger said.

As the tank drove away, Schlesinger placed his helmet on the machine-gun turret only to have it shot off by snipers. He survived with a small grenade splinter in the temple that a nurse later removed at a first aid station.

For his bravery, Schlesinger's superior awarded him the Iron Cross Second Class. One of his sergeants, however, protested on the ground that Schlesinger was a half-Jew. Nonetheless, Schlesinger's officers felt he deserved the medal and he received it. After this experience, his ethnicity likely became a topic of discussion. One day, one of his comrades said, "You know, there's something wrong with the Jews. But not you, Friedrich, you're all right."

By mid-1942, his unit participated in trench warfare at Shistra in northern Russia. At mail call, he received a letter from his mother, who wrote that she had not heard from his Jewish uncle Wilhelm since being sent to Theresienstadt. "I only found out after the war that the Nazis had sent him to Auschwitz from there. It sickened me to think that while I fought on the Russian front wearing the Iron Cross, my wonderful uncle was sent to the gas chambers in the east," Schlesinger said. One time he shared the story of his uncle's deportation with his commander, who expressed sympathy and could not believe the mistreatment.

During late 1942 and early 1943, Schlesinger's unit fought bitterly with the partisans. They were everywhere. "It became a nasty war and we hated them," he said. The partisans hurt the Germans a lot. Between August and November 1943, they blew up 200,000 rails, wrecked or derailed 1,014 trains with 814 locomotives, and destroyed or damaged 72 railway bridges.[34]

Friedrich Wilhelm Schlesinger taking a rest after watering two of his unit's horses. This picture was taken sometime in summer 1943 in northern Russia, probably near the town of Shistra.

Their hatred only increased the Germans' anger toward the Russians. The Wehrmacht commander for Belorussia claimed that in reprisals for partisan activities, "10,431 prisoners [were shot] out of 10,940 taken in 'battle with partisans' in October [1942] alone, all at the price of two German dead." This was just one of many "so-called 'anti-partisan campaigns.'"[35] The war in Russia turned into one without rules where each side often sought eradication of the other by any means.

In March 1943, Schlesinger's unit traveled away from enemy lines to a remote village to recuperate and receive new equipment. In his free time, Schlesinger read Heinrich Heine, the well-known German Jewish author. Although Propaganda Minister Joseph Goebbels had burned Heine's books, Schlesinger felt comfortable carrying around several of Heine's works with him. His comrades, instead of discussing the progress of the war, now just wished it would soon end. They now liked to talk in their off hours about how many girls they "had laid." "Few of us really faced what was happening. We just wanted to have fun and have peace like most young men do in any era," Schlesinger said.

In June 1943, after the army stationed his battery at Minsk in Ukraine, Schlesinger's superior told him he could not remain in the Wehrmacht because of his half-Jewish background. "I'd started to feel I was protected and had nothing to fear except Russian bullets. But when they explained I couldn't be a soldier, I became scared. I think I was more scared than when I was in battle. I almost cried when I was told to leave," Schlesinger said. His commander regretted the decision, but felt he could not go against the new regulations that banned half-Jews from the German service.

Schlesinger said his situation was strange. On the one hand, he felt pleased to finish his studies. On the other hand, he felt unprotected from Nazi attacks. His commander, Lieutenant Schlesremkämber, wrote Schlesinger a glowing letter of recommendation, dated 13 July 1943. Schlesremkämber stated that the "intelligent" and "brave" Gefreite Friedrich Schlesinger had received the Iron Cross and the Assault Badge and would have obtained the rank of "Unteroffizier long ago" had he not been half-Jewish. He also told Schlesinger that if he ever needed any help he should contact him.

Schlesinger returned to Karlsruhe, where he resumed his academic work with the support of the university's rector (president) Weigel. He continued to worry about his family and his own life. However, Schlesinger said that during this period, he knew nothing about the systematic murder of the Jews. "I should've known about it because of my situation," he said, "but even I didn't know what Hitler was really doing to the Jews."

He kept in touch with some of his Wehrmacht buddies, many of whom envied him. "It's strange to think that they fought in the east, with few of them ultimately ever returning home after 1943, while I had a good life from 1943 to 1945 studying engineering and sleeping with lonely women."

Having finished his studies and received his diploma at the beginning of 1944, Schlesinger started to work for I. G. Farben in Frankfurt. His boss knew about his background, but joked that he would protect him as his private "Jew."

As a civilian, people often asked him why he was not on the front. Just like Karl-Arnd Techel, Schlesinger had difficulties explaining his situation. He often told them he was in the reserves.

At the beginning of 1945 the Gestapo ordered him to report for forced labor to the OT. Ignoring the order, Schlesinger moved among different cities, where girlfriends hid him.

At war's end, Schlesinger welcomed the Americans in Frankfurt. He told the first soldier he met that he felt happy to see Germany free and Hitler dead. The soldier smiled and said, "Hey man, do you want a cigar?"

Schlesinger later encountered problems from the occupation forces because they did not realize that thousands of people of Jewish descent actually served in the Wehrmacht. One American officer challenged Schlesinger's service because he could not believe Schlesinger could be a soldier when at the same time his uncle was in Theresienstadt. This American officer plus countless other Allied personnel wondered why men of Jewish descent served under Hitler when they and their families were being persecuted. Yet, in the end many *Mischlinge* succeeded in explaining their situations adequately enough to get the papers they needed to be released earlier from prison or to work or study. Schlesinger eventually convinced this American officer to leave him alone and he soon returned to a normal routine. In late 1945, he started a business career and in 1955 joined the U.S. company W. R. Grace as a manager in Hamburg for one of its plants, where he worked for decades.

When asked about his religious beliefs, Schlesinger replied that although raised a Christian, he had "religious doubts" and that after his experiences during the Third Reich he did not believe in God. "If there's one," he said, "he doesn't care about us."

Schlesinger's experiences display the difficult situations of *Mischling* soldiers. On the one side, they felt good in the military and performed their duties well, but on the other side, they knew the Nazis persecuted and killed their families. And why, in the end, would God allow this?

Schlesinger echoes what many surviving *Mischlinge* feel about God. Several *Mischlinge* started out with strong faiths, but after having lost so many family members and seeing so much death in battle, most feel a strong aversion to religion and God. If God is just and merciful, they feel he must have been asleep during the war. Karl-Arnd Techel and Pinchas Hirschfeld, whose faith remained intact following the war, are exceptions to most of the men studied. The majority documented here have rejected religion and God. Schlesinger is typical in saying, "If God does exist, then He is a disgrace. He either chose not to prevent the Holocaust or he simply couldn't because he can't or because of the stupid rules He made for humanity not to intervene with free will. What a disgrace!"

Like Schlesinger, many *Mischlinge* express their disbelief in religion and God because a vast number of German Christians supported and even committed crimes against humanity. For example, the Protestant minister and leader as well as Nazi Party member Emmanuel Hirsch wrote of Hitler, "No other Volk in the world has a leading statesman such as ours, who takes Christianity so seriously." Hirsch believed "Hitler was a heaven-sent Christian leader" and that Jews were a "destructive force."[36]

Military reports and periodicals of the Third Reich era expressed the belief that "Providence has sent Germany the Führer at the right hour" or that the Wehrmacht's success was "redefined as a spiritual phenomenon, created by the Nazi party and directed by a God-sent Führer." Wehrmacht propaganda portrayed "Hitler and the Nazi creed as God's instruments charged with protecting German culture and blood, and communism as Satan's servant, unleashed from hell to destroy civilization."[37]

Not only the Wehrmacht but many churches also praised Hitler. Bishop Hans Meiser prayed in 1937, "We thank you, Lord, for every success . . . you have so far granted [Hitler] for the good of our people." Many churches extolled Hitler as the defender of Germany and, by extension, "Christianity from godless Bolshevism." The Catholic dioceses had church bells "rung as a joyful salute on Hitler's birthday on 20 April 1939 with prayers for the Führer to be said at the following Sunday mass." Some leading church scholars and leaders like Gerhard Kittel, Paul Althaus, and Emmanuel Hirsh supported Hitler and felt that God stood behind him.[38]

So when *Mischlinge* as well as other German Christians saw a large percentage of church leaders ignore Nazi persecution and apparently an indifferent God in the face of Hitler's atrocities, they rejected Christianity and its "pathetic god."

Many, like Helmuth Kopp, also believed that their religious Jewish relatives, with their intolerance and prejudice, were not much better. Religion, God, and their religious relatives and fellow citizens simply failed most of them in a miserable way. As historian Robert Ericksen argued, if rationalism, intellectual capacity, and religious belief failed to prevent distinguished religious leaders from supporting Hitler, then societies at large must be careful, especially those under the influence of fundamentalist religious groups, like the United States or Saudi Arabia, if they "desire the Hitler phenomenon not to recur."[39]

Schlesinger believed religion prevents the pursuit of tolerance and that this is one of the most important lessons to come out of the history of Nazism. He felt that since religion often causes divisions of hatred and frequently is resorted to by those in power only to push through their own agendas, it should be avoided. Furthermore, he held that if closely analyzed, all religious texts—including the Jewish Bible, the Christian Bible, and the Koran—support intolerance and should be avoided. When asked to extrapolate on this thought, he said that the Jewish Bible promotes genocide, as shown in Joshua when the Israelites murder whole cities of women, men, and children, and that both the Christian Bible and the Koran promote the belief that if you are not with them, you must be with Satan and be evil. Hitler's intolerance was no different, and he often invoked God's name in justifying his actions. In fact, Schlesinger noted, each of the religions just mentioned has perpetrated crimes on humanity similar to Hitler's.

In the end, what Schlesinger has expressed about religion is a common theme among many *Mischlinge* documented during the research for this book. The German Christian churches, both Catholic and Protestant, which should have been the most aggressive in defending the helpless and denouncing Hitler, failed miserably in this task and abandoned many *Mischlinge* like Schlesinger to suffer under the Nazis.

Conclusion

The men presented so far illustrate the emotional turmoil *Mischlinge* experienced throughout their early lives. Their families were divided on religious and ethnic grounds. Several Jewish families, like Kopp's and Meissinger's, did not approve of their children marrying gentiles. Likewise, gentile families like the Krügers, Meissingers, and Schefflers felt it disgraced the family to bring a Jew into the fold. Such intolerant, and one might add dysfunctional, families caused much pain and trauma.

The families' lack of unity affected the *Mischlinge* most when they needed to depend on relatives during times of danger. Members of many families have problems getting along, especially those who become related by marriage, but the unique stress these families experienced added a complicated dimension of dissension that distressed them. And sadly, many men, like Karl-Heinz Scheffler, Krüger, Scholz, Techel, and Schlesinger, felt embarrassed to have a Jewish background and tried to prove they were smart, strong, and honest, traits they had been conditioned to believe were the antithesis of being Jewish. Although most knew that the anti-Semites' theories were nonsense, they still wanted to prove they did not possess the negative traits the anti-Semites labeled as inherently "Jewish." In the end, they did much to disassociate themselves from such a persecuted minority. In order to do so, they sometimes changed their name, as we will see in chapter 5 with the Mendelssohn family, or performed brave acts in battle, as did Krüger, Günther Scheffler, and Schlesinger.

Due to the pressure to conform, many *Mischlinge*—like Günther Scheffler, Meissinger, Krüger, and Schlesinger—developed a deep sense of responsibility for their parents and a strong sense of self-reliance. In other words, many felt that when they were in the National Labor Service, the Wehrmacht, or out in society in school or at work, they had to do their best to prove to others and themselves that they were worthy human beings and honorable citizens. Most dramatically, one sees that when these men served, they did all they could to protect their families. Whether going on dangerous missions like Krüger or visiting a sick father in the Jewish hospital in uniform like Schlesinger, these men felt they needed to guard their loved ones.

Yet, just as they were establishing themselves in the military, the Nazis discharged many in 1940 with a new decree that prohibited *Mischlinge* from serving. The majority, like Meissinger and Krüger, felt that once discharged, they lost protection for themselves and relatives. Then, toward the end of the war, when deported to OT camps, they started to finally realize that they would never be able to live normally in Germany. In the camps, they sensed that the walls of Nazi Germany were inexorably closing in on them.

Shockingly, until then and even after, most did not truly know of the Holocaust, as demonstrated by Krüger, Meissinger, Schlesinger, and others. Karl-Heinz Löwy, the one person interviewed who did claim knowledge of the Holocaust, ultimately did not take any action because he felt he could accomplish little else than to save himself. Most half-Jews interviewed for this study echo Löwy in that they felt that even had they truly been aware of the genocide, they would have done nothing differently. Ultimately, had Germany prolonged the war or won it, the Nazis would have murdered half-Jews as well. This is what is tragic about most of these men's cases: they were moved along by events and oblivious of their final destination. Even those who understood more about Hitler and the camps behaved the same as the others. Most felt powerless to change the events and, whether in the Wehrmacht or OT, continued to serve a land that had abandoned them and had persecuted and murdered their families. These events show how powerful society is and the pressure it puts on us to conform even in the face of horrible discrimination.

3

Mischlinge Who Received the *Deutschblütigkeitserklärung*

No fewer than twenty-one generals, seven admirals, and one field marshal of Jewish descent served with Hitler's consent. And thousands in
the lower ranks of the Wehrmacht remained there because Hitler personally exempted them from the laws. Hitler did so mainly because they
looked Aryan (that is, had blue eyes and blond hair), had good military
records, had rendered Germany a unique service, or had come from distinguished families.

Two men in this chapter, Field Marshal Erhard Milch and General
Helmut Wilberg, were leading Luftwaffe personalities. Milch was second
in command and basically ran the Luftwaffe with the help of Wilberg
and a few other distinguished air force generals. Wilberg was a brilliant
tactician who developed the operational concept called Blitzkrieg (light-
ning war) today.[1] These men's accomplishments help explain why Hitler
Aryanized them.

Most who received Hitler's *Deutschblütigkeitserklärung* (declaration
of German blood) had distinguished themselves in war and proven their
worth as soldiers. As historian Omer Bartov wrote, "Both Nazism and
the military tended to idealize battle as the supreme test of the individual."[2] Admiral Bernhard Rogge would prove his value by becoming the
most successful surface raider captain during World War II, sinking or
capturing almost two dozen Allied ships with a combined total of
150,000 metric tons. Hitler awarded him the Oak Leaves to his Knight's
Cross (roughly equivalent to two Medals of Honor). Historian Martin
Gilbert wrote that Rogge's ship, the *Atlantis,* was one of Germany's
"deadliest" and most "effective" raiders.[3]

However, Hitler declared not only high-ranking officers like Milch
and Wilberg *deutschblütig* (of German blood), but also other, less distin-

guished *Mischlinge,* such as half-Jew Ernst Prager. Hitler moreover did not want seriously wounded *Mischling* veterans to suffer further discrimination. So on 4 May 1941, the Wehrmacht issued a directive stating that severely disabled *Mischling* veterans in the *Stufe* III category[4] who had received their wounds because of actions "above and beyond the call of duty" should apply for the *Deutschblütigkeitserklärung.*[5] In February 1942, the government wrote that Hitler had decided that half-Jews severely injured in war should be declared *deutschblütig,* because he did not want soldiers who had rendered the Reich such service to experience further difficulty. Although this declaration appeared to be automatic, most *Mischlinge* still had to apply before Hitler granted them clemency.[6]

Hitler also did not want to be "ungrateful" to *Mischlinge* who had made the ultimate sacrifice for their country. He decreed that those killed in battle were to receive the *Deutschblütigkeitserklärung* posthumously.[7] That meant Hitler should have given thousands of fallen *Mischlinge* the *Deutschblütigkeitserklärung.*

These actions show that Hitler granted exemptions only when military necessity or social stability indicated he should. Many wanted Hitler's exemption to protect their relatives and careers. However, this award did not protect a recipient's family as much as expected, as Prager's story demonstrates. Moreover, had Germany won the war, many who received these exemptions, as Colonel Ernst Bloch's story in chapter 5 illustrates, would have been discharged from the service and found their *Deutschblütigkeitserklärung* no longer honored.

Half-Jewish Field Marshal Erhard Milch[8]

Erhard Milch was a political animal and cared only about himself and his career. He was an opportunist and rarely worried about those he had to step on in order to climb the ladder of success. As a result, he had no problem becoming a Nazi Party member, and his actions also showed that he believed in many things the Nazis espoused. He was indeed an incredible organizer of the Luftwaffe, but also a nasty person and a hardcore Nazi.

Erhard Alfred Richard Oskar Milch, born on 30 March 1892 in Wilhelmshaven, became a powerful man of the Third Reich in contrast to

Half-Jewish Field Marshal Erhard Milch. Hitler declared Milch Aryan. He was awarded the Knight's Cross for his performance during the campaign in Norway in 1940. He was also a Nazi Party member.

most of the other men in this book. Milch also became a field marshal (the U.S. equivalent of a five-star general) who, according to historian James Corum, "ran the Luftwaffe and was its most powerful figure for personnel and planning issues, production and even strategy."[9]

His father, Anton, was a Jewish convert to Christianity. He ran a retail drug business and during World War I served as a quartermaster general for medical supplies. Milch's mother, Clara (née Vetter), was a gentile, although some people suspected her of being Jewish as well. In addition to

Erhard, Anton and Clara had five other children, three daughters and two sons.

Milch grew up in a strict family and did well in school. Although raised in the Protestant church, he later was agnostic. He was a passionate patriot and ambitious man. After completing high school in 1910, he enlisted as an officer candidate in the First Heavy Artillery Regiment in Königsberg, East Prussia, and was promoted to lieutenant a year later for his performance and leadership. Milch felt proud of his work and enjoyed the artillery since technical matters interested him.

When World War I erupted in August 1914, he served as a battalion aide on the Russian front. Although he liked the artillery, he transferred in 1915 to the Imperial Air Service and became a first lieutenant. The army awarded him the Iron Cross First Class in June 1916 for a courageous reconnaissance flight during the battle of Verdun. During a brief wartime General Staff course in 1917, he met Helmut Wilberg, a distinguished officer, who was also a half-Jew. He became friendly with Wilberg, who eventually made Milch a squadron commander. Since Milch excelled at navigation and reconnaissance, he successfully directed artillery fire. Due to his exceptional organizational talents, his superiors later assigned him to serve as a General Staff officer and air specialist. In 1918, they promoted him to captain.[10]

Immediately after the end of World War I, Milch commanded a flight unit of the Border Defense Corps, which worked with the Freikorps, the paramilitary groups formed after the war to fight Communist enemies both inside and outside Germany. In 1920, he moved to Königsberg and studied economics at the university there and later transferred to Danzig Technical University. Throughout the 1920s he worked in mail, transport, and travel service companies using airplanes. In 1926 Milch became one of three directors who merged several of these companies to form Lufthansa, Germany's national airline. One of the other directors was Martin Wronsky, another half-Jew. Under Milch's leadership, Lufthansa became one of the world's most modern and efficient airlines. As one of the leading personalities of Lufthansa, Milch also worked with the Reichswehr to prepare an air force. He supported the idea of converting airliners into bombers in case of war. And after Göring was elected to the Reichstag in 1928, Milch paid him 1,000 RM a month to lobby for

Lufthansa. When questions arose about whether this was legal, Milch arranged for Göring to receive 100,000 RM in one lump sum. And during the first speech Göring gave to the Reichstag, he supported higher subsidies for Lufthansa. Milch also attended parties where he met Hitler and other Nazi leaders.[11]

His support of the Nazis typifies how Milch operated. He was a skilled politician and intriguer and quite adept at getting along in the political world of Germany in the 1920s and 1930s. He behaved in a way that most professional officers did not respect, mixing with politics, something most Prussian officers' code of behavior prevented. But Milch simply saw that the Nazi cause furthered his ambition.

As the Nazis gained power, Milch often met with Göring to discuss a new air force. He granted the Reichswehr access to Lufthansa's archives to stay abreast of modern technology in airplane design and performance. In 1929 he told Göring that he was ready to join the Nazi Party. The fact that he wanted to join the Nazis at this time, when only a minority of Germans thought Hitler could come to power, shows he truly believed in the Fascists' ideals. According to James Corum, Milch was an officer who "fell completely under Hitler's spell." However, Hitler felt at that time they should wait to make him a member. The party issued him membership card number 123,885 but left it blank so Milch could claim it in the future. Only in March 1933 did he become a member retroactive to April 1929.

When Hitler took power in 1933, he wanted Milch to help build an air force and told him, "Now look, I haven't known you for very long, but you're a man who knows his job, and we have few in the Party who know as much about the air as you. That's why the choice has fallen on you. You must take the job. It's not a question of the Party, as you seem to think—it's a question of Germany and Germany needs you."[12]

Milch admitted later that this talk with Hitler convinced him to take the job but his ancestry still remained a thorn in his side. Göring, Hitler, and other high-ranking Nazis took care of this problem. Milch noted in his diary as early as 1 November 1933 that Göring had discussed his ancestry with Hitler, deputy head of the party Rudolf Hess, and the minister of defense, General Werner von Blomberg, and that "everything was in order."[13] Historian Klaus Hermann believes that the way he described his ancestry in his diary was "entirely self-serving . . . to prove beyond doubt his Gentile origin."

Once Göring took care of Milch's racial question, he decided to place Milch in a position of power with the up-and-coming air force. Göring knew that he did not have the abilities for organizing the Luftwaffe and felt Milch's record with Lufthansa made him the logical candidate to control the Air Ministry. So Göring appointed him secretary of state for aviation.

Future field marshal Milch's method of securing Aryanization was the most famous case of a *Mischling* falsifying a father's identity in order to gain exemption from the racial laws. In 1933, Milch's mother, Clara, gave her son-in-law, Fritz Heinrich Hermann, police president of Hagen and later SS general, an affidavit stating her uncle Carl Wilhelm Bräuer had fathered her six children rather than her Jewish husband, Anton. Both her uncle and husband were deceased at the time of her affidavit. She said that her parents had prohibited her from marrying her uncle because of the close bloodlines and that her Jewish husband knew about the relationship. She also claimed her Protestant church had denied her permission to marry Bräuer, although, according to the law, she could have done so. Some say she only married Anton, who really loved her, because she had become pregnant with her uncle's child.[14]

Only after the SA colonel and chairman of the Messerschmidt Airplane Development Company Theo Croneiss denounced Milch to Göring in 1933 did Göring take Milch's mother's affidavit to Hitler. Croneiss was not only an anti-Semite, but also jealous of Milch, feeling that Hitler should have picked him for the post of secretary of state for aviation. Croneiss made his accusation based on the knowledge that Milch family members were buried in the Breslau Jewish cemetery.

However, Croneiss's denunciation did not succeed. In 1935, Hitler accepted Clara Milch's testimony and instructed Göring to have Kurt Mayer, head of the Reich Office for Genealogy Research, complete the paperwork. On 7 August 1935, Göring wrote Mayer to change the name of Milch's father to "Carl Bräuer" in his documents and issue papers certifying Milch's pure Aryan descent.[15]

After the war, according to one of Göring's interrogators, John E. Dolibois, Göring felt proud that he had helped "the half-Jew Milch"

Berlin W 8, den 7. August 1935
Wilhelmstr. 68.
Fernspr.: A 2 flora 6841, 7071.

Streng vertraulich.

                    Der Führer und Reichskanzler hat auf meinen
        ihm gehaltenen Vortrag hin die arische Abstammung
        des Staatssekretärs und Generalleutnants
                    Erhard M i l c h ,geboren 30.3.1892 zu
                                Wilhelmshaven
        anerkannt.In Durchführung des Befehls des Führers
        ersuche ich Sie,die standesamtlichen Unterlagen
        dahin zu berichtigen,dass der Vater des Staatsse-
        kretärs,der verstorbene Baumeister Carl Bräuer,zu-
        letzt wohnhaft Berlin-Grunewald Königsallee 9,als
        solcher eingetragen wird.-Das gleiche gilt für die
        Geschwister.
                    Mit Rücksicht auf die Eilbedürftigkeit der
        Angelegenheit ersuche ich um umgehende Erledigung
        und Bericht an mich.

                                Heil Hitler!

An
    den Leiter der Reichsstelle
    für Sippenforschung.

            B e r l i n

One of Milch's Aryanization documents. On 7 August 1935, Hermann Göring wrote Kurt Mayer, head of the Reich Office for Genealogy Research, to change Milch's father's name in his documents and issue him papers certifying his pure Aryan descent. The letter reads: "Top Secret. Based on my explanation, the Führer and Reichkanzler has recognized the Aryan ancestry of Lt. General Erhard Milch, born 30 March 1892 in Wilhelmshaven. In fulfilling the Führer's order, I request you correct the official records by entering the State Secretary's [Milch's] father's name as the late architect Carl Bräuer, last residence at Königsallee 9, Berlin-Grunewald. The same should be done for [Milch's] siblings. Given the urgency of this matter, I request an immediate resolution and report to me. Heil Hitler!"

remain in "his Luftwaffe."[16] However, Göring's "act of generosity" was done more out of the need to have someone competent to build the Luftwaffe than to help Milch.

As previously mentioned, there were suspicions that Milch's mother was Jewish. Historian Robert Wistrich claims that she was indeed Jewish; however, he does not give his evidence for this. No known documents exist that prove Milch's mother was Jewish. If Wistrich is correct, then Milch would have been "100 percent" Jewish and not a half-Jew, making his position more precarious. In a rare moment of partially admitting his origins, Milch said at his trial in 1946 that "it is possible [my father] was partially Jewish, but of that I am not ashamed."[17]

Adding evidence that Milch was partially Jewish is the fact that his middle names—Alfred, Richard, and Oskar—were names of his Jewish father's nephews. These names came from the Jewish Wehlau family, sons of Sigmund and Fanny Milch Wehlau (Anton Milch's sister). As historian Klaus Hermann said, "I certainly find [these names] considerably more than just 'accidental.'"[18]

In Milch's case, the Nazis did not object to incest, but Jewish ancestry was indeed a problem. Milch's mother sacrificed her reputation as well as her husband's to protect her children. Without her lie, Milch might have lost his career and, along with it, his ability to protect his youngest daughter, Helga, who had Down syndrome, from Hitler's euthanasia program, which murdered at least 100,000 disabled people, among them Aloisia Veit, Hitler's own cousin.[19] Moreover, Clara Milch's affidavit allowed one of Milch's sisters to remain married to her husband, an SS general. Milch's mother did what thousands of other Aryan mothers attempted, most of them unsuccessfully, to do: erase their children's racial stigma. She also helped another son, Werner Milch, become a major in the paratroopers who would earn the Knight's Cross for bravery.

Milch "possessed tremendous drive." He wanted to build up Germany and create the most powerful air force in the world. He had a "thorough knowledge of the production capabilities of the German aircraft industry, a detailed understanding of its managers and designers, and perhaps most importantly, excellent connections within the political leadership" of the Third Reich.[20] After he put his "Jewish past" behind him and convinced the right people that he was indeed Aryan, he could pursue his dreams.

Since the Versailles Treaty was then still in effect, the building up of a Luftwaffe had to remain secret. In laying its foundation, Milch became adept at getting around most of the prohibitions of the treaty. One of the cleverest things he did was to found and promote the National Socialist Flying Corps, a large flying unit of the Nazi Party, which the Allies believed harmless. It not only stimulated interest in flying but also trained future Luftwaffe pilots. In addition, Milch developed close contacts with the Nazi elite, entertaining the likes of Himmler, Goebbels, Hess, and Blomberg at his home.[21]

In 1935 Hitler revoked the Versailles Treaty and announced the creation of the Luftwaffe. Now Milch did not have to worry about operating in secret. Most Germans welcomed the new military service and took pride in its development. Milch by this time had been promoted to the rank of colonel. According to James Corum, the greatest contribution Milch made "to the Luftwaffe was organizing the massive program of aerial rearmament." By 1936, under Milch's leadership, "the German air industry had become a first-class organization" producing modern aircraft for the Luftwaffe. Hitler had claimed in 1936 that "two names are . . . linked with the birth of our Luftwaffe," Göring and Milch.[22] On 1 April 1936, Hitler promoted Milch to general and on 30 January 1937 awarded him the Golden Party Badge. Milch felt that Hitler had done much for Germany, especially rebuilding the military and the country's infrastructure and putting millions of unemployed back to work. He firmly believed that Hitler was the right man to lead Germany into the future.

Probably because of the favors Hitler did for Milch and the recognition he received for his ambitious modernization plan, Göring became jealous of the subordinate who was running "his" Luftwaffe. He would later say to another general, "What is this Milch? A fart out of my asshole. First, he wanted to play the part of my crown prince, now he wants to be my usurper." Consequently, Göring designated General Ernst Udet head of the Technical Office, a position previously held by Milch.[23] Milch took this slight personally and felt deeply hurt. However, Milch found himself in a difficult situation. On the one hand, he felt that an injustice had been done, but on the other hand, he owed his livelihood and position to Göring, who had made sure he remained in the Luftwaffe despite his ancestry. Because of this and probably other reasons, he did not resign.

In April 1940, when the Norwegian campaign ran into difficulties, Milch's skills as an excellent organizer helped lay the "foundation for the success of airpower in Norway" and victory. If the Germans had not secured their northwest flank in Norway, Hitler would probably have been unwilling and even unable to launch his invasion of France one month later. Hitler therefore presented Milch with the Knight's Cross for his efforts during the Norwegian campaign. A few months later, after the successful conclusion of the war in France, Milch was one of three Luftwaffe generals Hitler promoted to field marshal.[24]

At the outbreak of war with Russia in June 1941, the relationship between Milch and Göring continued to be on the rocks. Göring was tired of always being in Milch's shadow. Milch wanted more power and freedom to enact policies he felt necessary, something Göring denied him almost categorically.

Nonetheless, although handicapped by Göring's unwillingness to give him more responsibilities, he continued to perform well. For his continued brilliance in organizing the Luftwaffe, Hitler gave Milch a present of 250,000 RM on his fiftieth birthday in 1942. From 1942 on, Milch worked more and more with Albert Speer, the minister of armaments. When subordinates claimed they could not do something in the years when Germany's fortunes took a turn for the worse, he would often reply, "The word 'impossible' does not exist."

In January 1943, when the Stalingrad battle was going poorly, Hitler called on Milch to relieve the Sixth Army, putting him in "charge of the entire airlift operation." However, it was too late for Milch to achieve this goal. Nonetheless, it was important to note that in this critical situation, Hitler called on Milch.[25] Hitler valued his skills and appreciated his loyalty.

When Udet died at the end of 1941, Milch took over as head of the Technical Office. It was only producing 1,000 aircraft a year under Udet. He had been a failure and committed suicide. He left a note behind that read, "Iron Man [Göring's nickname], you left me" and have "surrendered [me] to those Jews Milch and Gablenz."[26] (Carl-August von Gablenz was not a *Mischling*, but his wife was quarter-Jewish.)

Milch succeeded Udet and turned around Germany's lagging airplane production. Germany's defense against Allied bombing in 1943 and 1944 happened largely due to Milch's production program. Under Milch's foresight and leadership, and with Speer's support, the manufacture of aircraft by 1944 reached its highest level, and according to some figures, the Germans made more aircraft in one month in 1944 than in the entire year of 1940. In July 1944, 3,000 fighters were produced. Milch also stimulated the production of the V-1 flying jet-bomb, or in modern parlance, cruise missile.

Yet, for all his successes, Milch had several shortcomings. Early on, he believed that the Luftwaffe would only fight short, intense wars and never thought that Germany would fight four long years. With such beliefs, Milch helped cripple the Luftwaffe later in the war since he had not supported an expanded training program or expanded production plans in 1941. So, by 1942, when the Luftwaffe fought against England, Russia, and the United States throughout Europe and Africa, it found itself desperately short of planes and pilots. Production figures dramatically increased from 1943 to 1944, but the quality of pilots decreased significantly. By 1944, the average training of a pilot was 100 hours' flight time, compared with 400–450 hours for their Allied counterparts.[27]

Although he had been declared Aryan, Milch's Jewish past continued to haunt him. The later Bundeswehr general Johannes Steinhoff reported that when he went to receive the Oak Leaves for his Knight's Cross, Milch asked if he could do anything for him. Steinhoff first requested more ammunition. Milch said this would be done and asked if there was anything else. Steinhoff then requested help for the half-Jewish fighter-ace Feldwebel (staff sergeant) Rudolf Schmidt, whose Jewish mother and grandparents had been deported. He told Milch, "You, of all people, should know how difficult it's to fly missions against Russia all day fearing the Gestapo might be waiting to interrogate you when you land."[28] Milch's reply and what happened to Schmidt's relatives remain unknown.

By 22 February 1944, Milch ranked seventh among Hitler's subordinates. Immediately after the unsuccessful bomb attempt on Hitler's life on 20 July 1944, he sent Hitler a telegram: "[I cannot begin to express my] heartfelt joy that a merciful Providence has protected you from this cowardly murder attempt and preserved you for the German *Volk* and its Wehrmacht."[29] Perhaps Milch really believed what he said, or perhaps he only protected himself, knowing as he did that the events on 20 July made the situation for *Mischlinge* more precarious.

Contrary to expectations, this study has documented that some people of Jewish descent participated directly as perpetrators in the Holocaust, primarily because of their rank and responsibilities. But like most high-ranking Nazi officials at the Nuremberg Trials, Milch lied when he swore that he did not know about the Holocaust.[30]

When asked at Nuremberg about Nazi extermination policies, he denied all knowledge of the Holocaust and said that until after the war, he had only known about Dachau and Sachsenhausen. After hearing so many rumors about those camps from 1933 to 1935, he had asked permission from Himmler to visit Dachau. Himmler granted him permission and Milch visited the camp in 1935. Milch talked to many inmates and most were criminals. Several had participated in the Roehm Putsch (known as the Night of the Long Knives), during which people like Himmler and Göring murdered leaders of the SA and used treason as their justification. Milch claimed that nothing appeared abnormal to him, but did not know "if we were shown everything." He claimed he had no knowledge of what the Nazis did in other camps during Hitler's rule.[31]

But he had read reports from Sigmund Rascher, the notorious doctor at Dachau who conducted brutal experiments. Milch wrote the head of Himmler's personal staff, SS General Karl Wolff, on 20 March 1942 about the "interesting" experiments at Dachau. On 31 August 1942, Milch also wrote Himmler to express his interest in Rascher's high-altitude physiology tests in Dachau.[32] These tests were approved by the Luftwaffe and resulted in painful deaths for the human guinea pigs. Nonetheless, useful data were collected. Tests also involved immersing inmates in freezing water to see how long pilots shot down over the sea could live. All inmates died in these experiments and Milch was kept fully informed. Some inmates were actually turned over to the Luftwaffe testing facilities in Munich, where it conducted these tests itself.

When the Nazis conducted these tests, Milch and the Luftwaffe, not the SS or Dachau, were directly responsible for them. These experiments were done with Milch's support and on his initiative. As a result, according to historian James Corum, "This alone makes Milch a genuine war criminal." As the tribunal wrote of Milch, he was not upset about the in-humanity perpetrated by the Nazis. He was upset only by the fact that Germany was losing the war.[33]

Besides approving of these horrible experiments, Milch also served as cochairman with Speer on the Pursuit-Plans-Staff, which needed about a quarter-million slave workers. Milch knew of about 100,000 Hungarian Jews expected in Auschwitz whose labor his project could use.[34]

With respect to slave labor Milch (probably in 1942) told General Carl-August von Gablenz that he wanted him "to get in touch with [General Hermann] Reinecke concerning the French POW's. I demand that if the people refuse to work they immediately be placed against the wall and shot."[35] So Milch was guilty of war crimes.

In 1947, the Allies sentenced Milch to life in prison at the Second Nuremberg Trial for deporting and mishandling foreign workers and conducting criminal experiments on human beings. As historian Georg Meyer asserted, Milch can be considered a "German Jewish war crimi-nal."[36] However, his sentence was reduced and in 1954 he was dis-charged. He then advised the German air industry until his death in 1972.

As an incredibly gifted organizer, Milch helped the Luftwaffe develop into the menacing force that it became by 1939. Although half-Jewish, he did not let this get in the way of obtaining the power he so desperately craved within the Third Reich. He viewed his ancestry as a tiny speed bump in the race to the top of Hitler's regime. He believed in Hitler and his goals for the Fatherland and did everything he could to make sure Germany would win the war. He made a Faustian trade-off and had no regrets. Unfortunately, there were many like him at the top of the Wehr-macht and government. And if they did not support the regime like Milch, they were "forced to echo it and suppress their own thoughts." As philosopher Immanuel Kant rightly noted, "War is an evil inasmuch as it produces more wicked men than it takes away."[37]

Half-Jewish General der Flieger Helmut Wilberg

Helmut Wilberg was an officer and a gentleman. He radiated confidence, was built like a linebacker, and had clear blue eyes that stared out from

Half-Jewish General der Flieger Helmut Wilberg. Hitler declared him Aryan in 1935. (Military awards: Knight's Cross with Swords of the Royal House of Hohenzollern, Military Service Cross Second Class of the Grand Duke of Mecklenburg-Schwerin, Commemorative Flier Badge, EKI, EKII, and many others)

his square face. He was apolitical, a consummate professional, a devoted family man and patriot. Although he served in armed forces loyal to Hitler, he disliked the Führer. Like many documented in this study, he fought for Germany but not for the Nazis. Full Jew Edgar Jacoby (see chapter 1) gave the same explanation for why he served, and like Jacoby, Wilberg believed in his country.

Historian Matthew Cooper eloquently describes the dilemma in which Wilberg and many others found themselves under Hitler: "The generals who were faced with National Socialism were the prisoners of their own proud heritage. The tradition bestowed on them by their predecessors was one of unconditional personal obedience to, and identifica-

tion with, the autocratic Head of State, coupled with a self-imposed isolation from the world of politics—an isolation which, although elevated
to the status of a military virtue, took the form of political naivete and
ineptitude."[38] With this in mind, one can somewhat understand how officers like Prager, Rogge, and Wilberg served their nation with such passion and loyalty. It was a tragic situation for them. In hindsight, it does
seem they sold their souls in continuing their service.

Wilberg was born on 1 June 1880 in Berlin to a Jewish mother and a
gentile father, who was a famous painter of landscapes and buildings. He
had one brother, who died in combat in World War I. As a child, Wilberg
excelled in sports but not in school. His mother worried that he was not
intelligent. Considering Wilberg's later accomplishments, her concern
now seems absurd. He became one of the most distinguished airmen of
World War I, earning the Knight's Cross with Swords of the Royal
House of Hohenzollern (the equivalent of the U.S. Medal of Honor), the
Iron Cross Second and First Class, and the German Flyer's Badge.

Wilberg's father died when he was one year old and the family fell into
difficult times. With his background as a commoner, one might think it
surprising he became a General Staff officer. However, at that time, the
General Staff was becoming a meritocracy no longer limited to aristo-
crats. Yet, it was extraordinary that he ever became an officer, as he was
flat-footed, a condition that kept many from serving. However, Kaiserin
Auguste Viktoria, as a crown princess, had taken painting lessons from
his father and liked the family. Consequently, she looked after the
Wilbergs when the father died. When Wilberg finished his *Abitur* in 1898,
the Kaiserin fulfilled his wish to join the army, and he started training
with the Eightieth Infantry Regiment. Despite his Jewish mother and his
flat feet, the officer academy accepted Wilberg, and he performed well.
Later he received a special assignment as military tutor to the Kaiser's relatives, a position usually given only to officers of high academic standing.
Then in 1910, his superiors selected him to enter the General Staff Academy, a high honor and rare opportunity for any officer.[39]

He then became one of the first pilots in Germany; he held Imperial
Pilot's license number 26 and trained on the Wright B Flyer, a dangerous
plane that took the lives of many pilots. On completing the General Staff

Helmut Wilberg (right) in May 1912. Sitting next to him is Lieutenant Fisch.

course in 1913, he became the adjutant of the aviation branch. This important position put him in touch with central figures like Wilhelm Siegert, who built up German aviation. Before the outbreak of war in 1914, he served in the army's Aviation Inspectorate. During World War I, he gained valuable experience in aerial strategy and became a successful air commander. He was one of the leading experts on ground attack tactics and commanded the air units that supported the First and Fourth Armies. He also pioneered the use of radios in airplanes to coordinate strikes with the infantry, an ingenious use of the new technology at that time. During 1917–1918, he sometimes commanded over seventy squadrons.[40]

The army regarded him as one of the pioneers of ground support tactics who laid the foundation for the strategy later known as Blitzkrieg, as he was the first German air commander in World War I who employed whole squadrons for ground assaults. He was one of the senior officers of the Luftstreitkräfte (air force in World War I) and commanded over 700 planes on the Flanders front in 1917, one of the high points of German airpower during the Great War. At Flanders, under Wilberg's command, pilots used radios in the planes to coordinate attacks, used observation aircraft to drop supplies for forward units, and bombed en-

Helmut Wilberg was on the General Staff from 1920 until 1927; he had been personally selected by General von Seeckt. Wilberg commanded the secret Luftwaffe during this time. This picture from late 1920 shows Wilberg in his office, surrounded by military maps.

emy troops.[41] He was on friendly terms with the half-Jew and later field marshal Erhard Milch and gave him a squadron command. This relationship may have helped Wilberg in his career in the Third Reich when Milch rose in power within the Luftwaffe. His relationship with Milch was not unusual. Wilberg was on good terms with most air force leaders.

After the war, General Hans von Seeckt picked him as the commander of the secret Luftwaffe from 1920 until 1927. That someone as brilliant as von Seeckt chose him says a lot about Wilberg.

From 1923 onward, Wilberg organized and monitored German civil airfields, flight schools, aircraft factories, and repair shops as well as their equipment for an emergency air force in case France or Poland invaded. He became the Reichswehr's leading air theorist and successfully evaded most of the Versailles Treaty's restrictions on training pilots. He sent fighter pilots for schooling to the Russians at Lipetsk. As in the armor school at Kazan in Russia, the training program for Reichswehr airmen at Lipetsk provided unique opportunities for pilots between 1925 and 1933. Known as the Shadow Luftwaffe, Reichswehr officers were able to develop skills that could not be developed under the watchful eyes of the Inter-Allied Military Control Commission. At Lipetsk pilots trained for combat with the most modern equipment. More importantly, Wilberg cultivated a training at Lipetsk focused on maneuver warfare. German officers were thoroughly instructed in fighter tactics and ground attack operations, thus developing another key element for future Blitzkrieg success. In accordance with the emphasis on large-scale maneuvers, the Shadow Luftwaffe participated in Russian military exercises involving mobile ground forces. Much to the later regret of the Soviets, the Germans thus obtained practical experience in combined arms tactics.[42]

In addition, Wilberg encouraged future pilots to take up glider flying, another way of giving Reichswehr officers flying lessons. During the Weimar Republic, Wilberg often met with Milch, then one of the leading Lufthansa personalities, who gave him access to long-distance flight data. Without the training and research conducted by Wilberg, the Luftwaffe would not have grown at its incredible rate in the 1930s. He was a serious airpower thinker during the interwar period and widely respected in the aviation field. Corum argues that "Wilberg did a brilliant job at building up a shadow Luftwaffe and Göring had a firm foundation when he became air minister in 1933."

Though Hitler took over power in Germany in 1933, Wilberg entered the Air Force Ministry as a major general, indicating that having a Jewish mother, if known at the time, was not initially detrimental. Wilberg did not regard himself as a *Mischling*, which, even in 1933, he defined as the offspring of a black person and a Spaniard. Then, to Wilberg's great surprise, the 1935 Nuremberg Laws officially labeled him a *Mischling* because of his mother. But he continued his duties and later that year Hitler granted him "100 percent Aryan status."

Wilberg may have experienced a lot of mental anguish during that time. His son claimed that his father wanted to forget his Jewish past. In 1934 Wilberg had written in his diary that he had little hope for mankind

Helmut Wilberg (second from right, standing) with Göring (seated) and other Luftwaffe officers at Göring's estate at Karinhall, circa 1938.

and, without ever especially referring to his own situation, repeatedly discussed the Jewish problem. Corum wrote that Göring had taken his case personally to Hitler and obtained a signed order from him to Aryanize Wilberg. As Corum wrote, "Göring was not about to lose the services of a talented officer no matter how ardent the Luftwaffe's official commitment was to the ideology of National Socialism."

When the Luftwaffe was officially formed in 1935, Wilberg prepared the *Conduct of Air Operations* manual, which served as the Luftwaffe's "primary expression of battle doctrine" into World War II.[43] He had started work on this doctrine in 1934, when he took command of the Air Ministry. It laid out six missions of the Luftwaffe: to maintain air superiority, support ground troops, support the navy, disrupt enemy communication and supply, attack sources of enemy power, and destroy the enemy's governmental centers. According to Corum, this doctrine, also known as Regulation 16, "expressed Wilberg's balanced approach to air doctrine."

In 1935, he commanded the War College and in 1936, the military appointed Wilberg as the chief of staff for Germany's *Legion Condor* during the Spanish Civil War; he was responsible for arranging support and logistics for the whole operation.[44] Given only vague instructions by his government on 26 July 1936, Wilberg and the Luftwaffe general staff created Special Staff W (for Wilberg) in two days and started sending supplies and men to Spain. Within a week Luftwaffe pilots had already airlifted Spanish troops from Morocco to Spain to support Franco's forces.

From the end of July until mid-October 1936, the Luftwaffe airlifted 13,000 Spanish Nationalist soldiers along with a total of 271 tons of equipment, including artillery pieces, machine guns, and ammunitions, in what was "one of the decisive military operations of the Spanish Civil War." Wilberg made four clandestine trips to Spain from 1936 to 1938 to arrange support and requirements for the Condor Legion.[45]

To work with the Spaniards proved difficult because the whole infrastructure of the country had been destroyed. Also, Spanish military leaders lacked experience in modern warfare and thus, Wilberg had to teach them how to fight with the new technology the Germans provided. Hitler did not think much of the Spanish military leadership and even told Erwin Jaenecke, Wilberg's chief of staff and later a four-star general, that they "are dumb, lazy, arrogant and untrainable . . . it is regrettable that the Reds did not kill more of them."[46]

Untested when it entered Spain in 1936, the Luftwaffe left that country as a confident and well-honed air power, having helped Franco gain victory. In 1964, the Spanish government posthumously awarded Wilberg a distinguished medal for valor for his service in the *Legion Condor* and its support of the Spanish army in "its war against international communism." Jaenecke wrote of Wilberg at that time that he was one of the oldest and most famous officers of World War I and highly respected for what he was doing both abroad and domestically.

The German presence in Spain helped Franco's government maintain power and gave the Luftwaffe invaluable experience conducting almost every type of air warfare. During the Spanish Civil War, the Germans utilized and perfected "strategic bombing, interdiction campaigns, naval anti-shipping campaigns, close air support, and air superiority campaigns." The *Legion Condor* consisted of almost 5,000 soldiers and provided the testing ground for the Luftwaffe's most modern weapons.

While the legion's experience furnished necessary information for revising the Luftwaffe's operational air doctrine, it also provided the Luftwaffe with the most experienced corps of officers in the world. German officers spent between nine and twelve months with the *Legion Condor* and following their tour of duty, the military assigned them to various operational units of the Luftwaffe to disseminate the lessons learned. The Luftwaffe also practiced strategic bombing during this conflict, and the famous painting of Picasso's *Guernica* depicted the attack on this city and the killing of hundreds of its civilians there. Although the international press and Picasso described it as a terror bombing campaign, the Germans conducted this raid according to international law. They conducted this operational attack to close the retreat routes for the Basque army.[47]

Although Wilberg was by now a lieutenant general and one of the most distinguished Luftwaffe commanders, the Luftwaffe dismissed him in March 1938. His son said it happened because of his background. Supposedly, it occurred in connection with the Blomberg-Fritsch affair when Hitler got rid of several generals he disliked. Yet, Hitler recalled Wilberg as the Luftwaffe's chief of training right before he invaded Poland.

In June 1939, Wilberg had breakfast with Hitler. Although critical of the Nazis, he did not display such views in a letter he wrote to a close friend after the meeting. He described how freely the Führer discussed and developed his ideas. In September 1940, the Luftwaffe promoted Wilberg to General der Flieger (General of the Aviators—a three-star general).

Without Wilberg, the Wehrmacht might not have performed as well as it did from 1939 to 1941 invading Poland, France, and Russia. Many in the air force considered him the "natural commander of the Luftwaffe." General Jaenecke noted that "Wilberg, owing to his abilities and career, was the obvious choice to command the Luftwaffe, a position given . . . to Göring because of party politics. He was tall, good-looking, gifted and an officer who was a pleasure to work for, but, unfortunately, he was a 50 percent Jew." Jaenecke said that no one would see that Wilberg was "Jewish" in any way, referring to his supposedly German looks and behavior. Yet, his skills and reputation saved him, and Hitler granted him an exemption. But according to Jaenecke, Hitler still refused to allow Wilberg in his presence to seek advice even after his Aryanization. As a result, Jaenecke, chief of Wilberg's staff, often had to attend meetings with Hitler in place of his boss.[48]

Wilberg was an apolitical career soldier who did not like the Nazis. Nonetheless, he remained loyal to the Luftwaffe until his death in a flying accident outside Dresden on 20 November 1941.

Wilberg's tragedy was that he brilliantly served a nation controlled by Hitler. He hoped that Hitler's star would soon fall and that Germany would come under more honorable leadership. He loved his nation and to maintain his code of conduct, he had to serve Hitler. Unlike Milch, he was honest about his ancestry and hated the Nazi government. Yet, he was unable to act against the regime because of his upbringing and sense of duty as well as the threat of expulsion and death. That was a tragedy not only for Wilberg, but also for thousands of other German officers.

Half-Jewish Captain Ernst Prager

When Ernst Prager talked, he sounded like a Prussian officer. He loved the army and thrived in combat. Even after the war, he worked in the armament industry. He was rather short but stocky and athletic. With a clear voice, he balanced his thoughts in answering questions and never made decisions quickly.

Prager was born on 24 May 1909 in Kulmbach. His Jewish family had lived in Germany since at least 1598. Ernst was the second son of Heinrich Prager, a reserve army officer and director of a brewery, and Thekla (née Meseth). His father was a Jewish convert to Christianity and his mother was gentile and had been raised as a devout Protestant. Prager's parents raised him in a religious and patriotic home and he spent a lot of his childhood in a youth group similar to the Boy Scouts. He enjoyed camping, playing war games, and learning the history of his country.

His family had a strong military tradition. During World War I, his father had a company command and earned the Iron Cross Second and First Class and the Bavarian Military Service Medal with Swords, Fourth Class, as well. His father's brother Stephan became a major and earned the Iron Cross First Class, the Wound Badge, and the Bavarian Military Service Medal with Swords, Fourth Class. His grandfather Felix Prager had already served in the Prussian military and took part in the Franco-Prussian War from 1870 to 1871 as a lieutenant. All Pragers served their country in times of war.

After his *Abitur* in 1929, Prager entered a military flying unit. Crashing his plane in July, he broke his right foot. He worked hard during his rehabilitation and after several months returned to duty, and by 1933, the army had promoted him to lieutenant.

When Hitler came to power, Prager informed his superiors of his Jewish father. But Defense Minister General Werner von Blomberg reassured him that "nothing stood in the way of his promotion." Apparently, Prager's good standing with his superiors got him the required endorsements to convince Blomberg to retain him. However, this goodwill was short-lived; he had to leave the service in 1934 because of the race laws.

For the next seven years, Prager worked in the arms industry developing howitzers. But in 1941, Hitler granted him the *Deutschblütigkeitserklärung* after a long application process, and he returned to the army as an officer. Gaining reacceptance in the army took a lot of effort, and the trials Prager had to go through merit further explanation.

Prager's Jewish uncle Stephan helped with his application and knew how to work the German bureaucracy from his business experience. The family believed if Prager could get the *Deutschblütigkeitserklärung* it would protect them. This belief was common among *Mischling* families. However, Prager's situation is different from others in that he struggled to get clemency while outside the army.

On 19 July 1937, Prager wrote his uncle that the authorities had sent his case to the Reich Ministry of the Interior, but by late August, he still had heard nothing. Although this was disheartening, Prager's family worked on his case by writing to governmental officers, gathering documents, and seeking advice from lawyers and officers.

Luckily for Prager, he had the support of the famous World War I fighter pilot and well-known Luftwaffe general Wilhelm Haehnelt, friend of State Secretary Hans Heinrich Lammers, who asked Lammers and the Wehrmacht to help Prager. On 22 December 1937, Prager told his uncle Stephan that Haehnelt had heard that the bureaucrats had started to review his case. But on 14 February 1938, he informed Stephan that his application for Aryanization had been filed away because the government was not in a hurry to deal with him. Another possible reason Prager had to wait so long was that the authorities were being bombarded with applications and they did not have the manpower to process this new form of government activity. Prager continued trying to obtain the exemption throughout 1938–1941, but without success.

When the war in the Balkans broke out in spring 1941, Prager wrote the Wehrmacht's High Command again on 24 May 1941, emphasizing his family's Christian values and military tradition and his desire to go to the front. "I chose the career of a soldier due to my deepest conviction and with a firm desire to be the best that I could be," he explained. Prager also wanted to marry his fiancée, Hella Koberger, which he could only do if proclaimed *deutschblütig*. Without Hitler's approval, Prager could not legally marry an Aryan or have children with one. He had already lost one fiancée due to his racial status and did not want to lose another. A friend suggested that if he did not get clemency, then he and Hella could learn to "live for one another" instead of having children. Prager explained that such a position "contradicts the natural inclination of a woman. Hella loves children."

A few months later, Prager met with Hitze, who was working in Bernhard Lösener's office for racial matters in the Ministry of the Interior, to discuss his options. As he entered the office, Hitze said, "You came here, Lieutenant, because of marriage? You're making things difficult for yourself." Hitze explained that since Prager could not serve, he could not receive an exemption. Only when he had done something noteworthy as a soldier could he expect to get it. So since Prager could not serve, he would not be able to get an exemption. The meeting ended. "I then went to the district court," Prager wrote, "totally consumed by my worries, nervous, and held together only by my will and ability to pull myself together in the hope of finding out whether I could again serve."

In the court, a civil servant told Prager the situation was "hopeless. We

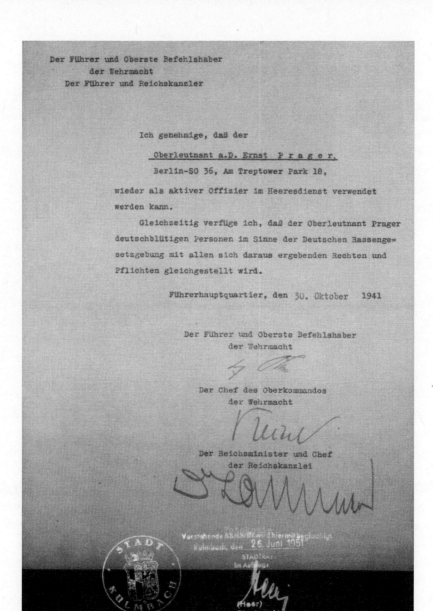

Der Führer und Oberste Befehlshaber
der Wehrmacht
Der Führer und Reichskanzler

Ich genehmige, daß der

Oberleutnant a.D. Ernst P r a g e r,

Berlin-SO 36, Am Treptower Park 18,

wieder als aktiver Offizier im Heeresdienst verwendet
werden kann.

Gleichzeitig verfüge ich, daß der Oberleutnant Prager
deutschblütigen Personen im Sinne der Deutschen Rassenge=
setzgebung mit allen sich daraus ergebenden Rechten und
Pflichten gleichgestellt wird.

Führerhauptquartier, den 30. Oktober 1941

Der Führer und Oberste Befehlshaber
der Wehrmacht

Der Chef des Oberkommandos
der Wehrmacht

Der Reichsminister und Chef
der Reichskanzlei

Vorstehende Abschrift wird hiermit beglaubigt
Kulmbach, den 26. Juni 1951
STADTRAT
Im Auftrag

(Haar)
terw. Oberinspektor

Half-Jew Captain Ernst Prager's *Deutschblütigkeitserklärung*, dated 30 October 1941, reads: "I approve that retired First Lieutenant Ernst Prager (Berlin-So 36, Am Treptower Park 18) may be used again as an active officer in the service of the army. At the same time, I declare that First Lieutenant Prager is of equal status with German-blooded persons with respect to German racial laws with all of the consequent rights and obligations. Führer and Supreme Commander Adolf Hitler, Commander in Chief of the Wehrmacht Wilhelm Keitel, Secretary of State and Head of the Reich Chancellery Hans Heinrich Lammers."

all had to fight, and the service of your ancestors will be considered, but I don't think it's enough for a *Genehmigung* to serve." Despairing, Prager believed he would not be able to pursue the career he so desired, marry the woman he dearly loved, and protect the family he cherished. However, on 26 June 1941, he informed his uncle Stephan that his application and that of another half-Jew had reached Hitler's adjutant, Gerhard Engel. If approved, they would be the first half-Jews to reenter the army.

At the end of October 1941, four months after the invasion of Russia, Hitler granted Prager the *Deutschblütigkeitserklärung.* It remains unclear why Hitler decided to give Prager the exemption. Perhaps it was because of the heavy officer casualties. Between June 1941 and March 1942, "no less than 15,000 officers were killed." In July 1941, there were 12,055 first lieutenants in the army, but by March 1942, "their number had diminished to 7,276."[49] Prager was also most likely brought back because State Secretary Lammers had recommended this case for his friend Haehnelt.

When Haehnelt heard about Prager's exemption he said, "Finally some good news during these shitty times." Prager wrote that Haehnelt cried because he was so happy for him. In his diary, Prager wrote, "I finally belong to the army again." He could legally serve, get married, and have children. After his wedding, he wrote his uncle Stephan and said, "Thank you for your good wishes . . . I know that you rejoice with me, and that a large stone has been removed from your heart." Prager's uncle could not travel to the wedding because Jews were banned from traveling in Germany. Prager believed his *Deutschblütigkeitserklärung* unique, a customary response of most who received it. Most simply thought their case was special. As he wrote his uncle Stephan, "We can once again hold up our heads with pride . . . This decision shows, especially during this particular time, the special handling of this case . . . This exemption would've been impossible without grandfather's, yours, and father's attitudes and convictions. This fact should always maintain you and father when you have problems."

On 26 November, Prager learned that at least two other *Mischlinge* had also received the *Deutschblütigkeitserklärung:* "another lieutenant with the same situation has been approved. A third one . . . was in China as an instructor . . . then he was in Spain and now he's a captain who re-

Ernst Prager and Hella Koberger at their wedding soon after Prager received his *Deutschblütigkeitserklärung* in late October 1941.

ceived the *Ritterkreuz* (Borchard[t]!). So, a well-deserved equalization [of a Jewish person with an Aryan]!"

Prager continued to talk to his uncle about his Aryanization: "Hella seems now to dream the most. That poor child has suffered so much. She could really only believe what had happened when Hitler's letter came in the mail. Along with the documents came the news that the Office for Racial Research will send me a certificate concerning my equality with Aryans. The letter further stated that I'm allowed to say I'm *deutsch-blütig* in questionnaires, as can my children." But Prager's Jewish uncle had to continue to wear the Jewish Star because Hitler's clemency gave only his nephew permission to declare himself non-Jewish. While Prager felt proud to once again serve, he was a nervous wreck and exhausted. The process to get the exemption had taken its toll. Once back in the military, his responsibilities snapped him out of his melancholy. Prager quickly adjusted to his duties as a company commander and was soon sent to Russia into the thick of battle, where warfare was often a "smoking chaos, a wellspring of continuous fear . . . and thousands of explosions."[50]

On 31 March 1942, Prager almost lost his life. Early in the morning, he and his men attacked an area around the town of Krasnaya Gora in Belorussia south of Smolensk. Two feet of snow covered the ground and a chilly wind blew the powder up in swirls. As they attacked, two Soviet T-34 tanks started to fire on their position. After a thirty-minute battle they destroyed one of the tanks, but the Russians opened up with an artillery barrage, killing many of Prager's men. Prager decided they must take over the position quickly or die. He led two platoons and moved forward.

Along with his men, Prager neared the Russian lines by crawling down through one of the tank tracks left in the snow. As they approached the Russians, a bullet grazed his forehead. As blood streamed down his face, Prager directed his men. Then a shell splinter hit him in the head. Although blood continued to drip on his neck and clothes, he organized his men in their attack. At that moment, a Russian tank started to outflank Prager's position and lay down enfilading fire. As Prager hit the ground, another bullet grazed his neck. Looking around, Prager found they had been cut off.

Prager's men lay helpless as the tank's cannon and its machine gun opened up, killing many. He unsuccessfully tried to get his men to fire into the tank's observation slots. In the chaos, Prager received his fourth wound, a bullet through his left shoulder. He wanted to return to headquarters to report the situation, but the tank prevented any movement. He worried that if the tank moved a few more meters in their direction, it would drive down the tracks in which they hid and finish them off.

Suddenly, the tank found their position and came toward them. Prager jumped out of the snow trench and landed in an artillery crater. When he did this, he received his fifth wound—a bullet through his neck, which knocked him to the ground. Remarkably, the bullet missed his arteries and veins. As he lay on the earth feeling the blood ooze down his neck and back, he tried to assess the situation. Suddenly, another bullet ripped through his left shoulder. He tried to bury himself in the snow and earth when he received his seventh wound—a bullet wound in the back of his head that only penetrated his skin and skull, but passed through without hitting his brain. Giving up for the moment, he rolled over on his back, pulled off his helmet, and awaited death. Examining his helmet, he saw that it had two bullet holes. After a few minutes, the will to live took over and he searched for better cover. He had now been in battle for over three hours. He crawled down to the bottom of the crater into a pool of cold water, hearing the pops and whizzes of the bullets flying overhead.

As he lay there hearing the battle travel west from his position, he knew the Russians had taken over the area and waited for the enemy to show up. Sure enough, three Russians walked up to him and pointed their rifles at him. He awaited the blackness of death.

Looking at the Soviets, Prager pointed to his wounds and the blood that covered him as if to ask, "What more do you want to do to me?" One Russian "with beautiful clear blue eyes" explained that he would soon be captured if he lived long enough. The Russians executed the other wounded Germans. Soon after this, Prager saw the Russian who had spoken to him get shot in the head and drop dead. Prager does not know why he was spared. He waited there for a long time hoping that the four Panzers would come soon. Unbeknownst to Prager, the Soviets had already destroyed three of the tanks and the remaining one was engaged in action far away from him. He was alone.

As he lay in the pool of water, he noticed ice forming around the edge of the crater. He struggled to stop his teeth from chattering as the sun set below the horizon. Watching the ice, he heard the sound of German Stuka dive bombers. This gave him strength, and he watched the planes rain down their bombs on the Russian positions. He thought about life and death, imprisonment and freedom. Prager wanted to live more than anything. After the planes left, some Russian soldiers returned to his position and plundered his belongings, and then one Soviet left a weapon with some ammunition next to Prager in case he wanted to commit suicide. Apparently, Prager looked quite bad and the enemy felt he would soon die, so why not spare him some misery? The Russians then left.

After a while, Prager crawled to his lines, which lay about 500 feet behind him. He came across three of his dead comrades, one of whom had his head crushed into a flat mess of flesh and brains by the tank. Every few meters, he had to stop to rest. His breathing was heavy and his pain horrible. He thought about his Jewish family and knew if he died, they would die also.

Ernst Prager, shown
a few days after
surviving an
engagement on the
Russian front during
which he was shot
seven times.
(Military awards:
EKI, EKII, and
Golden Wound
Badge)

After he struggled for hours to get to his lines, he yelled out for
someone to get him, and two comrades carried him to a first aid station.
Since many had witnessed the attack on Prager's position, they were
surprised he was alive. That night, a battalion doctor took care of Prager
and within a few days, he returned home to recover. Many of his comrades felt amazement at his heroic deeds. Other *Mischlinge* behaved
bravely on the battlefield as well, often, like Prager, feeling a deep compulsion to prove themselves. For example, quarter-Jew Artur Becker-
Neetz received the Knight's Cross in the fall of 1941 for preventing his
company from being destroyed even though he had taken a bullet to the

Prager was not alone in performing heroically on the battlefield. In 1941, quarter-Jew Unteroffizier Artur Becker-Neetz, who is mentioned in Prager's biography, prevented his company from being destroyed, even though he had taken a bullet to the head. It is very impressive that Becker-Neetz met with Hitler and also received the Knight's Cross. On 21 April 1943, Feldwebel Willy Moder (looking over Hitler's left shoulder); Artur Becker-Neetz (far right); and Göring (far left) are present at the presentation of a birthday gift from the army of military art to Hitler. Notice that Becker-Neetz is wearing his Knight's Cross. (Photo credit: Steve Sandman)

head. He received the award personally from Hitler as well as the *Genehmigung.*[51]

After Prager returned home, instead of receiving an award from the Führer like Becker-Neetz, he found out that, contrary to his hopes, Hitler really had no intention of protecting his relatives. Prager's father had to perform forced labor, and the Nazis had sent his uncle Stephan to Theresienstadt. Had Germany won the war or prolonged it, the Nazis would probably have deported Prager's father. After learning about

Prager's serious injuries, he said to his daughter-in-law, "If he dies, I'm finished."

When the Nazis persecuted Jews at home and deported them, they traumatized thousands of *Mischling* soldiers like Prager. During his trial in Israel, SS Lieutenant Colonel and Chief of the Gestapo's Evacuation Office Adolf Eichmann said that in 1941 and 1942, Hitler and General Wilhelm Keitel, the Armed Forces High Command's chief of staff, had expressed concern that when *Mischlinge* went on leave, they would become distressed to discover that their parents had been deported. The desk officer for racial law in the Reich Ministry of the Interior, Dr. Bernhard Lösener, also worried about this. On 4 December 1941, Lösener wrote that the government should grant special consideration to *Mischlinge* and their families, especially during the war. According to Lösener, it seemed illogical to let *Mischlinge* serve while the government persecuted their parents. Lösener described Prager's situation as an example of this problem. Even after Prager had received Hitler's *Deutschblütigkeitserklärung,* the police detained Prager's father and threatened him with imprisonment if the authorities saw him talking with an Aryan in public. The Nazis also required him to wear the Jewish Star and made him perform forced labor. Prager was lucky, though, in some respects. Many learned that a parent or grandparent had been deported and their fates remained unknown. At least Prager knew where his father was, and that he was alive.

After his return to Germany for recuperation, Prager helped a few of his relatives who were in danger. Prager actually met with Eichmann two and a half months after being injured and sent home. Although his doctors warned that traveling might kill him because of his wounds, he decided to leave Nuremberg for Berlin. Because of his serious wounds, Prager's wife, Hella, accompanied him to several SS buildings. When SS personnel learned that he had received Hitler's *Deutschblütigkeitserklärung* and was a decorated frontline officer, they treated him with the utmost respect and greeted him properly for his rank and status. Eventually, he was told to visit Eichmann's office. Surprisingly, Eichmann admitted him.

Wrapped in bandages, Prager marched into Eichmann's office with only a subtle hint of lameness. After an exchange of formalities, Prager explained the situation of his father, who was performing forced labor, and of his uncle Stephan and aunt Mathilde Blanck, who were incarcerated in Theresienstadt. According to Prager and his wife, Eichmann responded by describing Theresienstadt in positive terms as a new home for Jews where they were well treated and could decide their own fates. Prager became so irritated with Eichmann that he jumped up and said sarcastically, "Next you'll tell me you regret not being Jewish so you could spend a holiday in Theresienstadt." Eichmann then became serious and admitted that he could do nothing for Prager's father since he had not been deported yet, and thus fell outside of Eichmann's jurisdiction, but assured him that his uncle would be moved to the "Prominent Jews'" barracks where he would receive better food and not be deported to a death camp. Eichmann's promise to help Prager's uncle was carried out. Nothing was said about the aunt, whom the Nazis later murdered. Although Prager by now knew more than the average person about what the Nazis were doing to the Jews, he still failed to grasp the true extent. He later claimed, "It was all just too unbelievable."

As one can see, Prager's *Deutschblütigkeitserklärung* and his devout service did not prevent members of his family from being persecuted. Haehnelt again wrote Lammers on 2 April 1943 to help Prager when he heard about his plight, informing Lammers that Prager, an "outstanding soldier" who had been wounded several times and had proven his bravery, had experienced several problems. Haehnelt asked that Prager's father, Heinrich, remain protected, though his Aryan wife had died: "The son shouldn't have to continually worry about his father." Lammers answered Haehnelt on 8 April 1943 and told him that he had long been aware of Prager's case and assured him that he would help within the realm of possibility. Fortunately, his father was not deported and was only required to perform forced labor in his hometown of Kulmbach. Prager, with help from his friend Major Eberhard von Hanstein of the Wehrmacht's High Command, was also able to get support to protect his father. But, as we have seen, several other relatives did not benefit from Prager's unique status. Prager ended the war as commander of a replacement battalion in Bayreuth.

Prager's time in the military ended on a negative note. At the end of the war, four soldiers under his command deserted their post. He caught them and sentenced them to death. Before carrying out the sentence, Prager gave a speech in which he claimed he was a "convinced National Socialist" and that these men had behaved despicably. He had the condemned men stand before their coffins and then told those present that if any of them decided to abandon their comrades, they would meet the same fate. Then he had the four men executed. After the war, Prager was brought to trial for this action. Prager claimed he acted according to military law. He also justified his fanatical speech, saying that he did so to protect himself and his family. Eventually the court found him innocent, but this event indicates that when Prager was placed in a position to show mercy, he did not. For a man who owed so much to others for their mercy, Prager showed no empathy for men unwilling to continue serving a lost cause. Soon after the executions, the Americans entered Kulmbach.

Prager's story is absorbing. He struggled to conform to his society, and his Jewish family endorsed his decision to get back into the military. Yet, the Hitler exemption ultimately proved to be a pyrrhic victory in many ways, with Prager suffering horrible wounds and losing several relatives in the Holocaust. Many of his comrades, one of whom was a famous general and former head of the Bundeswehr, Ulrich de Maizière, recognized the horrible dilemma that Prager faced, and at his funeral, his comrades stated, "You had the courage while resisting the discrimination against your family to serve your Fatherland and go to the front to fight . . . you were a true, self-sacrificing comrade."

Many of those who, like Prager, sought the *Deutschblütigkeitserklärung* did so for the sake of their family members and girlfriends. They tried everything to be accepted by their tormentors, who continued to persecute them and their families. The political philosopher Isaiah Berlin eloquently described this situation when he wrote,

> I desire to be understood and recognized . . . And the only persons who can so recognize me, and thereby give me the sense of being someone, are the members of the society to which, historically, morally, economically, and perhaps, ethnically, I feel I belong. For what I am is, in large part, determined by what I feel and think; and what I feel and think is determined by the feeling and thought prevailing in the society to which I belong. So much can I desire this,

that I may, in my bitter longing for stature prefer to be bullied and misgoverned.[52]

Berlin's point that society determines a person's identity is shown dramatically with Prager, who was willing to go to the heat of battle in his desire to be accepted. He even went further at war's end when he carried out draconian measures against deserters in 1945 and attributed his actions to the need to protect himself and his family. According to his daughter, Thekla Pesta, Prager never got over executing the deserters. Prager's story displays the tragic events many *Mischlinge* experienced as they did their best to live under a brutal regime that rejected them.

Quarter-Jewish Admiral Bernhard Rogge

Bernhard Rogge stood six feet three inches tall and weighed 220 pounds. He carried his body with control and excelled at sports. His military bearing exuded confidence and he was a strong leader. His demeanor commanded respect, and he was the soldier-gentleman *par excellence.* He always wore neatly starched and ironed clothes, and his whole appearance, from his precisely combed hair to his manicured fingernails and spit-polished shoes, showed that he paid careful attention to the details of life. He was a machine who always did his duty with 100 percent of his being. He took responsibility for everything that happened to him and around him.

Bernard Friedrich Carl Edgar Rogge was born on 4 November 1899.[53] His mother was a homemaker and his father a government official. His maternal grandmother was Jewish, but her husband was Aryan. It appears he did not really care about his Jewish background until the advent of the Third Reich, when he was classified as a quarter-Jew. On the other side of Rogge's lineage, his paternal grandfather, Bernhard Rogge (1831–1919), after whom his parents named him, was a Lutheran who served as the clerical figure in the Kaiser's court.

The two things that charted Rogge's course through the dark and mysterious waters of the Third Reich were his faith in God and his unswerving dedication to the German navy even while it was under Hitler.

Quarter-Jewish Admiral Bernhard Rogge. Notice the Oak Leaves and Knight's Cross around his neck. (Military awards: Oak Leaves to Ritterkreuz, Ritterkreuz, Samurai Sword from the Emperor of Japan, EKI, and EKII)

Rogge's lengthy career spanned four navies. He served under the Kaiser, the Weimar Republic, the Third Reich, and the Federal Republic of Germany. At the age of fifteen, he volunteered for the navy and by 1917 had become an ensign. During World War I, he served on cruisers, including the *Moltke* during the great sea battle at Jutland in 1916, until the armistice was signed and hostilities ended in 1918. His generation witnessed the embarrassment of the mutiny of the navy, an event that career officers during World War II swore would never happen again. In 1919, he left the navy for a few months, then reentered in 1920 and served in different capacities throughout the Weimar Republic in a force

Bernhard Rogge as an ensign
during World War I, circa 1918.

dramatically weakened by the Versailles Treaty. The Allies had specified
limits on the quantity, offensive class, and armament of German ships.
The Versailles Treaty also imposed manpower limitations and prescribed
that officers would serve for twenty-five years to reduce the intake and
training of men. This resulted in the creation of a small cadre of highly
experienced and dedicated naval officers, such as Bernhard Rogge.

In 1933, the navy made the transition to the Third Reich. Rogge had
some trouble in 1934 when the Aryan Paragraph came out. He reported

to Admiral Hermann Boehm that he had a Jewish grandmother, but as a World War I veteran and a friend of Boehm, he avoided discharge. His half-Jewish mother, who died in 1924, was spared from experiencing the Third Reich.

Rogge's ancestry started to plague him in the early 1930s. He later wrote about his ancestry problems: "One could curse one's birth and ancestry; however, one cannot make it not to have happened. One can never step out of his family tree, no matter how much one wants to . . . He may keep it a secret, may hate it, may feel ashamed because of it; however, in his secrecy, his shame, his hate, he will in his disgust have to recognise it."

Rogge experienced great personal hardships during the mid to late 1930s from Nazi hardliners who wanted him out of the service until the grand admiral of the navy Erich Raeder took his case to Hitler. Raeder helped several *Mischlinge*. Besides wanting to keep qualified people, perhaps Raeder also helped because his own son-in-law was a *Mischling*. Raeder wrote after the war, "When individual cases came to my notice, I made use of my right to approach Hitler and various high Party authorities." Cases existed to which Raeder turned a blind eye, but he helped *Mischlinge* more than one would have expected.

Supposedly Admiral Karl Doenitz also took Rogge's case seriously and helped him. After being asked at Nuremberg in 1945 whether the navy supported any anti-Semitic policies, Doenitz said no and then continued,

> I had four Jewish high officers that I can think of at the moment. One was Rogge, a vice admiral who was in charge of the education of naval cadets all along until the end of the war. Another was a captain. I had an affidavit from Rogge for my defense. If any of those four Jewish officers had known about what was happening to the Jews inside Germany or elsewhere by Himmler and Hitler, they would surely have told me. There was a letter I received from Hitler once in 1943 saying that the party complained because a Jew was in charge of the education of naval cadets. He meant Admiral Rogge. I replied that he should mind his own business.[54]

So, besides Raeder, it seems other high-ranking officers helped Rogge.

Grand Admiral of the Navy Erich Raeder (left) walking with Hitler on a battleship, probably the *Scharnhorst*, circa 1939. Raeder took the cases of several officers, including Bernhard Rogge, to Hitler in order to help them get "Aryanized."

Soon after Raeder took Rogge's case to the Führer, Hitler in 1939 declared him *deutschblütig*. This change of status saved Rogge from great despair. Earlier in 1939, several Nazi Party officials had made Rogge's life a "living hell," and both his wife, Anneliese, and mother-in-law committed suicide due to the persecution. The prank and hate-filled phone calls they received and the constant worry about his career and their future had taken a dreadful toll on the family. It seemed, though, that Hitler's *Deutschblütigkeitserklärung* in 1939 prevented bureaucrats from further attacking Rogge, who accepted this "privilege" and carried out his duties as a typical Prussian officer. After the tragedy of losing his wife, all he had left in the world was his naval career and a dog, a small terrier named Ferry, who was often onboard with Rogge as a crew mascot. After 1939, available records indicate, Rogge faced little overt harassment due to his Jewish background.

Bernhard Rogge escorts Hitler in his inspection of the crew on the *Karlsruhe* in June 1936.

Although the Aryanization happened only in 1939, he did not have many problems conducting his military duties throughout the 1930s. In 1935 and 1936, he served as the first officer of the cruiser *Karlsruhe* during a world training cruise, which included a lengthy stay in Japan. Although the cruise stood him in good stead, his attitude toward the Nazis and their silly pageantry was displayed in a privately published book by Rogge and the captain of the *Karlsruhe*. As a humorous view of naval life, it included matters regarding the 1936 change to a flag bearing a swastika. The book included a drawing of Rogge marching down the corridor in a bathrobe mockingly making stiff arm salutes.

In the 1936 Olympics, Rogge served as a yacht sailing judge, and Admiral Raeder referred to him in his memoirs as "one of our best yachtsmen." From February 1938 until September 1939, he commanded the sail training ship *Albert Leo Schlageter,* the sister ship of the U.S. Coast Guard ship *Eagle.* Rogge's star seemed to be in the ascendant. He was one of the few officers to merit the distinction of having a book written about him. It covered his leadership of a sail training ship cruise with his main focus of teaching the men how to rely on one another during times of stress. In times of peace few military officers inspired anybody enough to become the subject of a book.[55]

After war broke out his duties changed. By winter 1939–1940, he prepared for his command on the ship *Atlantis* (formerly known as *Goldenfels*), built for the Hansa line in 1937. It was a rough start because the ship had to go through many stages of development before it was ready for war, but ultimately, this ship and its accomplishments would secure Rogge's name in the history books.

He moved to Bremen and took up residence in the Hotel Columbus, located right across the harbor from where the ship was berthed. He had to convert a cargo ship into a man-of-war called a surface raider.

The German navy responded to its material weakness with surface raiders. Since the German navy was numerically inferior to the British, it had to devise ways to compensate for this weakness. One of the obvious areas in which the Germans succeeded in doing this was producing hundreds of U-boats and attacking with them in numbers. Yet another less known but efficient way the Germans sank ships was with surface raiders, also called auxiliary cruisers or Q-ships.

These ships masqueraded as merchant ships until they got close to an enemy. Then they would drop hidden doors, revealing their guns, and order the opposing ship to surrender or be destroyed. To their enemies, they were known as "mystery ships" or "rattlesnakes of the oceans."

Rogge wanted "to harass and to do damage to the enemy for as long as possible and at constantly changing places, to disrupt his sea-borne trade and to tie up his forces." He further stated that their "task was not to sink every ship we sighted, but to spread alarm and despondency among the enemy, to force him to sail his ships in escorted convoys and to upset the economy of his dominions and colonies." The Germans had had a lot of success with such ships in World War I and wanted to use this type of warfare again. Yet the naval bureaucrats felt skeptical, thinking these ships would be decimated by the British, and thus called them "never-come-back liners."

Nevertheless, these ships lasted longer than any "paper pusher" imagined and spread confusion and fear among the Allies by disrupting their supply lines. This tied up many warships assigned to hunt them down. As historian of the German raiders August Karl Muggenthaler rightly noted, "the raiders constituted a serious threat and thus served their limited purpose extraordinarily well."[56] Rogge was the first World War II German surface raider captain to prepare a boat for war.

To transform the merchantman into a raider, Rogge had to have its entire inner structure reconfigured and the fuel capacity increased. The water tanks were increased to hold 1,200 tons, since 350 men would be sailing it instead of the usual crew of fewer than 50. A raider would have to stay at sea for several months if not a year or more, and therefore, Rogge had to change the ship dramatically.

The navy had to outfit the crew with several types of clothing to take care of them when they sailed in tropical seas of the Pacific and Indian Oceans or in the bitter cold seas near the southern regions of the navigable globe. The military supplied the crew with helmets, fur-lined watch coats, combs, erasers, jacks, lightbulbs, nails, boots, soap, papers and pens, razors, zinc oxide, toothbrushes, winter boots, and gloves as well as other items. The coal bunkers to fire the freshwater condensers had to be increased to 1,000 tons.

The refitters had to build sections within the ship to house prisoners,

Rogge and his officers of the *Atlantis*, circa 1940.

crewmembers, mines, sand ballast, chicken coops, torpedoes, and ammunition for the cannons. The engineers armed the ship with six 5.9-inch main gun batteries, cannons (one 75mm, two 20mm, two 37mm), and torpedo tubes. And Rogge and his men built a new ventilation system and a special compartment to house the ship's seaplane.

Since many raiders were originally built to carry cotton, sewing machines, sacks of cocoa beans, automobiles, cloth, and other items, the process of conversion took time and required much imagination and effort. Rogge involved himself with the work down to its tiniest details. One day during this process, Rogge wrote in the vessel's log, "We'll be proud of our ship by the time she has put on her makeup. But like so many ladies she takes an interminable time preparing."

Since Rogge had served in the navy's education department, he quickly realized that many shipmates assigned to him were substandard. Consequently, he sent half of them packing. Moreover many in the High

Command did not have much faith in the surface raiders and did not send their best officers there. After Rogge applied for new officers, the navy's personnel branch replied, "What! You want nineteen officers for drowning?" But Rogge finally got his officers, many of whom had already served under him.

Although a firm disciplinarian, Rogge treated his men well. He pushed himself and made sure his men knew he shared their fate no matter what. Sometimes during the cruise of the *Atlantis,* his exercise included stoning the ship decks (using rocks to smooth the wood surface) with the crew.

As one of the most chivalrous and honorable naval leaders of World War II, it was ironic that Rogge should be burdened with the "world opprobrium" of being a "pirate" captain. Surface raiders were indeed masters of disguise and stalkers of the sea. Their captains had to operate them according to strict codes, and although they were detested by the Allies, international law permitted such ships in times of war.

The *Atlantis* could change its appearance to mirror several ships from Japan, the Netherlands, and Norway, just to name a few. Using artificial stacks, masts, and superstructures, Rogge and his men could dramatically change the ship's appearance to confuse even the most experienced sea captain. Sometimes Rogge had "women passengers" with wigs and dresses pushing baby carriages on the deck to give the illusion to others that it was a passenger ship.

The ship started with a bad omen before reaching the open sea for its gunnery trials at Kiel—it ran aground while under the control of a harbor pilot. Many worried the navy would relieve Rogge, but the admiralty said, "It's not enough for a raider captain to have skill. He must have luck as well." The navy had faith in Rogge.

On 31 January 1940, Raeder came to see Rogge and his crew to wish them a successful patrol. Once properly disguised and armed, the ship left Germany for the South Atlantic on the last day of March, crossing over into the first day of April. Many felt that to leave on April Fool's Day was the second bad omen.

Disguised as the Russian ship *Kim,* the *Atlantis* made its way to the open sea. Since the British did not want to create any incidents with any of Stalin's navy, Rogge's masquerade provided good cover. Rogge rea-

The *Atlantis* in 1939.

soned that since the Soviets moved their ships around unaccounted for, and since a lot of political friction existed between England and Russia, the English probably would not interfere. And besides, Rogge noted, most English sailors did not speak Russian, so he did not have to worry about radio contact. Traveling through hostile waters full of enemy warships and mines, Rogge and his men continued to avoid danger. At first, a torpedo boat and fighter planes escorted them. The navy also sent a U-boat and a seaplane to help out.

By 16 April, Rogge sailed past the British blockade and into the open sea. He had just missed running into a formidable British force a week earlier. A lookout had spotted a British warship over the horizon and Rogge ordered his men to their battle stations and increased speed. The raider escaped this time.

Rogge did not like fighting England because of his profound respect for their government and people, but he had to do his duty. Now having reached the open ocean, Rogge headed to the South Atlantic to take pressure off the Germans in the north. The first ship they encountered was a sailing ship from a Scandinavian country. As an avid yachtsman, Rogge said that "even if she'd been packed with contraband, I still couldn't have sunk her." Besides, it was bad luck for a steamship to attack a sailing vessel. *Atlantis* let it sail on unmolested.

Though they had made it safely to the South Atlantic, they heard by radio that the British had reported a suspicious-looking Russian ship and, as a result, on 24 April, Rogge transformed the *Atlantis* to look like Japan's *Kasii Maru*. On 2 May, they passed the British liner *City of Exeter* and Rogge had his men go into action, having some of his shortest men dress up like Japanese women and push baby dolls in carriages. Several of the "Japanese sailors" even waved to the British. Although Rogge's men wanted to attack the liner, Rogge refused to be bogged down with so many prisoners so early in their voyage and before he arrived in his assigned operational area.

On 3 May 1940, one of the officers ran down the passage to the bridge yelling, "They've got one, they've got one just ahead to port!" "Buck-fever" ran high on the ship and many wanted action. Men hurried to their posts and waited for Rogge's command "*Enttarnen!*" which meant "Drop the hidden gates and fire." One of the officers measured the distance of the enemy through a range finder hidden in a water tank. Suddenly, Rogge raised the war flag and put out the signal "Heave to or I'll fire; you're prohibited from radioing." The British steamer *Scientist* refused to obey and continued on its course. Rogge ordered a shot over its bow. The vessel then started to radio the QQQQ message, meaning that a suspicious ship had stopped it. Rogge's ship opened fire and the shells tore into the steamer. The crew started to get into their lifeboats, and radio transmission stopped because the *Atlantis* had destroyed the wireless room. One of Rogge's most trusted officers, Adjutant Ulrich Mohr, got a boarding party together and they motored over to the smoking hulk. After looking through the ship, Mohr found that its captain had destroyed important documents and code books. There was little intelligence to gather.

As the ship sank, one of *Atlantis*'s crewmen said, "That's the stuff. That's how I'd like to see all their bloody old tubs go down." Overhearing him, Rogge shook his head and then said, "I don't agree. Let's just look at it as a necessary job. Ships are rather like human beings, you know. Each has a life of its own and each dies differently too. Yes, I'm sorry to see them go."

He took a total of seventy-seven prisoners. Rogge's crew gave them toiletries, soap, and blankets and they separated the black merchant sailors from the white. They were put to work, with the whites earning 40 pfennigs and the blacks 20 pfennigs a day. In those days, men were often segregated by race and nationality, not only by the Nazis.

On 10 May, Rogge approached the Cape of Agulhas off Africa on a clear night and dropped ninety-two mines in the shipping lane there. Afterward, Rogge proceeded to the Durban-Australia track but found no ships to hunt—the lack of ships there was due to the *City of Exeter*'s warning of a suspicious Japanese ship that might be a surface raider. As a result, Rogge quickly changed the *Atlantis* into the Dutch *Abbekerk* and moved it up to the Durban-Batavia and Mauritius-Australia shipping lanes. By now, reports of the victorious German armies in France had reached the crew. Many on board fretted that they might be robbed of glory. Others looked forward to what they would do with their lives once peace was declared. No one on board dreamed the war would last five more years.

On 10 June 1940, Rogge spotted the Norwegian ship *Tirranna*. Rogge flagged it to stop and then fired warning shots. Due to the fierce African sun the Norwegians did not see Rogge's warnings since his shells fell short. As a result, the ship continued and Rogge fired a few more shots. This time, the message was clear. *Tirranna* tried to make a run for it and radioed for help. The men on *Atlantis* jammed its signal and Rogge opened fire. The Norwegians tried to fight back with their single 4.7-inch gun while zigzagging wildly as they tried to escape. After *Atlantis* fired 150 shells, the Norwegians finally stopped. Although terribly mauled, the ship was captured as a prize.

When the Germans boarded the ship, they found its deck literally covered with blood. The Norwegian captain was on the verge of crying. Dazed, he said, "But Norway made peace with you today." *Tirranna* was a great prize, since among many other things it carried 3,000 tons of wheat, 178 trucks, 5,500 cases of beer, 300 cases of tobacco, 3,000 cases of canned peaches, and 17,000 cases of jam. In addition to this, it had plenty of fuel. With such booty, the *Atlantis* could continue hunting without many worries about fuel, water, and food. Rogge would repeat this technique with many ships, sometimes sinking them after he took their supplies, and other times sending them back to Germany, as he did with the *Tirranna.*

After this victory, Rogge learned that the actual *Abbekerk* had been sunk, so he changed his disguise to imitate another Dutch ship, the *Tariffa,* and moved to the Aden-Australia and Sunda-Strait-Durban sea lanes to find new prey.

On 11 July 1940, *Atlantis* sank the British steamer *City of Baghdad* and on 13 July 1940, the British passenger ship *Kemmendine.* On 28 July 1940, it sank the Norwegian ship *Talleyrand* and on 24 August 1940, the British steamer *King City.* On 9 September 1940, it sank the British steamer *Athelking* and on 10 September 1940, another English steamer, the *Benarty.* On 17 September 1940 it sank the French passenger ship *Commissaire Ramel,* which at 10,061 metric tons was the biggest kill to date. On 22 October 1940, it captured the Yugoslavian steamer *Durmitor.* On 8 November 1940, it sank the Norwegian tanker *Teddy.* On 10 November, it captured the Norwegian tanker *Ole Jacob* and on 11 November 1940, sank the British steamer *Automedon.* Rogge and his men seemed unstoppable. The significance of the loss of the *Automedon* was profound and only recently became the subject of study.

Before they sank the *Automedon,* Rogge's men seized several bags full of documents—some of which would prove invaluable to the war effort and allow Rogge to have a significant impact on the manner in which Japan conducted its invasion of Asia in 1941–1942. They were "highly confidential" documents drawn up by the British War Cabinet for its "Commander-in-Chief Far East," detailing the British military strength in East Asia, including the number of Royal Air Force units, the number and type of ships, an assessment of Australia's and New Zealand's military roles, copious notes on the Singapore fortifications, and an assessment of the feasibility of Japan entering the war. Most importantly, the secret documents made it clear that no effective reinforcement or counterstrike could take place for at least a year after a possible Japanese assault because the British Empire was under too much pressure nearer to home. Rogge turned these documents over to the Japanese, who, on be-

The Norwegian tanker *Teddy* shortly after being fired upon by the *Atlantis* on 8 November 1940. The tanker sank shortly after sustaining this major hit.

half of the emperor, awarded him a samurai sword for his contribution to their success. Besides Rogge, only Reichsmarschall Göring and Field-Marshal Rommel received such swords from the Japanese emperor. The Japanese war planners appreciated the confirmation that the only major credible military force that could oppose their expansionist aims in the Pacific was the American fleet based at Pearl Harbor. For his accomplishments, Hitler awarded Rogge the Knight's Cross, and Rogge continued his hunting.

Rogge had a lighter side to his personality. He often enjoyed a good joke and had fun with his men. For example, in the middle of war, during Christmas of 1940, he dressed up like Santa Claus and went around the vessel spreading good cheer. Yet, these moments of letting "his hair down" were rare, and Rogge never took his eye off his mission of creating fear and worry among the British High Command. Soon after Christmas, Rogge would strike again.

Atlantis spent Christmas of 1940 at sea in the remote Kerguelen Islands, which are the southernmost islands in the Indian Ocean. The ship needed to take on fresh water, change disguise, and give the men a rest. Unfortunately, two disasters marred the event. The first occurred while *Atlantis* made its way to a hidden anchorage where it struck a submerged pinnacle of rock and became impaled. It was likely that the ship would never leave the spot, as attempts to flood and counterflood, shift cargo, rock the ship, and all other means failed to free it. Eventually, a shift of wind saved the day and permitted the ship to swing free. Rogge himself went over the side as a hard hat diver on multiple occasions to plan for and inspect the progress of hull repairs.

A second incident cost the life of a crewman who fell from a stack while painting after engine exhaust cut the rope holding him. He was buried on one of the islands after Christmas. By January, Rogge and his men had left the island on their way to hunt Allied ships once again.

On 24 January 1941, Rogge and his men sank the British steamer *Mandasor*. On 31 January 1941, they captured the British steamer *Speybank*, and on 2 February 1941, the Norwegian tanker *Ketty Brövig*. In March Rogge helped the Italian submarine *Perla* with supplies under trying circumstances, for which Mussolini awarded him the Bronze Medal for Military Valor.[57] On 17 April 1941, during a brilliant moonlit night, Rogge observed a zigzagging ship that operated under black-out conditions. Fearing it was an auxiliary cruiser like his own, Rogge moved in for the kill and opened fire. Six shells from the *Atlantis* tore into the ship, hitting its engine compartment, radio room, and waterline. When the ship stopped and its identity became known, Rogge felt sick to his stomach. It was the neutral Egyptian steamer *Zamzam*, which had been a British troop carrier, but was now a passenger liner. There were 109 women and children on the ship out of 202 passengers, 140 of whom were Americans. Since Germany was not yet at war with the United States, the killing of that many Americans passengers was a potential international disaster similar to the *Lusitania* incident of World War I.

Even though the *Zamzam* had exhibited belligerent behavior and carried contraband cargo such as British-owned oil, steel, and ambulances, Rogge worried about world opinion. To make the situation even worse, 150 of the people were missionaries who belonged to the British-American Ambulance Corps. Most of the 107 Egyptian crewmen took to the lifeboats "in true cowardly fashion," while leaving the helpless people on board to fend for themselves.

Rogge ordered his men to drop their boats and assist the helpless people on the *Zamzam*. Luckily, they saved everyone from the "sinking ship." Now Rogge had to care for them. He had his crew make the people as comfortable as possible, even building a sandbox for the children. Soon after taking these prisoners, Rogge felt thankful that the supply ship *Dresden* rendezvoused with him so he could transfer most of his prisoners to this vessel headed for France. Unfortunately for Rogge, one *Zamzam* passenger was Time-Life photographer David Sherman, who left *Atlantis* with film of the raider hidden in a toothpaste tub. These photographs would later appear in *Life* magazine and make their way into the intelligence files of the Royal Navy.

Luckily, the *Zamzam* incident never caused the diplomatic problems Rogge had feared. Even if it had, this incident could not have made relations worse. Hitler went on to declare war on the United States in December 1941 regardless. It was also unlikely America would have gone to war over such a small incident, since the liner was not American. Lest one forget, it still took two years after the sinking of the *Lusitania* in 1915 and the Zimmerman telegram before America entered World War I.

On 14 May 1941, Rogge and his men sank the British steamer *Rabaul;* on 24 May 1941, the British steamer *Trafalgar;* on 17 June 1941, the British steamer *Tottenham;* and on 20 June 1941, the British steamer *Balzac.* On 10 September 1941, they captured the Norwegian ship *Sivaplana.*

On 22 November, Rogge was ordered to resupply submarine U-126, a dangerous job for a raider in the South Atlantic. This proved especially risky since the *Atlantis* had had engine problems and one of the motors was dismantled to replace a piston, thus dramatically reducing its speed. To make matters worse, the seaplane Rogge normally used for scouting was out of service, giving him no reconnaissance capabilities. If an enemy ship showed up, *Atlantis* was a sitting duck. Rogge hoped its disguise would hide it if a British man-of-war approached on the horizon.

Suddenly Rogge's worst nightmare became reality when the British cruiser *Devonshire* showed up at full steam and demanded Rogge identify himself. He cut the fuel lines to the submarine and the U-boat submerged. Rogge radioed he was a merchantman, but the cruiser saw through his subterfuge. The British captain had Sherman's photographs and, after communicating with the Admiralty, confirmed the ship was indeed the *Atlantis*. The English opened fire with 8-inch shells from 10 miles. As the shells tore into the *Atlantis,* Rogge made the order to abandon ship and scuttled the raider. He saved all his men except twelve. As the ship sank, the crew gave it three cheers. With tears coming down his face, Rogge saluted his ship as it went down.

Fearing the German submarine, the *Devonshire* departed after *Atlantis* made its way down to the ocean's floor. Soon the U-boat surfaced and divided the survivors into three groups. They put a group into the submarine, another group on the deck of the boat, and the rest in lifeboats. Two days later, the supply ship *Python* picked them up. Two days thereafter, on 26 November, the British cruiser *Dorsetshire* caught the *Python* supplying two U-boats. The U-boats dove and the *Python* was immediately scuttled to prevent casualties as shelling began. Rogge and his men found themselves in the water again after being sunk twice in four days.

Admiral Karl Dönitz sent more submarines to help with the rescue effort since there were now two crews to care for. Traveling home, Rogge fell into a deep depression. He knew he would no longer be master of his own little world on a ship and had to return to the land dominated by Hitler. He also was returning to an empty house, and his dead wife's ghost haunted him.

Rogge later wrote to a friend that he believed God was now taking care of his wife. He also mused that God gives people hardships to make them stronger.

After several weeks at sea being dragged in lifeboats by the submarines and undergoing a depth-charge attack, Rogge and his men arrived in occupied France. Still accompanying them was Rogge's dog, Ferry. After landing in Nantes, Rogge took his men to a local church to thank them for their service and God for keeping them safe.

Rogge was the most successful surface raider commander of the war, sinking or capturing twenty-two ships for a combined displacement of 150,000 tons while being at sea for 655 straight days (including 33 days spent being towed back to Germany) and traveling over 102,000 miles. *Atlantis* destroyed or captured "over twice as much tonnage as the notorious" pocket battleship *Admiral Graf Spee.* In the modern history of naval warfare, Rogge holds the record for staying at sea for the most days without docking in port. For 622 days, from 31 March 1940 until 21 November 1941, he raided Allied shipping lanes with his surface raider "Ship 16," taking twenty-two enemy ships out of commission.

When asked how he kept the unity and morale of his men intact for so long, Rogge said that many factors went into doing so, but foremost on the list was to respect every individual and make him feel part of the team. Rogge excelled at creating confidence, something he believed that no man could do without if he wanted to perform well and bravely. When someone had a birthday, he announced it over the loudspeaker, and if someone became ill, he had people visit him in sick bay. He also focused on making sure no one was bored, believing this was the worst enemy for a serviceman. Rogge was a master at human relations in creating an environment where everyone felt he was invaluable.

Many recognized his leadership and accomplishments. On 31 December 1941, Hitler awarded him the Oak Leaves to his Knight's Cross at a reception in Berlin for successfully disrupting the Allies' shipping lanes and capturing valuable goods for Germany. The Naval High Command initially did not think the raiders would succeed, but Rogge gave them a shining example of the effectiveness of these ships.

From April 1942 until September 1944, Rogge served as education inspector for the navy, a position that, according to Admiral Oskar Kummetz, he fulfilled with professionalism and skill. On 1 March 1943, he became a rear admiral. From October 1944 until the end of the war in May 1945, he ran the education department.

He also commanded the First Battle Group (or Force 1) in the Baltic in late 1944 and early 1945 and helped the army with fire support, especially around Riga and the Kurland pocket. Without Rogge's support of the army in the Baltic, the Kurland pocket would have never continued its resistance, tying down thousands of Russian soldiers in 1944 and

Bernhard Rogge receiving the Oak Leaves to his Knight's Cross from Hitler in 1942. From left to right are Hitler, Rogge, and U-boat officers Heinrich Lehmann-Willenbrock and Schoen.

1945. By keeping a 30-mile corridor open at Riga, he helped twenty-nine divisions and much of their equipment to escape Russian encirclement in 1944.[58]

The troops knew that if they had the support of a warship, the Russians would stay away. As Guy Sajer, who was stationed at Memel on the Baltic Sea during the encirclement there, wrote: "Two warships were standing close by the shore. One of them was the *Prinz Eugen.* The other was a ship of the same size. To the desperate defenders of Memel, they were a source of support we had never hoped for. The tanks respected their large guns, and kept their distance."[59]

Rogge also used his ships to cover the millions of refugees leaving Prussia under the savage advance of the Soviet army, especially around Danzig in 1945. In fact, the atrocity stories about the Soviets at Danzig were so horrible that many "civilians in and around" the city committed

The heavy cruiser *Prinz Eugen*. Rogge commanded a fleet of ships at the end of the war and this was his flagship.

suicide instead of falling prey to the Russian onslaught of terror.[60] On 1 March 1945, he became a vice admiral. At this time, Rogge took charge of Battle Group "Rogge" (Task Force 3), which included the battleship *Schlesien*, heavy cruiser *Prinz Eugen*, light cruiser *Leipzig*, and escorts. His flag flew on the *Prinz Eugen*.

After the war, the Allies took him prisoner and then released him in September 1945. But they later brought him up on criminal charges. One charge claimed he had machine-gunned survivors of a ship he sank. This charge turned out false. The other claim stated that he, just like Prager, executed several men for desertion. This charge was true. He was brought to court, but found innocent. Though Rogge had received much help from others, he did not show mercy for those who no longer wanted to fight for Nazi Germany. Rogge claimed he carried out the executions to follow orders and maintain discipline. Others have found this argument difficult to follow. Historian Georg Meyer said in respect to this situation: "Rogge was hard as steel." This is the only event where some might question Rogge's judgment. Placed in perspective, however, his actions may not seem so extreme when compared with the mutiny at the end of World War I, and when one considers the rescue and evacuation mission assigned to Rogge's battle group.

After the war, Rogge fell in love again and married his second wife, Elsbeth, who adored him. In turn, he cherished her and felt sad that he was unable to have a family due to complications.

After the new German military (Bundeswehr) came into being in 1955, he became the commander of NATO forces for the State of Schleswig-Holstein in 1957, holding that position until 1963. He commanded all land, sea, and air forces composed of German and Allied personnel. During the major flood there of 1962, Rogge was responsible for 8,000 soldiers who conducted the rescue efforts. Interestingly, Rogge worked closely with Hamburg's mayor, the later chancellor Helmut Schmidt (who also was a Wehrmacht officer and a quarter-Jew). For Rogge's efforts, the government awarded him the Great Service Cross of the Federal Republic of Germany in 1962. The next year, he retired after a bitter fight with Defense Minister Franz-Josef Strauss.

In retirement, he pursued his passion of sailing while administering the largest school system for sailing, based in Hamburg. He also co-managed the Hamburg-Atlantik line, "a merchant shipping business," and served as consultant for civil defense matters for the government.[61] Being religious, he also busied himself with church activities, believing "that our destiny lies in God's hands and this knowledge is our strength." When asked about his successes, he said his leadership philosophy was responsible for his accomplishments, and stated, "How does one exert leadership? Well, with a Christian respect for the human qualities of others, conviction and trust in oneself." On 29 June 1982, he died and was buried in Reinbeck outside Hamburg with full military honors. Over 600 people attended his funeral service. The stone above his grave bears the carved likeness of a sail training ship underway.

In an article Rogge wrote for the February 1963 issue of the *U.S. Naval Institute Proceedings*, he attempted to explain the leadership style he used to keep the peace among over 350 officers and men away from home in time of war on board the *Atlantis* for more than a year. Among many other profound statements, one comment he made sheds some light on his personality. Rogge quoted Baron von Stein's address to young Prussian officers, "Take careful note of the fact that your rights are not being discussed. Fulfilling your obligations entails establishing your rights, so it can be said that it is your foremost right to do your duty." Rogge noted that such convictions had become unpopular after the war, but they remained sound in his opinion. Rogge's conflict with the Nazis, who attempted to destroy his naval career because of his Jewish background, may demonstrate how perfect a creature of duty Rogge had become. He remained loyal to his country and his duty and adhered to his Christian principles in spite of the fact that many Germans then considered him inferior by the circumstances of his birth.

After Rogge received his *Deutschblütigkeitserklärung* in 1939, it appears he did not have to deal with his Jewish past again. The Nazis did continue to harass him throughout the Third Reich for his religious convictions and for not adhering to Nazi ideals. All in all, it seems that Rogge concerned himself little with the "Jewish Question." Had it not been for the Nazis, he would have given little thought to his Jewish ancestors. He kept this secret from most, even close friends. It just seemed irrelevant in his life.

As a private man, Rogge shied away from the spotlight. Due to the trauma of experiencing devastating defeats in two world wars, the loss of his wife, the loss of his mother in a mental institution, and Nazi discrimination during the 1930s, he probably wanted to put his past behind him and do his best to live a peaceful life. Everyone interviewed who knew Rogge, both foreign and German, spoke highly of a "true gentleman." Yet, in many of the pictures of Rogge, as well as the letters he wrote, one picks up on a deep sadness. As mentioned above, many things haunted Rogge.

In a sense, the life of *Atlantis* mirrored Rogge's own life in that what you saw on the outside did not mirror the inside. During the Hitler years, he never quite escaped persecution for his ethnicity and religious beliefs. After the war, he sometimes had a difficult time shaking his "Nazi" past and "criminal acts" as a raider captain who served under Hitler. Although he was anything but a Nazi and hated Hitler, he still had to answer several questions about his background after the war. Also, he never recovered from his wife's suicide, often blaming himself for it. And he regretted the fact that he could not have children. Often, when he fell into depression, he must have feared sharing the same fate as his mother, who after suffering her mental breakdown never recovered. The fact that Rogge did not let his trials break him is a testament to his mental fortitude. He was not only a giant among World War II commanders, but was also a strong human being who, although often knocked down by life, refused to let it defeat him. He wrote his own obituary when he said, "If God decides to call me home, I should not quarrel with my destiny. I have been thankful for every day I have had on this earth. I have lived a full life."

Conclusion

The *Mischlinge* who received Hitler's *Deutschblütigkeitserklärung* have presented difficult problems for the general public. People often ask how these men could serve under Hitler. Wilberg and Rogge served for several decades and in World War I before Hitler ever came to power; serving their nation as warriors was the only profession they knew. In the case of Prager, although he was not a World War I veteran, the life of bearing arms for Germany was his calling. Milch was unique out of all of them in not being a career soldier, but when his nation called him, he gladly served and, as shown, did well.

Prager's life also illustrates that sometimes a man pursued this clemency not only to fulfill his calling, but also to protect his family. All these men, especially those with families, believed clemency would protect their immediate relatives to at least some degree.

Although Milch, Rogge, and Prager served until the war's end, the Nazis dismissed many with the *Deutschblütigkeitserklärung* after the 20 July 1944 bomb attack on Hitler. He needed to blame someone, and the *Mischlinge* provided him with an easy target.[62]

Since Wilberg was dead by 1944, this new change of policy did not affect him. Moreover, Wilberg, like Milch and Rogge, probably would have remained untouched had he remained alive since it seems this purge only affected active army officers. This all goes to show how fickle Hitler was with his convictions about "Jewish" soldiers.

Obtaining a *Deutschblütigkeitserklärung* was a complicated process and for readers today, it is simply confusing. Although all these men fit the Nazi definition of true Germans and brave warriors, thus granting them the right to apply for clemency, ultimately how and why Hitler went about giving these men such exemptions does not mirror his hard-core ideology. As is often the case with Hitler, it is difficult to find rational explanations for his behavior. His unpredictability with *Mischlinge* all seemed to stem from his being influenced by their connections, their family backgrounds, their social rank, their military experience, and their phenotypical traits. In other words, Hitler employed no logical and systematic process to determine their racial pedigree, even though Nazi language at the time tried to make the whole "race science" a logical and clear-cut discipline.

That Hitler involved himself so intimately with this process, though, shows how obsessed he was with his racial ideology and how he believed that only he could truly decide who was Aryan. In the end, the power to discern a person's true genetic, racial, and spiritual worth during the Third Reich was left in the hands of an uneducated fanatic Austrian named Hitler. Erich Maria Remarque, author of *All Quiet on the Western Front*, had it right when he wrote, "It is very queer that the unhappiness of the world is so often brought on by small men."[63] Hitler's exemption process for *Mischlinge* shows how deranged and small the dictator of Germany had become and how his decisions grew out of his pathology, irrationality, immorality, sadism, and racism.

4

Mischlinge and the Process of Getting a *Genehmigung*

In addition to the *Deutschblütigkeitserklärung*, other *Mischlinge* could receive another less sweeping form of clemency called the *Genehmigung* (special permission) to stay in the armed forces. The stories of Oberge-freiter Dieter Fischer and Obergefreiter Horst Geitner demonstrate how difficult and time-consuming it was to acquire one of these special ex-emptions. Thousands tried to get this coveted exemption, and many felt desperate and awaited the outcome as if it were a matter of life and death.[1] Only a small percentage succeeded. The lucky few awarded this exemption were told that if they continued to perform well, they would then be declared of German blood after the war. This gave hope to many that their nation would recognize them as full citizens.

Both men discussed in this chapter had a diverse and complicated ex-perience with the *Genehmigung* process. We will meet Dieter Fischer, who received special permission only to have it rescinded late in the war. Horst Geitner's story illustrates the frustration several felt at being re-jected after meeting the requirements for it.

It seems strange that men like Fischer and Geitner wanted to remain in the service with Hitler's permission, but many wanted to do so because they believed it was the best way to protect themselves and their families, to prove their worth as Germans, and to get clemency. These men would have been surprised had Hitler won the war to learn that their *Genehmigung* would not shield them from further persecution and the death camps.

Half-Jewish Obergefreiter Dieter Fischer

When interviewed, Dieter Fischer had difficulty hearing as a result of combat injuries. When he was young, he exuded confidence and was a handsome man with soft brown hair and thoughtful gray-brown eyes. He looked like a typical soldier and not like the Nazi description of a "Jew." His looks and behavior proved the unscientific and unrealistic nature of the Nazi racial theories. Fischer did not boast about his life or accomplishments. He was a quiet type, lived a humble life, and had served God as a pastor.

Dieter Fischer was born on 14 December 1916 in Mainz. His Jewish mother, Clara Hirschhorn, married his gentile father, Erwin Fischer, in 1903. His father had been a lieutenant colonel and during World War I was chief of the General Staff of a large army corps under General Strantz. Before he married Clara, she had to prove she was Christian, because of her Jewish name, although her parents had already converted. As his superiors told Fischer, a Prussian officer was not allowed to marry a Jew. Once proven she was indeed a Christian, they married.

However, the marriage was unhappy and Dieter's parents divorced in 1918, only two years after Dieter, one of four children, was born. His father had been caught sleeping with another man and admitted he was homosexual. Captain Ernst Roehm, the notorious homosexual and later SA leader, had been Erwin's subordinate and may also have been one of his lovers. He pleaded with Clara not to leave him but, disgusted, she got a divorce. Later, Erwin became a Nazi Party member with the Golden Party Badge, a special designation awarded to the first 100,000 members, or to other individuals at Hitler's discretion. After the divorce Dieter only saw his father once or twice a year under strict supervision.[2]

In 1918 Clara fell in love with and married Dieter's godfather, Professor Heinrich von Mettenheim. Many in Professor Mettenheim's family were furious with him over this because not only was she a divorcée with four children, she was also Jewish. Some relatives cut off relations with him. Nonetheless, Clara and Heinrich remained happily married and started a family of their own with two children, Hans-Heinz and Amelis von Mettenheim.

Professor Mettenheim ran a medical clinic in Frankfurt. He was a kind man who treated Clara's children from her previous marriage as his own. Clara busied herself with her six children, encouraging their intellectual pursuits, athletic participation, and church activities. She strongly believed in the message of Christ, and often attended Bible classes with them.

But when the Nuremberg Laws came out, Dieter Fischer thought they were just for the Jews and he agreed with the laws in how they viewed Polish Jews. He remembered that his family disliked *Ostjuden*, Orthodox Jews from the east who did not speak German, who "committed street crimes" in the big cities, and did not assimilate.[3] He believed the Nazis directed their racial policies at them rather than at Germans with Jewish ancestry.

Fischer's mother did not talk about her Jewish past. Even in the 1980s, shortly before her death at the age of 96, she wanted her Jewish maiden name left off her gravestone. Her parents had converted to Christianity and had her baptized as a child, and that remained her world. She simply did not feel Jewish. Her parents had converted for economic and social reasons, helping her father conduct his business. He raised his family in a strong patriotic home. Their conversion also allowed Clara to marry an officer and she raised her children as loyal Christian Germans. So Judaism did not play a role in the family until 1936.

When Fischer turned 18 in 1936, his mother told him about her background. It took "me a long time to get my life back in balance," Fischer said. He now knew he no longer belonged in Germany because of the new government.

In 1937, Fischer started his seven-month National Labor Service. Afterward, he began his theology studies in Wuppertal as he wanted to become a minister.

In July 1939, the army drafted him into the medical corps. He enjoyed soldiering and resented the fact that his superiors would not promote him because of his Jewish mother. As Hitler prepared for war, the Wehrmacht moved Fischer's unit to the Polish border along with 1.5 million other soldiers, and on 1 September 1939, they invaded.

Fischer fought in the forward lines and remembered officers feeling excited about the war. "It was their chance to get their medals. It was disgusting to see how some of them misused their men to get their Iron Crosses," he said. The "apparent triviality of playing to the vanity of men by offering them medals" made many act courageously as well as foolhardy in combat.[4] Fischer recalled that his Frankfurt division lost 25 percent of its officers, many to snipers noticing rank insignia on their uniforms. He pointed out that "stupid courage" got many killed. One day

Half-Jewish
Obergefreiter Dieter
Fischer. He received
Hitler's *Genehmigung*
in October 1941.
(Military awards: EKII,
Wound Badge, Assault
Badge, and Eastern
Campaign Medal 1941–
1942)

several officers drove up and asked for a status report. Fischer explained they had spotted a Polish tank down the road and should not go further. "Are you a coward?" one of the officers asked. They drove on and a few minutes later, the tank blew up the car. Every officer inside died.

Although Fischer's two brothers and his half brother, Hans-Heinz von Mettenheim, also served, his family, like many with half-Jewish sons, continued to suffer discrimination in school, work, and church. On 8 December 1939, Dieter's mother sent a letter to Army Commander-in-Chief General Walther von Brauchitsch asking him on behalf of all "half-

Jewish" soldiers to work together with the Nazi Party to alleviate the problems of families like hers:

> I speak to you as the mother of three soldiers, and as an old soldier's wife [of Lt. Col. Erwin Fischer] . . . The boys are soldiers from head to toe. The godfather of one of my boys [Adalbert Fischer] is Germany's former Crown Prince, and my old friend [General von] Seeckt held the other one [Dieter] at his Christening. My sons are *Mischlinge* because of me. During the war, when my sons were fighting in Poland, we were tortured here on the home front as if there were no more important tasks to be done during the war . . . Please stop this mistreatment of half-Jewish soldiers and their parents.

She described how angry it had made Dieter when he returned from the war to find that his sister had been expelled from certain organizations, and his mother was constantly being maltreated. For example, Dieter accompanied his mother to the Office for Jewish Affairs on Hermesweg to pick up her Jewish identification papers. His uniform with military decorations, which he wore because he was about to return to his unit, shocked those in that office. He returned to the front upset and worried about his mother. Clara enclosed her son's picture in her letter to Brauchitsch "to show that my son doesn't racially degrade the Wehrmacht . . . I beg you to use your influence to make sure the Party leaves those [*Mischlinge* and their relatives] alone . . . These men already have it bad enough being treated as second-class soldiers, they shouldn't also have to worry about their families at home while they're fighting a war."

The army wrote back on 16 December inquiring how "non-Aryan" she was. She answered, and on 24 December, General Keitel informed her that the offices responsible for such cases would look into what they could do to help Jewish parents of soldiers. In January 1940, Clara received a letter from General Hermann Reinecke in the Armed Forces High Command stating that the Ministry of the Interior, rather than the army, was responsible for these issues. Clara then forwarded her request.

Perhaps annoyed by such protests, on 16 January 1940, Hitler ordered the Wehrmacht to ascertain the number of *Mischling* soldiers to "get a

Clara von Mettenheim
(née Hirschhorn),
mother of Dieter
Fischer.

clear picture of the situation."[5] On the same day, Hitler decided that those married to quarter-Jews could serve in the war but could not become regular officers. On 20 January, the military then ruled that *Mischlinge* could also remain in the Wehrmacht, but not hold ranks higher than sergeant. However, this rule was not enforced.

At the beginning of 1940, the armed forces and government struggled with unclear policies governing *Mischlinge*. Although Hitler had drawn lines of enforcement, he issued new decrees regarding *Mischlinge* at a frequency that made it difficult for government agencies to avoid implementing outdated, and thus conflicting, policies.

In March 1940, the military future for half-Jews looked bleak. At that time famous Evangelical theologian Heinrich Grüber, an enemy of Hitler and a good friend of Clara's, tried to discuss her sons' problems with some of the military contacts he had, "but I didn't find the officers very understanding." According to a memorandum of 26 March 1940, the chief Wehrmacht adjutant, Colonel Rudolf Schmundt, had told Hitler that Fischer, decorated in Poland for bravery, was shocked at how his mother had been treated when he accompanied her to get her Jewish identification card. Hearing this story, Hitler announced that such events were intolerable. Either all half-Jews must immediately leave the Wehrmacht or the government must protect their Jewish parents. Since he did not want to protect full Jews he ordered half-Jews discharged.[6]

After the Poland campaign, Fischer's company was sent to the Eifel region to prepare for the war with France. Though accepted by his comrades, Fischer feared that he would soon be discharged. When, in March 1940, he and his fellow soldiers had to sign ancestry declarations, Fischer reported his background honestly.

Nonetheless, his commander treated him with understanding. His comrades also did not seem to care. But in May 1940, his commander received Hitler's new order discharging half-Jews and he told Fischer that he must leave the army. However, after talking with Fischer, the commander agreed to keep him after Fischer pleaded with him to say, if challenged, that he had not received the order.

During the French campaign, Fischer took care of many wounded while under fire, earning the Iron Cross Second Class, a rare decoration for a medic. He also was awarded the Infantry Assault Badge (again rare for a medic) and the Wound Badge.

But after the conflict with France ended, the army discharged Fischer in June 1940. This hit him hard. When Fischer left his company, his comrades and unit commander accompanied him to the train station. He felt nervous about his uncertain future, as other Mischlinge did.

The future also looked bleak for other members of Fischer's family. His half brother Hans-Heinz von Mettenheim was discharged and spent a few weeks in jail because the Nazis found negative comments about Germany and the war in his diary.

Fischer's brother Eberhart Fischer also had the Iron Cross; he served as a spy on the Romanian border with Russia to help prepare reports for the army in preparation for the Russian invasion. While he was rescuing a fallen comrade in battle in 1941, a sniper killed him. On hearing how he

died, Clara wrote, "he didn't have to stay out there . . . he only did it because he wanted a medal to compensate for his blemish (me!), or possibly he wanted to die to escape everything."

After Fischer returned home in 1940, he decided to apply for an exemption from Hitler. Fischer felt that if at least one of Clara's sons remained in the army, then this would protect their mother. This was a
common feeling among *Mischlinge*. "I actually wrote a letter saying that
I was willing to fight and die for Hitler," Fischer admitted. In his application, Fischer enclosed recommendation letters from his officers, teachers, and family friends and the required face and profile photos. Hitler
placed great importance on how *Mischling* soldiers looked. If a soldier
looked "Jewish," Hitler usually rejected him without further consideration.[7] In the military office where Fischer had to go to submit his application, the soldiers there told him about Hitler's close involvement in
awarding clemency and the important role pictures played.

On 21 October 1941, Commander Richard Frey in the domestic office of the Armed Forces High Command (OKW) informed the family
that Fischer had received Hitler's *Genehmigung*. Fischer then quickly
returned to the army. "I had mixed feelings about the *Genehmigung*," he
said. "I was happy to serve once again and be able to study in the universities which the clemency permitted. It also, at least I thought, would
protect my mother."

Although Fischer now had Hitler's *Genehmigung*, he was sent to a
Frontbewährungseinheit (frontline probation company), a penal unit
that allowed for the possibility of rehabilitation—this was a grim assignment. The troops called these units *Himmelfahrtskommandos*—"tickets
straight to heaven." Most in such units did not survive. In October 1941,
Fischer was sent into Russia near Ladoga Lake with 1,000 men. In December, when his unit had only 35 men left, he took a grenade splinter to
his back and was sent home to a hospital.

From his experience in the hospital and the war, Dieter realized more
strongly than before that he wanted to live his life for God. He worried
whether he would be permitted to study theology and feared the Nazis
would not let him, a *Mischling*, become a minister who would take care
of hundreds of Aryan families. He points out that the Nazis had forgotten that Jesus was a rabbi and was a Jew in everything he did.

Many Nazis denied the fact that Jesus was a Jew. For instance, commander of the SS Heinrich Himmler claimed that Jesus was not Jewish.[8] He was joined by several theologians throughout Germany who claimed Jesus came from "non-Jewish blood."[9] Julius Streicher, head of the notorious newspaper *Der Stürmer,* called Christ the "greatest anti-Semite" ever.[10] Regardless of the nonsense the Nazi religious elite preached, the Jew Jesus, the central figure in Christianity, presented Hitler with a dilemma: either exempt him from his racial ideology or face millions of angry Christians who believed the Bible when it said Jesus was Jewish. Hitler therefore dubbed Jesus an Aryan, and Nazi Christianity made images of Jesus look more Nordic and no longer described him as the advocate of love, but as the bearer of the sword for the rebirth of the *Volk.*[11] Hitler believed Jesus did not practice Judaism, but was the greatest early fighter in the war against the Jews. Nor was he, according to Hitler, the apostle of peace. Hitler believed that Jesus preached against capitalism and this was why the Jews, his archenemies, killed him. What Christ had started, Hitler said he would finish.[12]

Hitler also approved of the formation of the Institute for the Research and Elimination of Jewish Influences on Christian Living. This institute claimed Jesus was Aryan and published a "de-Jewified" Bible. Hitler Aryanized Christianity to make it conform to his weltanschauung. He also declared the Germans the chosen people, claiming, "there cannot be two chosen people. We are the people of God. Does that not explain it all?"[13] Fischer worried about such developments, but thought God would eventually help him live a pure religious life.

Fischer also described how war, in a strange way, made him feel alive. It brought him close to the grave and made him appreciate the life and beauty that "God has given mankind." Evading the clutches of death so often made him want to live life more fully.

When Fischer's wounds had healed, he returned to Russia in April 1942 with another infantry probation battalion. His unit fought south of Ladoga Lake, where a thick layer of snow remained on the ground. The Germans' gray summer uniforms made them easy targets against a background of white. Remarkably, they had a lot of success, and nearly every day they took over a town. "We always tried to conquer a village every night so we had a place to sleep," Fischer said. However, they had a difficult time sleeping because of lice. If they found a warm place to rest, the lice bit them and sucked their blood. If they slept in a cold place, the lice did not bother them as much, but they could not sleep in the chill, which made them shiver violently.

Sometimes the temperature dropped to –35 degrees Fahrenheit. When this happened, the men would be combat ineffective, since their gasoline froze and "oil became first a paste and then a glue, which entirely blocked the mechanism [of rifles, cannons and automobiles]."[14] They frequently went hungry, and to wash themselves, they often had to use snow. "Let me tell you, that was a cold business," Fischer said with a laugh. After the first winter in Russia, Fischer and his comrades knew Hitler would not win. They often told each other in 1942–1943, "Enjoy the war, the peace will be terrible."

During that time, the Nazis continued to persecute Fischer's family. The Gestapo arrested Fischer's brother Adalbert for *Rassenschande*. Disobeying the Nuremberg Laws, he had become engaged to an Aryan. They released him only when he agreed to spy for them. He did so, but fed them false information, for which they then sentenced him to several years in prison. The Americans liberated him in 1945.

As the Nazis persecuted Jews, it seemed that Fischer's service indeed protected his mother. When the Gestapo interrogated Clara, she told them that she had sons who served. This surprised the Gestapo men, who, somewhat bewildered, usually released her. It seems that most Nazi officials and police agents just did not know how the government dealt with *Mischlinge* in general.

The Gestapo tried to persuade Fischer's stepfather to leave Clara, but he refused to do this. Had he divorced her, the Nazis would have deported her. Many factors came into play to save Clara's life.

"I lived with the situation and did my best," Fischer said, talking about these difficult circumstances.

As a medic, Fischer not only dealt with victims of tank attacks but also took over the responsibilities of the battalion doctor when the doctor was killed. Tending to the wounded, he could wrap their wounds but often had no drugs to dull their pain. The wounded screamed in agony and yelled for their mothers. "It was a horrible sight and I could do nothing," Dieter said with sadness. Sometimes he would lay a wounded soldier in the snow to stop the bleeding.

Working within frontline hospitals was hazardous. One day, he remembered seeing a relative of Keitel, who died before his eyes. While tending the wounded, he talked with this officer, when suddenly, an artillery shell exploded nearby, and the officer disappeared. All that remained was some of his blood and brain matter on Fischer's jacket.

Fischer himself was wounded again during an artillery attack and was sent to a hospital in the Saarland and from there to Frankfurt to be near his family. To his surprise, the army issued him new papers, which did not mention his background.

In January 1944, Professor von Mettenheim, Clara's husband, died during an air raid on Frankfurt. Since Clara thus lost the protection of her privileged mixed marriage, she went into hiding in February 1944 and survived the Holocaust. When asked what she was hiding from, Fischer responded that they knew things were bad in the camps and did not want the Nazis to deport her. That the Nazis would have gassed her was something Fischer simply could not imagine back then.

After July 1944, the army discharged Fischer again on the grounds that he had not proven worthy of Hitler's exemption. Most other half-Jewish soldiers with exemptions, except high-ranking active officers, remained in the service. Returning home, he found odd jobs to support himself. In late 1944, the *Volkssturm* (Auxiliary People's Army) drafted him. At the same time, the Gestapo ordered him to report to a work station at the Nordhausen concentration camp, where German scientists assembled the V-2 rocket. But Fischer decided to go "underground" in a church near Marburg where he hid until war's end.

He said he did not feel embarrassed about his Jewish past, which he described as a rich past that he could trace to Jesus. He added, though, that he would be lying if he said he had not wished his Jewish background away during the Nazi years.

Asked about his ethnicity, he said that though Halakah considers him a Jew, "I don't feel Jewish." He did not believe in Halakah and considers Judaism only a religion. "Only in the Old Testament sense," Fischer continued, "do I feel Jewish." He strongly emphasized that there is no such thing as race and that those who believe there is are wrong. He also believed the differences between religions create problems between people. "Shockingly, the difference between Catholics and Protestants is not nearly as great as that of the Jewish Orthodox and Reform groups. These differences create more hate than love," Fischer said.

Could he still believe in God after the war and the Holocaust? He answered by saying that Jesus also felt abandoned by God when he was on the cross, saying "My God, My God, why have you forsaken me?" "I have also felt this way many times but God was always there," Fischer said.

When asked what he knew of the Holocaust, he said he always served with the front troops and never knew what happened behind the lines in the death camps. However, he and his comrades knew that they fought for something that "wasn't right. We hoped that it would all end soon. I was a medic. The others fought and we cleaned up the mess," Fischer said. "The Russians were tough and good soldiers and I didn't like going against them," Fischer continued. "I hated being in battle when we knew the Soviets attacked our positions with Panzers, because when the Russian tanks drove over our foxholes, they would twist their treads violently until the Germans there were mashed into the earth. I hated burying those guys because they were balls of jelly."

Fischer said that by 1941, he knew the Nazis treated people horribly in the east but he could not imagine systematic extermination. After the war, he learned that he had lost his aunt, May Salomon, in a death camp. Fischer then also discovered that well over a dozen other relatives had died in the *Shoah*.

When asked whether he felt close to Israel, he said, "I realize that I'm related to those people. However, Israel does some of the same things from which Jews suffered during the Holocaust."

Fischer said his time as a soldier taught him to hate war. After 1945, he became a pacifist and a minister. He died of bone cancer in 2002.

Like Karl-Arnd Techel, Fischer was glad that he worked as a medic. This allowed him to care for others during the trials of combat. He could serve without killing and at the same time help protect his family. He did the best with what he felt was presented to him, hoping that one day he could put all his efforts into serving God. Interestingly, the only two medics in this story, Fischer and Techel, both became Protestant ministers.

Half-Jewish Obergefreiter Horst Geitner

Horst Geitner is a man torn in two. He struggles with his past and trauma. He thinks about this history often and fights to make sense of it. Dark, pensive eyes stare out from his wrinkled face. He carefully weighs his words and his voice often breaks with emotion. His body took a lot of shrapnel during one battle, but he believes that these little pieces of iron have added to his longevity since iron, he claims, is responsible for healthy blood and brain activity. After the war, he became a judge.

Geitner was born 31 March 1922 in Berlin to Olga Geitner, a Christian mother, and Arthur Moses, a Jewish father, who were not married to each other. Since Geitner's father insisted on raising Horst Jewish, he had Horst circumcised according to Jewish tradition.

Arthur Moses, a journalist, was married to a Jewish woman with whom he had a daughter, Ruth. Yet even though he and Geitner's mother loved each other, Arthur refused to divorce his wife. Although married, he often spent weeks living with Geitner and his mother. "It was a strange situation," Geitner says, "but back then I thought it was just the way things were. I had a mother and a father who weren't married, and my father called someone else his wife."

Geitner learned his prayers and on the Sabbath and holidays attended the Orthodox synagogue at Fasanenstrasse in Berlin with his father. This all changed when he turned 11 in 1933, when the Nazis took power and Geitner's mother felt that Geitner should convert to Christianity. She believed the Nazis would not harm him if he became a practicing Christian. His father agreed and in 1933, Horst was baptized a Catholic.

From 1933 to 1936, Arthur Moses moved around throughout Holland and France with his Jewish wife, children, and mistress. They knew they had no future in Nazi Germany.

Olga grew tired of their transient life and decided to return to Germany with her son in 1936. Although she left her lover in France, she often returned and spent time with Arthur. In Berlin Geitner stayed with his gentile grandparents. They did not like their daughter "living in sin"

After World War II, half-Jewish Obergefreiter Horst Geitner (right) became an officer in the Bundeswehr. Here he is receiving an award from his superior. Since the Nazis had prevented him from becoming an officer during the Third Reich, becoming an officer later helped him prove to himself and others that he was indeed worthy of such a distinction.

with a married man. To their relief, relations between Arthur and Olga cooled and the love affair ended after 1936.

Although he lived with his gentile family, Geitner also spent time with his Jewish relatives. He often visited his Jewish half sister, Ruth, who was one year younger than he, and his father's Jewish wife, whom he called Auntie. He also spent some time with his Jewish grandmother. But she, he remembered, did not like him because he was the son of "that woman" and a *Goy*. His Jewish grandfather had died in 1922. "It was a blessing that he died before Hitler," Geitner said. "He didn't have to die a murderous death in Auschwitz, unlike his wife and family."

Geitner lived a fairly normal life for a couple of years following his return with his mother to Germany in 1936. He felt sad when he learned that his father had died by suicide in Metz on 23 December 1938. Before he killed himself, Arthur wrote a friend asking him to help his former lover and his son. This man honored Arthur's request.

In 1939, rumors of war circulated. Geitner felt afraid that, as a half-Jew, he might not be allowed to finish his *Abitur*. He had heard that if he volunteered for the Luftwaffe, he would get his *Abitur*. Also, if he volunteered, he was informed, he would not have to serve the customary two years required of most, so he decided to volunteer. His mother signed the required release forms because he was only seventeen years old, and in 1940, he officially reported for duty to Regiment 11 at Schönewalde.

During his initial medical examination, the doctor approached Geitner, looked at him strangely, and whispered, "Are you Aryan?" Geitner told him the truth about his circumcision. The doctor smiled, walked away, and the issue never came up again.

His superiors treated him well. His Unteroffizier (NCO) Paul Ammer knew about Geitner's Jewish background but protected him. He told him, "I couldn't care less that you're Jewish. You're one of the best soldiers here." "He was good to me," Geitner said, "and he would die in the war. Such a loss for me."

One day in 1940, Geitner's first sergeant asked him if he was Aryan. Geitner answered truthfully, and the other man made a note in a file, told him everything was fine, and ordered him to return to his unit. During Geitner's meeting with the sergeant, Ammer had lined up the men and was asking each about his ancestry. They all were replying "Aryan." As Geitner took his place in line, Ammer ignored him and most did not notice that Ammer never asked him about his ethnicity. "My superiors protected me," Geitner said.

After boot camp, Geitner wanted to become a fighter pilot. But when he told this to the recruiting officer, the officer said, "You want to be a fighter pilot, hey? Well, that's out of the question for a half-Jew. Dismissed." Geitner left the office deeply depressed.

Since Geitner was also one of the best goose-stepping marchers in his company, his superior selected him and five others to join a special guard detachment in Berlin. They guarded special monuments there, performed military ceremonies, and acted as Göring's personal bodyguards when he was in town.

At Göring's Berlin home, Göring would exchange jokes with Geitner and the other guards or talk about their careers. Often, Geitner was posted right outside Göring's sleeping quarters. He was afraid that as a half-Jew he would immediately be suspected if something happened to Göring. When he told his commander, Lieutenant Ladach, about his concerns, Ladach just winked at him and said, "Nonsense." Geitner remained at his post until 1941, and luckily for him, nothing ever happened to Göring.

Göring also had them stand guard at the grave of his beloved first wife, Karin, at his estate, Karinhall, outside Berlin. Geitner and his comrades hated this duty. One day, one of them fell asleep while on guard. Threatened with punishment, the soldier shot himself. Afterward, Göring allegedly cracked, "It's sad that we lost a 35-cent bullet on this soldier." Geitner would soon leave his guard duties for more hazardous surroundings.

At the end of 1941, Geitner's battalion became a Panzer-killer unit for knocking out tanks with mines, bazookas, and cannons. During the winter of 1942, the Wehrmacht sent it to the Russian front. "We immediately entered battle," Geitner said, "and we took several casualties. We had no clue what to do." Eventually, he helped his unit knock out several tanks. During the constant grind of war, he remembers his fatigue the most. When not fighting or eating, they tried to find a few minutes here or there just to sleep. Whenever he had time to shut his eyes, he immediately fell asleep. After a few months of fighting near Moscow, he caught spotted fever and was sent back to a Berlin hospital.

After he recovered, he was promoted to Obergefreiter (corporal) and moved to train soldiers in Fürstenwalde. In June 1942, Geitner guarded a train transporting gasoline to the Ukraine. When his train stopped outside of Tychy near Auschwitz, he noticed the SS offloading several Jews there. When he and others walked over to learn what was going on, an SS soldier stopped them and asked what they wanted. They asked what those people were going to be used for. "Oh," the SS soldier said, "they're Jews from the Reich sent here to work for the Wehrmacht. They'll eventually be sent to Auschwitz." Geitner added, "Only after the war did I learn that my whole family would be gassed there. Probably as I talked to that SS man, my relatives were already in the camp dying."

Half-Jewish
Obergefreiter Horst
Geitner, circa 1943.
(Military awards:
EKII and Silver
Wound Badge)

Returning to his training unit in Germany, Geitner became bored with his duties. One day, "General [Eduard] Dietl came to our base to put together a new division. He told us that he needed brave men to be part of his antitank outfit. I immediately stepped forward." Geitner then joined the First Tank-Destroyer Company in the Sixth Luftwaffe Field Division and went to the northern front of Russia in winter 1943. One morning, he awoke with a feeling that something dismal was going to happen. Before leaving for his duties, he wrote his mother about his thoughts, sealed the letter, and then prepared for battle. He often thought that he would love to have a *"Heimschuss"* (a bullet wound to send him home) and would even sacrifice a leg or an arm to get out of combat. Many Germans yearned to go home with a *Heimschuss.*

At Velikiye Luki near Pskov, Geitner engaged in local attacks against T-34 tanks with antitank weapons. At this battle, the Soviet tanks machine-gunned several Germans to pieces. One man who tried to make it back to a trench was cut in half by the bullets. As his body fell, blood and guts poured out of his torso and onto the earth. He screamed and then rolled over, lifeless. Explosions rocked the ground as men tried to kill the "iron beasts." When one tank came down on them, Geitner got behind the tank and took it out with a bazooka. As the tank erupted into flames, he yelled in triumph.

Then an artillery shell hit their position, and the blast slammed Geitner to the ground and pain traveled through his body. His head alone had received over twenty metal splinters. Three of his comrades immediately died. Luckily for him, he was extricated from the battlefield. He later received the Silver Wound Badge.

Geitner was the first in his battalion to receive the Iron Cross for bravery in taking out the tank, though the officer awarding it knew about his ancestry. Geitner felt proud of his decoration and thought that no one would harm him now. "I had proven that I was brave and earned my equality," he said. He felt the authorities would now see he was a worthy German and not view him as half-Jewish or as a "second-class" soldier anymore. Many *Mischlinge* felt this after serving bravely.

The military gave Geitner a strong sense of security. In the armed forces, he looked like everyone else, and this had a strong psychological effect on him. "I would be lying to you if I told you I didn't like being a soldier. It was an honor to serve," he said.

After his severe injury, Geitner entered a hospital in Brest, Poland, and then one in Reutlingen, Germany. While still recuperating, he was placed in a desk job. One day early in 1944, he noticed a red folder in the office entitled "*Mischlinge* in the Wehrmacht." "I read that if a *Mischling* had proven himself in battle, then Hitler would declare him 'Aryan.' I wanted to send in an application. I felt I had earned it," Geitner said. He later asked his officer about applying. The officer replied that the regulations had since changed and that he should not try. He further explained that Hitler now would decide these matters after the war and that Geitner should wait.

However, Geitner did not want to wait. "I had shed blood for Germany and proven myself in battle . . . I was a worthy soldier," he said. As a result, he put his application together and sent it to the authorities. A few weeks later, he reported to his new duty station in Oldenburg. Three days after arriving, his commander requested his presence.

Inside the office, the commander said, "Your application has been rejected. You're to leave the Luftwaffe immediately." Shocked, Geitner did not understand why this had happened. He requested one month's leave to try to find a job since he had no money or clothes. The commander regretted that he could not give it to him and dismissed Geitner. Later, in the privacy of his quarters, he could not stop his tears.

A few days later, arriving in Hamburg, Geitner received his discharge papers. Luckily, he still could wear his uniform and decorations, giving him some protection. He now believes his discharge probably spared his life because the Russians destroyed his entire division during the Soviet offensive in the summer of 1944. Out of around 18,000 men, he heard, only 500 made it out alive. At that time though, he wished he could have remained. The failure to get an exemption happened to many half-Jews.

Geitner's future looked dismal after his discharge, and he thought about killing himself. After contemplating it for a while, though, he remembered his mother and knew she needed him. As a result, he chose to live.

He later returned to Berlin, where he started to study chemistry because he wanted eventually to become a doctor like his Jewish uncle. He also found odd jobs at a Catholic church that helped half-Jews. The church employed him until the end of the war. A few weeks before the Nazis surrendered, he went into hiding in a bunker.

He did not know about the systematic extermination of the Jews—including over two dozen of his relatives—until after the war. He heard about shootings, but not in much detail. While Geitner served in Russia, his Jewish sister, Ruth, uncle Wilhelm Auerbach, and aunt Erna Auerbach (née Moses) all died in Auschwitz. Geitner is now the last living member of his Jewish family, which had been in Germany for over 200 years.

After the war, Geitner studied law and became a judge. He also became a reserve lieutenant colonel in the Luftwaffe because "I wanted to prove that I was indeed worthy of becoming an officer for my homeland." At the end of his professional life, he served as vice president of the Supreme Labor Court of Baden-Wuerttemberg.

A few years after the Third Reich, Geitner visited his father's grave in the Jewish cemetery in Metz. It made him reflect again about his Jewish identity. When asked whether he is Jewish or Christian, Geitner said that he does not know. "The good Lord has been so good to me," he said, starting to cry. "He has saved my life many times, especially during the horrible war. I hope he approves of me. I hope he will bless me. I've had a wonderful life. I have two great daughters. I was an honest and respectable person. I don't know whether I'm Jewish or Christian. I feel Jewish, but I also know and accept a lot about the Christian religion. I just don't know who I am." After he said this, Geitner wiped the tears from his eyes and shook his head.

Geitner explained that discussing his past is painful but talking about *Mischlinge* is necessary, he says, since "no one to date has attempted to explain their experiences and the suffering they underwent in the Third Reich."

Geitner's life is unique for its breadth of experience. He is also unique for becoming a Bundeswehr officer after the war to prove that he could. It was a rank he felt he had deserved in the war and he was determined to end this chapter of his life on a good note. As a soldier, he also followed the Prussian ideal that you serve your nation, just as Ernst Prager and Karl-Arnd Techel felt they should.

Having such convictions proved devastating to Geitner when he was discharged from the Wehrmacht. He felt no longer like a worthy German. Many *Mischlinge* felt similar emotions after their dismissal.

Geitner's struggle with identity mirrors the experience of several men in this study. The trauma they experienced under Hitler left psychological scars. Just like Horst Geitner, many felt torn in two by their experiences as *Mischlinge*. Frequently, they use the term "schizophrenia." Geitner ended our interview by saying, "I have never healed from that time and will die with many questions about myself and people."

Conclusion

The process of getting a *Genehmigung* was convoluted and often unsuccessful. Frequently, the process could drag on seemingly forever and even if approved, as with Dieter Fischer, it meant going to a punishment battalion. As these clemency documents stated, Hitler wanted to give these men an opportunity to prove their Aryan background in the face of combat.

Fischer was lucky to get away relatively unscathed. These battalions were "widely feared and resented as a virtual death sentence" and, thus, one sees what the Nazis wanted to do to such *Mischlinge*.[15] In general, men who applied for the *Genehmigung* were not like Fischer—the majority, as was true for Horst Geitner, had no luck obtaining clemency.

Ultimately, these *Genehmigungen* would not have helped the *Mischlinge* in the long run. Yes, some of those who received it felt like it would protect them and their families, but by war's end, as seen with those with *Deutschblütigkeitserklärungen,* most were rejected, just like Dieter Fischer.

Hitler's policy with the *Genehmigungen,* as with many of his racial decrees, shows how cruel and deranged he was when dealing with this population of faithful soldiers and citizens. Hitler knew no loyalty, especially when looking at those *Mischlinge* with exemptions. They were his creations and he could play with their status and futures as he pleased. Feeling himself as a god, Hitler believed he could fashion a new humanity, the Aryans, who were in reality a non-people made in the image of what his disturbed mind felt were the super-beings, the blond and blue-eyed perfect humans of a mythic past. Dealing out *Genehmigungen* and *Deutschblütigkeitserklärungen* illustrates just how unrealistic was Hitler's goal of creating a population dominated by recessive traits and, thus, expressed by a minority of humanity. One just has to remember that, having dark hair and standing at 5 feet 7 inches, Hitler himself failed to meet the criteria of the tall, blond "Aryan." In the end, the *Genehmigungen* were an abysmal failure for Hitler and for the men who received or tried to receive them.

5

Mischlinge and Uncommon Rescue Stories

Mischlinge often helped family members in need, but many regret what they didn't or couldn't do. Most do not feel guilty for serving but wish they had done more for their persecuted relatives. Several thought that by performing their military duties well, they could protect their families. A few actually secured the release of a relative from a Gestapo office or deportation station, but most were away in combat and unable to take such action or simply did not dare to do so.

Nonetheless, most claim today that had they known what lay beyond deportation, they would have done more to find a hiding place for their loved ones or help them emigrate. Many justify their position by claiming they were also mistreated and did not have the means to resist.

In this chapter of the Holocaust, there were a few *Mischlinge* who helped Jews survive. Quarter-Jewish Oberbaurat (naval engineering captain) Franz Mendelssohn and half-Jewish Colonel Ernst Bloch were part of a small group who helped save Jewish lives. The story of Bloch goes into much detail about the larger moral issues these rescue stories from the Holocaust raise, including inquiries into whether the people saved even deserved it. Both Mendelssohn's and Bloch's stories give a better understanding of what it was like to live not only as *Mischlinge* in the Third Reich, but as individuals who took the rare action to rescue lives even when doing so meant compromising themselves.

Quarter-Jewish Oberbaurat Franz Mendelssohn

Franz Mendelssohn was born 25 July 1887 in Potsdam to a half-Jewish father and a gentile mother. He was the great-great-great grandson of the eminent German Jewish philosopher and leader of the *Haskala* (Jewish Enlightenment) Moses Mendelssohn and took great pride in his ancestor.

He was educated in a strict Prussian school and learned to repress his feelings. His father believed in this philosophy of self-control and was tough on his son. If Mendelssohn did not perform well in school, his father punished him.

In 1906, when Mendelssohn turned nineteen, he entered the navy, studied shipbuilding, and became an engineer. After the outbreak of World War I, he built submarines and zeppelins. Numerous cousins of his lost their lives during the Great War, and he felt lucky to have survived.

After Germany's defeat in 1918, Mendelssohn stayed in the navy for two more years. In 1920, the military placed him on leave in the course of the personnel reduction under the Versailles Treaty. He then lived in Danzig and started a business importing American cars. He also arranged several race car events. After 1933, when Hitler came to power, Mendelssohn encountered problems, mainly because of his name. Local Nazis called him a "dirty Jew." Although he felt proud of his ancestry, he had limited contact with German Jewry except for his Jewish relatives who were converted Christians and knew little about Judaism. Yet, many of his colleagues thought Mendelssohn was Jewish and denounced him. Soon after Hitler came to power, the Nazis pressured the German automobile organization ADAC (Allgemeiner Deutscher Automobil-Club) in Königsberg to dismiss Mendelssohn as racially inferior. Mendelssohn was deeply upset by this event.

Either out of conviction or the mere desire to be accepted by his society or both, Mendelssohn joined the Nazi Party in 1934. It is unclear why the party accepted him, but his move later helped him keep his job in the military. At the same time, Mendelssohn, who had married a gentile woman, cautioned his two daughters against disclosing their Jewish past.

Demoralized and without a job or money, Mendelssohn left for Berlin in March 1935. A few navy comrades got in touch with the authorities at the navy's Supreme Headquarters, who reactivated him. According to his daughters, an admiral in Hamburg told Mendelssohn, "We [his navy buddies] will protect you." He became a Marine-Baurat and later Oberbaurat (an engineering rank equivalent of a navy captain).

Quarter-Jewish Oberbaurat Franz Mendelssohn (far right), who joined the Nazi Party in 1934, at the wedding of his daughter Eva-Irene Mendelssohn and Werner Müller-Thode. At far left is Marine-Baurat Müller-Thode, the groom's father.

In spite of his name, the authorities could not prove Mendelssohn's Jewish ancestry. Also, Commodore Ernst Wolf and Admiral Eugen Lindau staved off Nazi officials and protected the unemployed engineer. They assigned him to building torpedo-boats and submarines and transforming luxury liners into supply and hospital ships.

But the name "Mendelssohn" continued to cause problems for his two daughters. For one daughter, Eva-Irene Eder-Mendelssohn, it proved hard to explain to people that she "wasn't as Jewish" as they thought. "I'm proud of the name," Eva-Irene said, "but I always had to explain our situation to the authorities. It was crazy. I often would get asked, 'Do you descend from that horrible Jew?'"

Many encouraged Mendelssohn to change his name, but he refused, though his brothers, Alexander and Ernst, did. Their lives were made easier after changing their name from Mendelssohn to Leyden. Mendelssohn did not want to abandon the name of his ancestors and viewed such a move as something he could not do. His brothers not only changed their name, but that of their entire families. Three of Mendelssohn's nephews, one of whom died fighting in Russia, served in the Wehrmacht.

One can understand the actions of Mendelssohn's brothers. Having the name "Mendelssohn" in the Third Reich was like wearing a sign on your forehead that read, "I'm a Jew." One wonders why Mendelssohn also did not change his name instead of joining the Nazi Party—one would think that would have been easier. This is especially the case since Mendelssohn continued to encounter problems because of his name.

One evening, when Mendelssohn attended a party, he entered the foyer with a nobleman who was short, fat, and unkempt but, nonetheless, Aryan. Without even thinking to ask, the maître d'hôtel introduced the fat man as Mendelssohn, and Mendelssohn, who was 6 feet 3 inches tall, slender, and handsome, as the nobleman. When the men clarified who they were, not only did it embarrass all parties concerned, but it also deeply troubled Mendelssohn. He felt he could never escape the constant cloud of oppression and discrimination.

When Mendelssohn rejoined the navy in 1935, he felt secure that he could support his family and pursue a career he had trained for and liked. Furthermore, the navy offered a place of security, and he felt comfortable in its surroundings. He continued to experience problems but carefully falsified his ancestral records. His thick personnel file testifies to what lengths he went in order to "prove" his "Aryan" ancestry. He signed a document in April 1935 in which he said that careful research did not disclose any Jewish ancestry. He knew that if he admitted he was a quarter-Jew, he would not be allowed to serve and unable to support his family. After the initial trauma of 1933–1935, life for the Mendelssohn family settled down.

Mendelssohn was probably left alone because the navy needed experienced engineers to build the navy Hitler had ordered Raeder to create. Hitler, having done away with the Versailles Treaty, now allowed the navy to make as many ships and submarines as possible. Mendelssohn, as an excellent engineer, had plenty of work to do. The shipbuilding program called for eight new battleships, three aircraft carriers, eighteen cruisers, forty-eight destroyers, and seventy-two submarines to be completed in fifteen years.[1]

Mendelssohn believed the military provided his only chance for a normal existence. He did not have many other options. Some asked why he did not sabotage any naval projects he worked on. But this was something he would have never done. According to his daughter Eva-Irene, her father "was too Prussian and his dedication to duty and country would have prevented him from doing anything against Germany." As a result, both serving the navy and living in Germany required that he obey the law. Although he had to disobey the law in falsifying his ancestry, he could not falsify his duty. He had to perform not only in the military, but also in society, even if he did not believe in its institutions. Consequently, it was not surprising that in 1937, he signed a document like other officers swearing that he would be "true and obedient to . . . Hitler." Most officers at this time had to sign similar documents and the procedure was quite routine.

In light of the Holocaust, one may find Mendelssohn's actions shocking. However, he simply "didn't think it would get as bad as it did." Yet Mendelssohn tentatively tried to get out of Germany, especially after his wife mentally collapsed following Reichskristallnacht in November 1938. He thought of emigrating but did not have the necessary funds. He spoke fluent English, but receiving permission from the U.S. or British emigration authorities was difficult. His whole life had been dedicated to building ships, and in Germany particularly, the only shipbuilding done from 1935 until 1945 was for the navy.

In 1941, Mendelssohn used his position to save a few Jews. In January of that year, while stationed in Paris, he learned that the Gestapo had arrested Mr. René Fould, a French Jew who had built ships and supported de Gaulle. After Fould's family pleaded for Mendelssohn to help them, he decided to do so, even though Fould's reputation was one of a tough, greedy businessman. Mendelssohn hesitated but did intervene on Fould's behalf, though it could have jeopardized his position. On 30 January 1941, Mendelssohn secured the release of Fould from prison. Fould then hid in southern France with his family and survived the war.

Mendelssohn probably helped Fould for many reasons. He had worked with Fould for years and had developed a friendship with him. Perhaps he felt a need to rescue Fould not because of their relationship, but because of his own Jewish past. Maybe he sympathized with Fould

French Jew and businessman René Fould, whom Franz Mendelssohn rescued from the Nazis.

and recognized that what happened to Fould could happen to him. Like Fould, Mendelssohn felt persecuted, and if a few officers had not helped him, he too would have suffered under the Nazis. He would have been jobless, labeled a *Mischling*, and stripped of his military status and benefits. Before he left the Fould family, Mendelssohn claimed he had done what he thought was possible and right and nothing more. He then explained to them that it would be too dangerous for them if they asked for help again. In other words, this was their only opportunity to escape the Nazis.

Toward war's end, especially after the Normandy invasion, Mendelssohn's work seemed to deteriorate and the admiral for St. Nazaire wrote in July 1944 that Mendelssohn was incompetent, weak, and lazy. Mendelssohn said this negative report was motivated by his superior's feelings of inferiority. Mendelssohn was better educated and better looking than his commander and refused to take part in his superior's drinking parties. Consequently, his superior resented him and expressed his anger in his reports.

Later in the summer of 1944, Mendelssohn refused to destroy the shipyards in Bordeaux before the Allies overtook them. He left with the army, marching at night and hiding during the day to avoid Allied planes. In late August 1944, the Allies took him prisoner. In September 1944, the Allies first shipped him to England, and then on to America to a POW camp.

Unlike many Jewish families, the Mendelssohn family survived the Third Reich and World War II intact. After Mendelssohn's imprisonment, he returned to Germany and resumed building ships, this time for a British ship-building branch in Hamburg.

His daughters said that neither they nor their father knew about the Holocaust. After the war, they were horrified to learn what had happened to the Jews. Asked what she thought Moses Mendelssohn might have thought about the situation, Eva-Irene Eder-Mendelssohn said, "On the one hand, he probably wouldn't have promoted Jewish emancipation as much as he did had he known what would've happened to his family during the Third Reich. On the other hand, his efforts to emancipate the Jews allowed most of his descendants to become Christians and marry gentiles and thus, they survived the war because most weren't Jewish enough to be sent to the camps. It was a strange paradox." His daughter Eleonore Barz-Mendelssohn said that her father's actions might prove difficult to understand today but asked, "Can you understand how a person feels who's trapped and yet has to do something to protect his family?" She believes that her father was forced to make a Faustian bargain that he never would have made had Hitler not threatened his family's livelihood. He did not want to support Hitler's navy, but felt he had to do so.

Mendelssohn displayed amazing courage in keeping his name during the Third Reich even though he did everything else to hide his Jewish background. Luckily for him, he got away with it. Often *Mischlinge* with Jewish-sounding names like Levin, Cohn, or Mendelssohn had a harder time blending into German society than those with names like Geitner, Krüger, or Meissinger. As historian James Tent wrote, "*Mischlinge* who had the misfortune to carry a name that the Nazis could immediately stereotype as sounding 'Jewish,' often faced severe persecution."[2]

Mendelssohn's case also shows that people could help rescue others during the Third Reich, but most of those in positions to do so often failed to act. Mendelssohn's rescue efforts, though limited, are noteworthy.

Rebbe Schneersohn and Major Bloch: Moral Issues of Holocaust Rescues

In 1939, a half-Jewish Wehrmacht officer, Major Ernst Bloch, rescued the ultra-Orthodox Jewish leader, the Lubavitcher Rebbe Joseph Isaac Schneersohn, a true but seemingly incredible story.[3] A narrative as much about Bloch as about the Rebbe, it raises several troubling issues surrounding religion, identity, and moral decisions during the Holocaust.

Germany's quick defeat of Poland prevented most of the 3.3 million Polish Jews from fleeing.[4] The SS immediately started committing crimes against humanity. To end a situation he felt disgraced Germany, Admiral Wilhelm Canaris, head of the Abwehr, tried to have SS formations removed from Poland. But Hitler asserted, "Our struggle cannot be measured in terms of legality or illegality. Our methods must conform to our principles. We must prevent a new Polish intelligentsia taking power and cleanse the Greater Reich of Jewish and Polish riffraff." He told his generals the SS would not only continue but intensify its work.[5]

The Nazis killed nearly all the Jews in Poland, but a few managed to escape. One of the most spectacular escapes of World War II was assisted by Abwehr officers, who enabled the fervently Orthodox Jewish leader the Rebbe Schneersohn to leave Poland in 1940.

The Rebbe served as high priest of the Lubavitcher movement, an ultra-Orthodox Hasidic Jewish sect, a kind of Jewish "pontifex maximus." What makes this story amazing is that Wehrmacht officers played a central role in rescuing the Rebbe.

Schneersohn, the leader of the Chabad sect of Hasidism until his death

Half-Jewish Lieutenant Colonel Ernst Bloch. The horrible wound on his face is quite pronounced although he had several surgeries to repair it. He received Hitler's *Deutschblütig-keitserklärung*. (Military awards: EKI, EKII, Wound Badge, War Service Cross Second Class, and War Service Cross First Class)

in 1950, was born in Lubavitch, Russia, in 1880. He was a scion of the founder of this Hasidic sect, Rebbe Schneur Zalman, whose five generations of descendants had guided the movement.

In 1920, on his father's death, the Rebbe, a rather portly man standing 5 feet 8 inches, took over the movement. Light blue eyes peered out above his red and silver beard. Many Lubavitchers believed him to be endowed with mystical powers, without sin, and blessed with the holy spirit.

After the October Revolution in 1917 when Russia sank into chaos,

Rebbe Joseph Isaac
Schneersohn, the
sixth Lubavitcher
Rebbe (1880–1950),
at his desk in
Brooklyn, 1949.
(Photo credit:
Eliezer
Zaklikovsky)

the Rebbe devoted himself to restoring religious life in Russia. Communist hostility toward religion, Schneersohn felt, would make Russia inimical to his movement. Throughout the 1920s the Soviet authorities often
arrested the Rebbe and in 1927 even sentenced him to death, but thanks
to the intervention of people such as U.S. senator William Borah, the Soviets released him.[6] Later that year, Russia exiled him, and he set up his
new headquarters in Poland.

In 1929 the Rebbe traveled to the United States to campaign for funds.
He met many dignitaries, including President Herbert Hoover. On his
return to Europe, he continued his work to invigorate Orthodox Judaism.[7]

When Germany invaded Poland on 1 September 1939, the Rebbe's
followers tried to convince him to escape. He agreed, but not with the

timing. He would not desert his followers in a time of danger.[8] But finally, on 4 September, Schneersohn, realizing the futility of staying, left by car for Warsaw with his family in hopes of traveling from there to Riga. Dead horses and the charred remains of buildings lined the road to Warsaw as the Luftwaffe continued to rain explosives on the roads leading to the capital. Yet, the Rebbe survived.

On reaching Warsaw, Schneersohn helped his students escape to neutral countries and save his yeshiva's documents. When he finally wanted to leave in late September, it was too late. The Wehrmacht had encircled the city.[9]

Nazi bombing raids forced the Rebbe to move around. When news of Russia's invasion of Poland reached the Lubavitchers on 17 September, they panicked. They knew if the Soviets got their hands on the Rebbe again, they could not rely on international support to save him. Yet staying in Warsaw was perilous as the Nazis tightened their coil around the city.

On 25 September, Hitler ordered Warsaw leveled to the ground. More than 500 tons of high explosives and 72 tons of incendiary bombs accompanied by heavy artillery fire fell on the city. Yet, the Rebbe escaped death again. On 27 September, Warsaw capitulated to the Nazis. After visiting Warsaw, which had been nearly half-destroyed, Hitler told a foreign correspondent, "Take a good look around Warsaw. That is how I can deal with any European city."[10]

During that grievous time, Lubavitchers and prominent New Yorkers urged Senator Robert Wagner to ask Secretary of State Cordell Hull to request information from the Germans about the Rebbe's whereabouts and his safe passage out of Poland.[11]

Wagner wrote Hull again three days later to ask the U.S. foreign minister in Riga to locate Schneersohn, emphasizing that many U.S. Jewish organizations were concerned about him. Hull acted and received a reply from the American Legation in Riga on 30 September that the Rebbe was in Warsaw.[12]

After receiving inquiries about the Rebbe, U.S. Supreme Court Justice Louis Brandeis asked Benjamin Cohen, Roosevelt's advisor, for help. Cohen informed Robert T. Pell, the assistant chief of European Affairs in the State Department, who had cultivated important contacts with influential German officials.[13]

Pell agreed that it would be a tragedy "if any harm befell one of the leading Jewish scholars in the world." Pell knew Helmut Wohlthat, chief administrator of Göring's Four-Year Plan, an expert on international industry and economics and a Nazi Party member, whom he met after the Evian Conference in 1938, at which Germany had insisted that the world take its Jews, a demand the world, including the United States, rejected. After this conference, Wohlthat assured Pell that in a special case in which American Jewry was "particularly interested, he would do what he could to facilitate a solution." Pell forwarded Cohen's request to Wohlthat, who kept his promise. "In every instance," Pell wrote, "Wohlthat acted quickly and favorably."[14]

Pleas to save the Rebbe continued to pile up on Hull's desk. The Lubavitchers had informed the U.S. authorities that their community was in part made up of 160,000 Jews in North America. This was a lie intended to influence the government. Hull then told the U.S. Postmaster on 2 October 1939 that the State Department would ask the U.S. Vice Consul in Riga to ascertain the Rebbe's situation at the expense of interested citizens.[15]

On 3 October 1939, Hull approved a telegram from Pell to Raymond Geist, the U.S. Consul General in Berlin, asking to rescue Schneersohn.[16] On behalf of the White House, Geist therefore asked Wohlthat to help Schneersohn leave Poland. "I turn to you," Geist wrote Wohlthat, "because I know you, and you may be assured of the absolute discretion of the . . . State Department. I am aware of the considerable risk to any German persons intervening in this matter." Geist then telegraphed Hull and Pell to report that he had met Wohlthat, "who promised to take the matter up" with the authorities.[17] Wohlthat agreed that pressure from such influential sources to save a well-respected international figure warranted action. Once again Hull made sure that the rescue's cost would not be supplied by the government, but by the Lubavitchers. The mission's success now depended on Wohlthat, a Nazi. Whom he contacted and how he conducted the plans would decide the rescue.

Though Wohlthat believed the Rebbe's rescue would serve Germany's interests, he knew that Nazi authorities would not allow it.[18] The situation looked grim. Hitler had taken Poland and the SS had started the ghettoization and murder of Jews.

Wohlthat knew one man he could turn to: Admiral Wilhelm Canaris, chief of the Abwehr. They were friends, cognizant of one another's views. In 1939, Canaris, like Wohlthat, did not approve of all of Hitler's policies and employed *Mischlinge* in his department.[19] Canaris also disapproved of the plan to exterminate Polish Jewry.

The day after his conversation with Geist, Wohlthat met with Canaris and told him about the case. Canaris agreed to help and promised to send some of his officers to Warsaw to rescue Schneersohn.[20]

In so doing, he risked not only his own position and life, but also those of the soldiers he assigned to this task. But he knew the murderous danger the Rebbe faced and acted quickly.[21]

He entrusted the mission to Major Ernst Bloch, who knew Wohlthat and had often dined with him and Canaris.[22] He shared their animosity to the Nazis' anti-Semitic policies. Perhaps Canaris had ordered Bloch to save the Rebbe not only because he was an excellent soldier but also because his father was Jewish.

A contemporary photograph reveals a man of strong build and dark eyes exuding self-assurance. Bloch knew his place and his duty. Yet his most striking feature was his scarred face. During the battle of Ypres in 1915, an enemy bayoneted Bloch through his lower jaw into his skull, removing large portions of his chin and several teeth. The next thing Bloch remembered was waking up in a hospital. Although his family feared he would never function normally again, he did not suffer any brain damage and returned to war a few months later to fight in the battles of Verdun and the Somme in 1916, Champagne in 1917, and Flanders in 1918. Known as a competent officer, he ended the war with both Iron Crosses and the Wound Badge and remained in the army from World War I through the Weimar Republic into the Nazi Reich.[23]

The Nazi rise to power did not immediately affect Bloch. In 1935 Canaris recruited Bloch for the Abwehr and placed him in charge of the economic division, which gathered data on the industrial capacity of foreign countries.[24]

The half-Jewish Bloch could remain and was promoted in the army because Hitler had declared him *deutschblütig*. Canaris had brought Bloch's case to Hitler late in 1939, and had Hitler personally sign papers declaring him of "German blood."[25] Bloch and his family were therefore generally protected. Under Canaris, Bloch had nothing to fear and was even picked to rescue Jews—all under the nose of the SS.

Back in America the Chabad's U.S. office telegraphed the Rebbe's secretary in Riga that the German authorities in Warsaw were "desirous of cooperating" and had sent an officer to locate the Rebbe and accompany him to Riga. Two days later, Pell, who also received this information, told the U.S. chargé d'affaires in Germany where they might find Schneersohn. Wohlthat then notified Washington on 4 November 1939 that Bloch had been given the responsibility of helping the Rebbe escape.[26]

Daily, Bloch combed the Orthodox Jewish neighborhoods and asked for the Rebbe. Most faced the German major with fear and told him nothing.

At that time, Max Rhoade, a Jewish lawyer in Washington, D.C., had taken charge of the legal aspects of this rescue and handled the relations between the Lubavitcher community and the government.

Rhoade encouraged Cohen to ask the State Department to have the consulate in Warsaw urge Schneersohn to cooperate with Bloch.[27] Rhoade believed that, if the consulate could communicate with the Rebbe, he would then follow Bloch.

Meanwhile, Bloch and his group discovered that Schneersohn had registered with the police, but his address had been destroyed during the siege of Warsaw. Bloch and his men now walked from house to house asking scared and hungry Lubavitchers about the Rebbe, yet no one wanted to talk. But Schneersohn was still in Warsaw, having escaped from his building seconds before airplanes destroyed it.

On 25 November 1939, the Germans found the house where the Rebbe lived.[28] They knocked on the door and an old man answered. His red, bloodshot eyes stared at Bloch and his group with fear. Bloch explained that, despite their uniforms, they truly wanted to help the Rebbe get out of occupied Poland.

Chaim Liebermann, the Rebbe's secretary, later reported that when the soldiers came, the Rebbe was "living in the house of Rabbi Hirsch Gurary. Suddenly there came uniformed Nazis to the door and asked about the Rebbe. The owner of the house feared the worst from these soldiers and told them that none by the name of Schneersohn lived there." After Bloch left, the Rebbe instructed his followers that should the officer return, they should give him "truthful information."[29]

Soon someone informed Bloch that he had in fact located the Rebbe's house. Bloch returned and forced his way inside. Eventually, after Bloch explained his mission, the Rebbe accepted his help.

Meanwhile, in America, Pell informed Rhoade on 27 November that the Germans had found the Rebbe. He pointed out that Wohlthat had done an extraordinary thing in arranging a military escort for foreign "Jewish" citizens.[30]

Wohlthat and the Abwehr had agreed on an escape route from Warsaw to Stockholm via Berlin and Riga, and on to the United States. But visas were still needed for the Rebbe's group.[31]

While Rhoade struggled with the visa division and the State Department, the German officials involved had made a great deal of progress. Bloch procured a truck and a wagon to take the group outside of Warsaw to a train so they could leave from there for Berlin and then for Riga. This rescue operation required arranging for automobiles and the coupons for refueling them, as well as railroad tickets and passes. More importantly, Bloch needed security clearances, especially for passing through newly conquered Poland, where no one could travel without being checked by military police and the SS.

After many months of planning, the American embassy in Berlin reported on 22 December 1939 that a week earlier, not only Schneersohn but also his family and some of his followers had left Warsaw for Riga via Berlin.[32]

A Lubavitcher described the journey: "Even the chief of intelligence [Bloch] had difficulty in conveying the Rebbe and his family to Berlin. There were many roadblocks manned by German military police . . . Whenever they saw the car with bearded religious Jews in it, they stopped it. [Bloch] pretended that they were his prisoners and that he had orders to take them to Berlin. Finally, they made it to Berlin, the very heart of the evil Nazi kingdom."[33]

Bloch succeeded in bringing the Rebbe and his group into Berlin, where they stayed at the Jewish Federation. The next day delegates from the Latvian embassy came and accompanied them to Riga.[34]

On 13 January 1940, the State Department finally approved the issuance of visas for the group.[35] While the group waited in Riga for the U.S. visas, the Swedish ocean liner *Drottingholm* was chosen to carry the Rebbe and his group to their new home.

The Rebbe and his entourage left Riga on 6 March 1940, traveled to Stockholm, and from there by train to Göteborg, where they boarded the *Drottingholm* to New York. It crossed the Atlantic at a time when German U-boats sank many Allied ships. The group arrived in New York City on 19 March and was greeted by over 1,000 of Rebbe Schneersohn's followers singing and dancing on the pier. After Schneersohn's arrival, he tried to rescue some of his followers abroad, but unfortunately failed in saving most throughout 1940–1941.[36]

The Rebbe never mentioned Bloch or the other Germans who helped him, but did thank Hull: "You can imagine how happy . . . we were to walk again on the friendly soil of [America] . . . especially after all the terrible experiences . . . under the Nazi regime."[37]

But giving thanks for his rescue did not save others. Instead, the Rebbe approached the politicians who rescued him only to ask to save his library of 40,000 books. One might understand this somewhat if the books were spiritual, but many were about the Communists and there was even Dante's *Inferno* in the mix. In 1941, he succeeded in getting, with much time, effort, and expenditure, all 40,000 books out of Europe.

Most troubling were the Rebbe's reasons why Hitler was murdering the Jews. He explained in 1941 that the persecution was God's punishment for Jews' "transgressions" of not observing religious laws. When asked why European Jews, who were by and large "more Torah-observant and God fearing" than American Jews, had been chosen to bear the brunt of God's retribution, the Rebbe replied that the "pious" suffered "on account of the others." The Rebbe added that this "bloodbath" would force Jews to return to the Torah, and thus clear the path for the Messiah. He claimed that the "suffering of world Jewry today is a voice from heaven calling" upon Jews to repent for straying from *Yiddishkeit*. All they could do for those suffering was to be more religious. He said, "do not be deluded into thinking that we Jews can be helped only by mortals and politics. The 'wise and understanding people' must not be influenced by such foolishness. We Jews will be helped by repentance, Torah and *mitzvos* [good deeds]."[38]

Even though "mortals" like Bloch, Canaris, Pell, Rhoade, and many others had rescued the Rebbe by working through a maze of "politics," the Rebbe simply saw it largely as an act of God. Mortals were merely instruments of divine will.

Religious leaders have often espoused the view that God orders catastrophes to punish "sinners" for not accepting God's commandments. The Rebbe of the Satmar Hasidic sect claimed that Zionists brought on the Holocaust. And more recently, after the 9/11 terrorist attacks, the Reverend Jerry Falwell declared to religious television host Pat Robertson that God was punishing Americans because of abortionists, pagans, feminists, gays, and lesbians, saying, "I point the finger in their face and say 'You helped this happen.'"[39] Both Falwell and the Rebbe understand God as both omnipotent and intimately involved in human affairs.

Ironically, the Rebbe's view of the Holocaust turns men like Hitler into instruments of divine will, a horrifying proposition. Distinguished rabbi Ken Roseman differs: "That one believes the Holocaust comes because the victims merit it is obscene."[40]

The Rebbe's thoughts about the Holocaust raise several troubling issues about God. As Karen Armstrong, a teacher at Leo Baeck College for the Study of Judaism, wrote, "If God is omnipotent, he could have prevented the Holocaust. If he was unable to stop it, he is impotent and useless; if he could have stopped it and chose not to, he is a monster."[41]

The Rebbe's opinion of why God allowed Hitler to perpetrate evil creates more problems than it solves. As renowned author Rabbi Harold Kushner said, "The idea that God gives people what they deserve, that our misdeeds cause our misfortune, is a neat and attractive solution to the problem of evil . . . but it has a number of serious limitations . . . it teaches people to blame themselves. It creates guilt even where there is no basis for guilt. It makes people hate God, even as it makes them hate themselves. And most disturbing of all, it does not even fit the facts." Prominent rabbi Chaskel Besser chose to believe that to truly understand God and why He allows bad things to occur is beyond human comprehension: "I'm not in Heaven and I'm not a prophet so I cannot comment on why God did what he did . . . I only know that the Holocaust makes me want to be a better person every day."[42]

Rabbi Norman Lamm, chancellor of Yeshiva University, blamed the

Rebbe outright for committing blasphemy. What the Rebbe said "is re-
pugnant to me and bespeaks an insufferable insensitivity." And he adds
that to point the finger at others as the Rebbe did "is an unparalleled instance of criminal arrogance and brutal insensitivity . . . How dare anyone, sitting in the American or British or Israeli Paradise, indict the
martyrs who were consumed in the European Hell?" He fails to see why
God would order the Nazis to kill anyone to punish the Jews for their
transgressions—he speaks from a position of pain since the Nazis murdered his grandmother. Saying such a thing is "unforgivable," Lamm explains that one should not forget that Moses was punished by God for
"making offensive statements" against His people. In the end, Lamm
concludes, "small-minded people blame others, not themselves."[43]

It is difficult for Lubavitchers to accept the Rebbe's limitations, yet
history shows that Schneersohn made mistakes. Focusing on a theology
of condemnation, the Rebbe missed out on opportunities to save lives
and offended many. Consequently, according to well-known rabbi Alex
Weisfogel, the Rebbe was a "moral failure."[44]

Ultimately, the Rebbe considered his coming to the United States "a
mission to make the country into a . . . dwelling place for Torah." Until
his death in 1950, he dedicated himself to leading the Chabad's world
headquarters in New York and never spoke publicly about his escape
from Warsaw.[45]

Bloch did not talk about it either. Working in the secret service, he had
been trained never to discuss his work, even with his wife. Had he survived the war, perhaps he would have told her. After rescuing Schneersohn, Bloch returned to his espionage work and was promoted to
lieutenant colonel in 1940. He continued to provide the military with information on the industrial capabilities of other countries, utilizing German companies to place spies under cover abroad.[46]

Bloch worked in the Abwehr until the army granted his request on 1
May 1943 to serve on the Russian front.[47] In the spring of 1943, the
Wehrmacht urgently needed his experience in the field preparing for the
battle of Kursk.

Both Bloch's son and his secretary said he left the Abwehr because his
only opportunity for promotion lay on the eastern front. He commanded a battalion and later a regiment and fought in many battles

around Kiev. For exemplary service, Bloch was promoted to colonel and awarded the Iron Cross. By 1945 Bloch's regiment had been decimated, leaving only a handful of men alive. But Bloch was by then no longer in the army.[48]

In September 1944, Heinrich Himmler, the Reichsführer of the SS, demanded that Bloch be discharged because of his ancestry. In the middle of that month, an SS officer in Himmler's office wrote General Wilhelm Burgdorf requesting Bloch's dismissal and deportation to a forced labor camp. Bloch had to leave on 27 October 1944, and on 15 February 1945, he was discharged.[49] Stunned and disappointed, he returned home a retired officer. A few months later the Volkssturm (a paramilitary organization for civilian fighters formed at war's end) drafted Bloch to train civilians.

In late April 1945, when the Russians closed in on Berlin, Bloch continued to fight. After repelling several attacks, he reportedly led a counterattack, throwing grenades at the Soviet lines and firing his submachine gun as he advanced. Then a mortar shell landed behind Bloch, killing him. A few days later the war ended.[50]

It is easy to look at Nazi Germany in black and white categories of good and evil, victims and perpetrators. However, such a two-dimensional view of Nazi Germany fails to account for the complexity of human society demonstrated by the story of Bloch's rescue of Schneersohn.

American officials failed to respond not only to thousands of desperate pleas from Jews who wished to escape the Nazis, but also to Germany's own self-serving request at the Evian Conference in 1938 to let them immigrate. Extremely influential politicians, such as Secretary of State Hull and Pell of the State Department, along with a supporting cast of several senators and Justice Brandeis, banded together to push Schneersohn's case successfully through the bureaucratic Bermuda triangle. Yet, without such a powerful lobby in Washington, what chance had the average European Jew to come to America?

The motives of the U.S. politicians, whose support was essential for the approval of Schneersohn's visa, also deserve a searching look before we hold them up as heroes.

Rhoade constantly emphasized the Rebbe's spiritual significance for Jews all over the world, and often compared him to the Pope to convince officials of the tangible results their intervention in this case would have for them. They could proudly prove their humanitarian concern for European Jews under Hitler and leave a favorable impression with a large block of voting American Lubavitchers, whose numbers Rhoade (with false information from Chabad) exaggerated.

U.S. officials knew how much the Jews suffered under Hitler. However, their inaction, even after acting favorably with the Rebbe, confirmed to some Nazis the apathetic attitude with which the Western powers approached the persecution.[51]

On the other side of the two-dimensional view stand the Germans. Even Hitler made a distinction between the army and the SS. In August 1939, he informed Himmler that "Poland will be wiped off the map of nations. What will happen behind the Wehrmacht front may not meet with the approbation of the generals. The army is not to take part in the elimination of the Polish cadres and the Jews. This will be the task of the SS."[52] Hitler did not expect all high-ranking officers in the military to support the extermination of Jews; but it was surprising that Wohlthat, chief administrator of Göring's Four-Year Plan; Canaris, head of the Abwehr; and Bloch and others risked their careers and perhaps their lives to rescue a group of ultra-Orthodox Jews.

Admittedly, Wohlthat and Canaris did not act on their own initiative. Wohlthat saw an opportunity to foster goodwill in Washington. At that time, Germany, not at war with the United States, hoped to have Britain ignore Germany's actions in Poland and join it as an ally. Canaris, too, had expressed reservations about Hitler's regime to Wohlthat and others for a while before the Rebbe's case landed on his desk. He had used his office to protect several "half-Jewish" officers, including Bloch, and promote them.

Had Bloch known about the Holocaust, would he have continued to fight? As a high-ranking Abwehr and combat officer, he must have known more than the average soldier. However, most soldiers do not spend their days engaging in political thought or moral consideration during a war. But the question of what Bloch and others could have done to stop the Holocaust if they had known about it is compelling.

Unavailable documentation makes it difficult to reconstruct exactly what Bloch thought or believed. *Mischlinge* express the entire spectrum of motivations for serving. Why Bloch did what he did will never be known, but after a decade of researching his case, I can make an educated guess.

Bloch was a professional soldier and learned at an early age to obey orders. He would have found the systematic extermination of the entire Jewish population of Europe unbelievable. If he saw any evidence of it, he must have ignored it to survive. Still, the paradox that Bloch fought to support a regime that may have killed half-Jews had Germany won the war is itself tragic.

Almost all *Mischlinge* were Christians who came from assimilated families and served because they were drafted. Some enlisted because they wanted to have a military career; they trained themselves for war, and when it came, they did their duty.

Bloch wore the German uniform, swore an oath of allegiance to Hitler, gathered valuable wartime data on enemy countries for Hitler's war machine, and fought on the Russian front against one of Germany's archenemies, the Soviets. The real question is why Bloch was unable or unwilling to fight the Hitler regime. The answer is buried in the battlefield, where Bloch gave his life defending his country—a country ruled by the Nazis.

The rescue of Schneersohn represents the complexity of life in Germany, not just a curious anomaly. It shows that America should and could have done more to help rescue Jews. But it also demonstrates how many U.S. Jewish leaders, even those who were aware of Hitler's extermination policies like the Rebbe, did not push the American government enough to help those Jews still stranded in Europe.

What could or should have been done now seems so obvious, as hindsight always is, but one must realize that, as historian Walter Laqueur notes, "Nothing is easier than to apportion praise and blame, writing many years after the events . . . It is very easy to claim that everyone should have known what would happen once Fascism came to power. But such an approach is ahistorical." Laqueur explains the world's inaction during the Holocaust as follows: "Few come out of the story unblemished. It was a story of failure to comprehend, among Jewish leaders and communities inside Europe and outside, a story of failure among non-Jews in high positions in neutral and Allied countries who did not care, or did not want to know or even suppressed the information."[53] The Rebbe's followers worked hard to put a name, a face, a great reputation, and a large following in front of powerful politicians. Although politicians might ignore the faceless masses without a surfeit of guilt, leaving a person they had come to know well and valued as a great leader in Hitler's clutches was simply unthinkable. Thus they worked tirelessly to rescue the Rebbe, while those unnamed Jews under Hitler were left to suffer and die. Hopefully, civilized humanity can learn to be quicker in the future to recognize the signs of genocide and stop it.

This story shows how much good can be achieved when a small group stands together to do the right thing. The Talmud says, "If you save a life you save the world."[54] This remarkable rescue saved over a dozen lives, and all it took was initiative and imagination—letter writing, a few thousand dollars, and the courage to speak up. How sad that the 6 million Jews who died in the Holocaust were not afforded the treatment the Lubavitcher Rebbe met with in 1939.

Conclusion

Rescue stories such as the two in this chapter were rare during the Third Reich. Yet, they both show that some lived by a moral code to save lives when they could. Moreover, they illustrate that opportunities did exist to successfully get people out from under the dark cloud of Nazism even after war erupted in 1939. Of course, Mendelssohn, Bloch, and Canaris operated from differing motivations, but ultimately, they all found ways to help people in mortal danger.

Due to a personal relationship and after recognizing the threat, Mendelssohn went out of his way to rescue and then facilitate the escape of René Fould. One only wishes more men during the Third Reich who thought about helping would have been as courageous as Mendelssohn.

Although Canaris ordered Bloch to rescue Schneersohn, he seemed to have no problem carrying out this order and even sympathized somewhat, it seems, with the Rebbe's plight and persecution. Either due to the successful job he did or letting Canaris know he would take similar assignments or both, Canaris allowed or ordered him to conduct other missions that rescued other Jews.[55]

Some may find puzzling Bloch's decision to continue active military service, ultimately losing his life only days before war's end. Yet, Bloch

may have fought at war's end because he regarded the Soviets as "no better than the Nazi loser," as historian James Tent said. Perhaps he had become so apathetic with life and with the uncertain future he faced that he
actually looked forward to dying "with the last bullet in the last battle of
the war and be done with it."[56] While Bloch fought in this battle,
Schneersohn busied himself building up his Hasidic movement, which
today probably numbers over 200,000.

What is remarkable about the Rebbe's rescue is that it was accomplished by men who, had they known the Rebbe's true personality,
probably would not have tried to save him. In this respect, the Rebbe's
followers and lawyer skillfully put on the Rebbe's best face to convince
people to save him. There is little to admire about Schneersohn unless
you are a devout Lubavitcher, since Schneersohn obviously had little use,
love, or respect for the very ones rescuing him. From the fact that he
thought secular and reform Jews, just like Brandeis, Cohen, and even
Bloch, caused the Holocaust, one realizes he did not admire much if anything about these men. The people he felt caused the Holocaust were the
very ones who saved his life, yet the Rebbe failed to see this irony.

Since Schneersohn felt God stood behind the operation, he dismissed
the incredible risks many undertook to rescue him, especially Bloch and
Canaris. Neither during nor after the war did the Rebbe thank the families of his rescuers. The Chabad organization has failed to acknowledge
them as well, nor has it ever criticized the Rebbe for condemning others
from the safety of the United States and for focusing on his books when
he should have focused on saving lives. Most who learn about the Rebbe
feel confused about why anyone would want to rescue him.

So these rescue stories are complicated on many levels. Whether it was a
"Nazi" naval captain saving a rich, secular businessman or secret service
German agents rescuing a prominent rabbi, these stories present the reader
with difficult questions about moral responsibility. The only reason why
men decided to help these Jews is that they saw that their lives were in
peril. There was no discussion about whether the person was worthy or
unworthy of such a rescue. As Holocaust survivor Victor Frankl said, the
best of humanity did not survive the Holocaust, and one could argue that
both Fould and Schneersohn were not the best of humanity.

Conclusion

"Who is a Jew?" "What is Jewish?" The different laws and definitions, religiously and historically, greatly complicate the issue, especially when studying the Third Reich and the Holocaust. Many German Jews and *Mischlinge,* including Oppenfeld, Krüger, and Jacoby, wanted nothing to do with Jews or their own Jewish past. After the war, neither Jewish identity nor Jewish loyalty played any role in their lives. Some, such as Scholz, Löwy, and Hirschfeld, embraced their Jewishness and now call themselves Jews. Others, among them Meissinger and Techel, acknowledge their Jewish roots, but would not call themselves Jewish in any sense of the word. The group represented by Kopp and Geitner has wrestled with questions about themselves and their role in society in light of their Jewish background throughout their lives. These men acknowledge their Jewishness, but feel bewildered as to what this means in practical terms. Jewish identity is complicated and may be best summed up as historian Jonathan Steinberg claimed: "A Jew is a person who asks himself his entire life what it means to be a Jew."

These men's stories illustrate the wide range of experiences of German soldiers of Jewish descent, a group that probably numbered over 150,000. The trauma thousands of mothers, sisters, wives, girlfriends, and children suffered by being connected to them broadens the scope of the tragedy of this chapter of the Holocaust. The lives of many *Mischlinge* and some Jews in the Wehrmacht were traumatic, filled with difficult choices and painful experiences. Some came from families with strong military traditions, a background that encouraged them to accept service under the Third Reich as natural and honorable, which is strongly illustrated by Techel and Prager. Their fathers and uncles had served in World War I, and a few, like Milch, Wilberg, Rogge, Mendelssohn, and Jacoby, had even distinguished themselves in this very conflict, giving them a strong foundation of military service before Nazism. The majority of their families and most of these men had the customary rights of German citizens, only to have them quickly taken away once Hitler came into power.

These case studies show in vivid detail that these men fought for a government that took away their basic human rights and sent their relatives to extermination centers. Nevertheless most continued to serve, since any open resistance would have cost them their lives. Further, they mistakenly hoped their service would protect themselves and their families. For some, military service delayed the deportation of a relative, and some *Mischlinge* received special treatment for some period of time. However, most ultimately lost their relatives to the genocidal Nazi machine, and most *Mischling* soldiers surrendered more and more of their rights as the Nazis years wore on.

The fact that their Aryan superiors courageously helped many of them added to their belief that their service would help protect them. As in the cases of Günther Scheffler, Wilberg, Mendelssohn, Fischer, and Geitner, their superiors disregarded the Nazi racial laws, valuing a trained soldier and true comrade more than Nazi regulations. This helps explain why many of these men remained loyal.

The passionate patriotism felt by many *Mischlinge* is ironic. When drafted, most thought it their duty to obey, even though the Nazis persecuted them and their families. As half-Jew Dieter Bergman said, "I loved my Fatherland, and most half-Jews I knew all believed they were fulfilling their duty to Germany. We loved Germany and wanted to see her become great again. Unfortunately, we were lied to and were abused by the very country we held so dear."[1] Nazi policy toward *Mischlinge* gradually worsened and pushed them toward the world of the Holocaust.

Hitler refused to use these patriotic citizens to help win the war. This demonstrates how Hitler valued racial purity over military victory. From 1942 to 1944, Hitler assigned hundreds of trains to move "millions of Jews across Europe to the death factories in Poland" when the army could have used those trains to move "troops and war material." Despite the constant labor shortage, Hitler exterminated millions of Jews who could have worked in factories.[2] Hitler had discharged tens of thousands of half-Jews from military service by late 1942, when Germany encountered severe setbacks at Stalingrad. He could have recalled these men, and most would have fought bravely. Did Hitler have nothing better to do at the height of the battle of Stalingrad than to examine applications from *Mischlinge* to see if they were worthy of Aryanization? Only he could grant such an exemption, since he believed only he, like God, could discern a person's true racial makeup. Hitler's racial policies turned most *Mischlinge* against him and his government. The majority of them looked forward to the day of Hitler's demise. Krüger admitted that had Hitler not discriminated against him, he probably would have become a Nazi. When asked why, he simply explained how difficult it is today for people to understand how attractive the movement was to young men. In front of "the evil goals of the Nazis stood the wonderful activities for young men of camping, war games, and community. It all just felt so good."

Just as shocking as Hitler's perverse racial policies with respect to partial Jews in the Wehrmacht is that most *Mischling* soldiers did not know Hitler was murdering millions of Jews, including their relatives. Like most other Germans, they knew about Nazi deportations, but what happened at the deadly destinations lay beyond their knowledge or imagination. Oppenfeld, Günther Scheffler, Kopp, and others knew about executions in the east, but not the systematic killing of millions in gas chambers.

The most convincing proof that these men did not know what was happening is the story of half-Jews in the OT forced labor camps. Had half-Jews known about the Holocaust, one would expect them to have done everything they could to avoid deportation. But as this book shows, most reported when called. Holocaust historian Yehuda Bauer wrote, "The Jews were the products of a civilization which stood in stark contradiction to all the premises of Nazism. It was totally incomprehensible to them that people should exist who denied the sanctity of human life, or who excluded some people from humanity altogether. They were therefore outwitted at every point, easily misled, and murdered precisely because they could not accept the reality of the world in which such murder was possible."[3] If Jews did not know the endgame of the Nazis, their *Mischling* relatives remained at least as ignorant of what Hitler's plan would do to them.

The story of *Mischling* soldiers illustrates how corrupt and demeaning the Nazi government was and how confusing its racial laws were. These *Mischlinge* fought for a regime that repaid their service by murdering their relatives and persecuting them. Furthermore, had Germany won the war, its leaders probably would have slaughtered half-Jews *en masse* too—something many came to realize in their OT camps or after the war. Hitler's constant attention to the details of *Mischling* policy support the assumption that he was at least as intimately involved in the policies that affected them as in those that affected the Jews.

The story of the *Mischlinge* sheds light on the Pandora's box Hitler opened when he tried to split his society between desirables and undesirables. It demonstrates how miserably Hitler failed at this as he destroyed the lives of individuals and millions of families, both Jewish and Aryan.

Yet the *Mischling* story offers much more than copious evidence of Nazi discrimination, persecution, and injustice. Many *Mischlinge*, among them Fischer, Meissinger, Krüger, and the Scheffler brothers, did a great deal to protect their relatives. Mendelssohn, Bloch, and others saved Jews to whom they had no previous connection. We also see courage, generosity, and self-sacrifice in the face of great danger.

Unfortunately, we also see evil in the lives of some *Mischlinge*. Field Marshal Milch, a Nazi, represents a *Mischling* who turned himself over to Hitler and his goals. In the end, he served time as a Nazi war criminal. Luckily, this disgusting person was a member of a tiny minority among the *Mischlinge*.

In the end, the Third Reich cannot be limited to extremes. Not every soldier was an archetypal Nazi, nor was every soldier a pure Aryan. History does not fit into simple black and white categories. We must struggle to understand the gray middle where real life happens. The *Mischling* stories show how complicated and varied the racial laws and their effects were, especially in the military.

The *Mischlinge* lead us beyond the Third Reich into a discussion of identity both as individuals and as members of society. Identity can be fluid and is often forced upon a person. Who we are can be a reflection of how people view and treat us, rather than how we want to be perceived. The dramatic identity crises of the men in this book should remind each of us to ask, "Why are we the way we are?" The way we understand ourselves directly influences how we interpret history. More importantly, the way we view ourselves affects how we treat others. This lesson should never be lost on students of the Holocaust. In other words, we need to constantly monitor ourselves for how we talk about and treat others. Genocide—including the post-Holocaust genocides in Bosnia, Rwanda, Sudan, and Iraq—begins with discriminatory and prejudicial thoughts long before anyone dies. How we learn to think about others and their worth makes all the difference. The *Mischlinge* remind us how important it is to fight vigilantly against our tendency to denigrate others in order to bolster our own faltering self-esteem.

NOTES

The quotation on page v is from Judah Goldin, ed. and trans., *The Living Talmud: The Wisdom of the Fathers* (New York, 1957), 86. For abbreviations see Bibliography.

PREFACE
1. BA-MA, BMRS, interview with Hugo Fuchs, 8 July 1995.
2. BA-MA, BMRS, interview with Joachim Schmidt, April 1995.

PROLOGUE: A BRIEF HISTORY OF THE WEHRMACHT
1. Wilhelm Deist, "Einführende Bemerkungen," in Rolf-Dieter Müller and Hans-Erich Volkmann, eds., *Die Wehrmacht: Mythos und Realität* (Stuttgart, 1999), 39; Fritz, *Frontsoldaten*, 3, 12.
2. Ian Kershaw, *The Hitler Myth: Image and Reality in the Third Reich* (Oxford, 1990), 138; John Wheeler-Bennett, *The Nemesis of Power* (New York, 1980), 425.
3. Matthew Cooper, *The German Army 1933–1945: Its Political and Military Failure* (New York, 1978), 159.
4. Gilbert, *Second World War*, 11, 214–15; Kershaw, *Hitler Myth*, 153.
5. Kershaw, *Hitler Myth*, 1.
6. Michael Geyer, "German Strategy, 1914–1945," in Peter Paret, ed., *Makers of Modern Strategy from Machiavelli to the Nuclear Age* (Princeton, NJ, 1986), 588; Hitler, *Mein Kampf*, 660–66; Kershaw, *Hitler Myth*, 237–38; Michael Burleigh, *Ethics and Extermination: Reflections on Nazi Genocide* (New York, 1997), 42.
7. Fritz, *Frontsoldaten*, 10.
8. Cooper, *German Army*, 285; Alexander Werth, *Russia at War: 1941–1945* (New York, 1964), 143.
9. Burleigh, *Ethics and Extermination*, 41.
10. Ibid., 43.
11. "U.S.A. Military Tribunals: Case No. 12—German Generals," in Office of the U.S. Chief Counsel for Prosecution of Axis Criminality, ed., *Nazi Conspiracy and Aggression*, Vol. 2 (Washington, DC, 1946), 10120; Gilbert, *Second World War*, 296, 311–12, 366.
12. Werth, *Russia at War,* 131; Geyer, "German Strategy," in Paret, *Makers of Modern Strategy,* 566, 590.
13. Gerhard L. Weinberg, *A World at Arms: A Global History of World War II* (New York, 1994), 281–82.
14. Alan Clark, *Barbarossa: The Russo-German Conflict 1941–1945* (New York, 1985), 250.
15. Werth, *Russia at War,* xiv.
16. Fritz, *Frontsoldaten*, 31.
17. BA-MA, BMRS, interview Reiss, 15 October 1994; Sajer, *The Forgotten Soldier,* 223.
18. Fritz, *Frontsoldaten*, 31.

INTRODUCTION

1. BA-MA, BMRS, Heinz Bleicher, 4.
2. Adolf Hitler, *Mein Kampf* (Boston, 1971), 248–49, 400–402.
3. James F. Tent, *In the Shadow of the Holocaust: Nazi Persecution of Jewish-Christian Germans* (Lawrence, KS, 2003), x.
4. Stephen G. Fritz, *Frontsoldaten: The German Soldier in World War II* (Lexington, KY, 1995), 1.
5. John Keegan, *War and Our World* (New York, 1998), 46.
6. Ernst Behler, ed., *The German Library*, Vol. 13, *Kant, Philosophical Writings* (New York, 1986), 242.
7. John Stuart Mill, *On Liberty with the Subjection of Women and Chapters on Socialism*, ed. Stefan Collini (Cambridge, 1991), 8.
8. BA-MA, BMRS, Dieter Bergman, Diary, 19 July 1941, 31 May 1942.
9. BA-MA, BMRS, Gerlach, Gerlach to Rust, 11 May 1941, 4.
10. Fritz, *Frontsoldaten*, 24; Isaiah Berlin, *Four Essays on Liberty* (Oxford, 1969), 24. See also Erich Maria Remarque, *All Quiet on the Western Front* (New York, 1982), 12, for a description of this obedience.
11. Verordnung zum Reichsbürgergesetz, 14 Nov. 1935, Reichsgesetzblatt (RGBL) 1, no. 135 (1935), 1333–36; Raul Hilberg, *Destruction of the European Jews* (New York, 1961), 48; *The Holocaust*, Vol. 1, *Legalizing the Holocaust—The Early Phase, 1933–1939*, Introduction by John Mendelsohn (New York, 1982), 31; H. G. Adler, *Der Verwaltete Mensch: Studien zur Deportation der Juden aus Deutschland* (Tübingen, 1974), 280; Hilde Kammer and Elisabet Bartsch, with Manon Eppenstein-Baukhage, *Nationalsozialismus: Begriffe aus der Zeit der Gewaltherrschaft 1933–1945* (Reinbek bei Hamburg, 1992), 39–40; Ian Kershaw, *Hitler: 1889–1936: Hubris* (New York, 1999), 572; Norman Rich, *Hitler's War Aims* (New York, 1974), 1–2; Nathan Stoltzfus, *Resistance of the Heart: Intermarriage and the Rosenstrasse Protest in Nazi Germany* (New York, 1996), xxv; Marion A. Kaplan, *Between Dignity and Despair: Jewish Life in Nazi Germany* (New York, 1998), 191.
12. Martin Gilbert, *The Holocaust* (New York, 1985), 45–47.
13. Berlin, *Four Essays on Liberty*, 26; Rolf Vogel, *Ein Stück von uns* (Bonn, 1973), 238.
14. Karl-Heinz Maier, *Und höret niemals auf zu kämpfen* (Berlin, 1994), 27–51, 165–66.
15. Bryan Mark Rigg, *Hitler's Jewish Soldiers: The Untold Story of Nazi Racial Laws and Men of Jewish Descent in the German Military* (Lawrence, KS, 2002), 51–67.
16. Arthur Ruppin, *The Jews in the Modern World* (London, 1934), 329; Ruth Gay, *The Jews of Germany* (New Haven, CT, 1992), 139; Beate Meyer, *Jüdische Mischlinge: Rassenpolitik und Verfolgungserfahrung 1933–1945* (Hamburg, 1999), 20; Deborah Hertz, "The Genealogy Bureaucracy in the Third Reich," *Jewish History* 11 (Fall 1997), 1; Hitler, *Mein Kampf*, 120; Joseph Walk, ed., *Sonderrecht für den Juden im NS-Staat: Eine Sammlung der gesetzlichen Massnahmen und Richtlinien: Inhalt und Bedeutung*, Law from 4 October 1936 (Heidelberg, 1981).

17. Martin Gilbert, *The Second World War* (New York, 1989), 351; Geoffrey Hartman, ed., *Holocaust Remembrance: The Shapes of Memory* (New York, 1994), David Tracy, "Christian Witness and the Shoah," in Geoffrey H. Hartman, ed., *Holocaust Remembrance: The Shapes of Memory* (Oxford and Cambridge, 1994), 83; Aleksandar-Saša Vuletic, *Christen Jüdischer Herkunft im Dritten Reich: Verfolgung und organisierte Selbsthilfe 1933–1939* (Mainz, Germany, 1999), 6; BA-MA, BMRS, Hans Günzel and interviews with Dieter Bergman, 10–16 September 1996; Leni Yahil, *The Holocaust: The Fate of European Jewry* (New York, 1990), 73; Chaim A. Kaplan, *Scroll of Agony: The Warsaw Diary of Chaim A. Kaplan* (New York, 1965), 78–79.

18. Rigg, *Hitler's Jewish Soldiers*, 168–69.

19. Institut für Zeitgeschichte, N 71–73.

20. Hilberg, *Destruction of the European Jews*, 309.

21. Ibid., 152; Noakes, "The Development of Nazi Policy towards the German-Jewish 'Mischlinge' 1933–1945," *Leo Baeck Yearbook* 34 (1989), 338; Kurt Pätzold, ed., *Verfolgung, Vertreibung, Vernichtung: Dokumente des faschistischen Antisemitismus 1933 bis 1942* (Leipzig, 1984), 249, 264–65.

22. Rigg, *Hitler's Jewish Soldiers*, 168–69.

23. Ibid., 156–71.

CHAPTER 1. JEWS AND *MISCHLINGE*
HIDING THEIR IDENTITIES

1. Unrecorded interviews with Simon Gossel, 11 January 2005, 27 January 2005.

2. James Bradley, *Flags of Our Fathers* (New York, 2000), 58; Albert Seaton, *The Russo-German War 1941–1945* (London, 1971), 586; Gilbert, *Second World War*, 746; Keegan, *War and Our World*, 12; Fritz, *Frontsoldaten*, viii, 138.

3. See Stoltzfus, *Resistance of the Heart*.

4. John Keegan, *The Second World War* (New York, 1989), 198; Werth, *Russia at War*, 324.

5. Guy Sajer, *The Forgotten Soldier* (New York, 1971), 302.

6. Hans Ulrich Rudel, *Stuka Pilot* (New York, 1979), 80.

7. Sajer, *Forgotten Soldier*, 337, 373.

8. Jews or people of Jewish descent committed the Nazi crime of *Rassenschande* when they indulged in sexual activity with Aryans. Rigg, *Hitler's Jewish Soldiers*, 22–23.

9. Werth, *Russia at War*, 765–66.

10. Sajer, *Forgotten Soldier*, 316.

11. Gilbert, *Holocaust*, 329–30.

12. Sajer, *Forgotten Soldier*, 94.

13. Elon, *The Pity of It All: A History of Jews in Germany 1743–1933* (New York, 2002), 81–90.

14. Ian Kershaw, *Profiles in Power: Hitler* (London, 1991), 149.

15. Seaton, *Russo-German War*, 245–48.

16. Fritz, *Frontsoldaten*, 54.

17. Beate Meyer, *Jüdische Mischlinge: Rassenpolitik und Verfolgungserfahrung 1933–*

1945 (Hamburg, 1999), 20–21, 92; Adler, *Der verwaltete Mensch*, 280–81; Kaplan, *Between Dignity and Despair*, 148–49.

18. Gilbert, *Second World War*, 351.

19. Akten der Parteikanzlei der NSDAP, 107-00398, 107-00407–408; Stoltzfus, *Resistance of the Heart*, 54; Vuletic, *Christen Jüdischer Herkunft im Dritten Reich*, 21; Hilberg, *Destruction of the European Jews*, 49; interview with Colin Heaton, February 2004.

20. From Association of Soldiers of the Former Waffen-SS, *Wenn alle Brüder schweigen* (Osnabrück, 1973).

21. Hannu Rautkallio, *Finland and the Holocaust: The Rescue of Finland's Jews* (Helsinki, 1989), 198–201.

22. Gottlob Herbert Bidermann, *In Deadly Combat: A German Soldier's Memoir of the Eastern Front* (Lawrence, KS, 2000), 94, 236.

23. Omer Bartov, *Hitler's Army: Soldiers, Nazis, and War in the Third Reich* (New York, 1991), 34–35.

24. Charles Sydnor, *Soldiers of Destruction: The SS Death's Head Division 1933–1945* (Princeton, NJ, 1977), 313–46.

25. Wolf Zoepf, *Seven Days in January: With the 6th SS-Mountain Division in Operation NORDWIND* (Bedford, PA, 2001); Johann Voss, *Black Edelweiss: A Memoir of Combat and Conscience by a Soldier of the Waffen-SS* (Bedford, PA, 2002).

26. Judah Goldin, ed. and trans., *The Living Talmud: The Wisdom of the Fathers* (New York, 1957), 88.

27. Behler, *Kant, Philosophical Writings*, 65.

28. Johann Wolfgang von Goethe, *Faust* (Franklin Center, PA, 1979), 48.

29. Unrecorded interviews with Frau Karl-Heinz Löwy, 25 August 2005, 10 September 2005.

30. Unrecorded interviews with Simon Gossel, 11 January 2005, 27 January 2005.

31. See Rigg, *Hitler's Jewish Soldiers*, 80–85.

32. Fritz, *Frontsoldaten*, 187.

33. Gilbert, *Second World War*, 38.

34. Keegan, *Second World War*, 70.

35. Bartov, *Hitler's Army*, 14.

36. Clark, *Barbarossa*, 143; Cooper, *German Army*, 325.

37. Bidermann, *In Deadly Combat*, 43, 49.

38. Geyer, "German Strategy," in Paret, *Makers of Modern Strategy*, 592.

39. Cooper, *German Army*, 331.

40. Fritz, *Frontsoldaten*, 107.

41. Sajer, *Forgotten Soldier*, 30.

42. Bidermann, *In Deadly Combat*, 62.

43. Cooper, *German Army*, 283.

44. Keegan, *War and Our World*, 215.

45. Clark, *Barbarossa*, 207; Werth, *Russia at War*, 703–708; Bartov, *Hitler's Army*, 83, 87.

46. Clark, *Barbarossa*, 207.

47. Ian Kershaw, *Hitler: 1936–1945: Nemesis* (New York, 2000), 5.

48. Werth, *Russia at War*, 397.

49. Bidermann, *In Deadly Combat,* 57.
50. Sajer, *Forgotten Soldier,* 220–21.
51. Ibid., 438–39.
52. Cooper, *German Army,* 434.
53. Fritz, *Frontsoldaten,* 3.

CHAPTER 2. HALF-JEWS, THE WEHRMACHT,
AND OT FORCED LABOR CAMPS

1. SA stands for Sturmabteilung (Storm Detachment), a Nazi Party paramilitary formation.
2. Rigg, *Hitler's Jewish Soldiers,* 107, 200.
3. Bartov, *Hitler's Army,* 36, 38–39.
4. Gilbert, *Second World War,* 746; Seaton, *Russo-German War,* 586.
5. Fritz, *Frontsoldaten,* 90, 95.
6. BA-MA, BMRS, Florian Stahmer.
7. U.S. National Archives, Box 329, AE 501661, Fritz Bayerlein, 1–155.
8. BA-MA, BMRS, Herbert Lefévre, 15, 61, 80.
9. Keegan, *Second World War,* 426–27.
10. Weinberg, *A World at Arms,* 894; John W. Dower, *War without Mercy: Race and Power in the Pacific War* (New York, 1986), 47; unrecorded interview with Gerhard Weinberg, 2 September 2005.
11. Dinah Shelton, ed., *Encyclopedia of Genocide and Crimes against Humanity* (New York, 2005), 171.
12. Ibid.
13. Honda Katsuichi, *The Nanjing Massacre: A Japanese Journalist Confronts Japan's National Shame* (London, 1999), 287.
14. Tent, *In the Shadow of the Holocaust,* 30.
15. Keegan, *Second World War,* 160–72.
16. Ibid., 165–66.
17. Ibid., 166.
18. BA-MA, BMRS, Moshe Mantelmacher.
19. *Sammlung wehrrechtlicher Gutachten und Vorschriften,* no. 2, 27.
20. Tent, *In the Shadow of the Holocaust,* 163.
21. Rigg, *Hitler's Jewish Soldiers,* 45.
22. Saul Friedman, *No Haven for the Oppressed: United States Policy toward Jewish Refugees, 1938–1945* (Detroit, 1973), 12; Yehuda Bauer, *American Jewry and the Holocaust: The American Jewish Joint Distribution Committee 1939–1945* (Detroit, 1981), 26; Rigg, *Hitler's Jewish Soldiers,* 59–65.
23. Remarque, *All Quiet on the Western Front,* 101.
24. Jonathan Steinberg, *All or Nothing: The Axis and the Holocaust, 1941–43* (New York, 2002), 50–51; Kaplan, *Between Dignity and Despair,* 184, 227.
25. Kaplan, *Between Dignity and Despair,* 194.
26. Keegan, *War and Our World,* 3, 11.
27. Gotthold Ephraim Lessing, *Nathan the Wise, Minna von Barnhelm, and Other Plays and Writings,* Peter Demetz, ed. (New York, 1991), 214.

28. Cooper, *German Army*, 279.
29. Clark, *Barbarossa*, 181.
30. Ibid.; Cooper, *German Army*, 333; Rudel, *Stuka Pilot*, 50.
31. Sajer, *Forgotten Soldier*, 37, 334.
32. Fritz, *Frontsoldaten*, 117.
33. Ibid., 109, 112–13.
34. Werth, *Russia at War*, 194, 717, 768.
35. Bartov, *Hitler's Army*, 83–84.
36. Robert Ericksen, *Theologians under Hitler* (New Haven, CT, 1985), 148, 154, 166.
37. Bartov, *Hitler's Army*, 121–22, 124.
38. Kershaw, *Hitler Myth*, 105, 111, 116; Ericksen, *Theologians under Hitler*, 25.
39. Ericksen, *Theologians under Hitler*, 27.

CHAPTER 3. *MISCHLINGE* WHO RECEIVED THE *DEUTSCHBLÜTIGKEITSERKLÄRUNG*

1. See James S. Corum's books *The Roots of Blitzkrieg: Hans von Seeckt and German Military Reform* (Lawrence, KS, 1992) and *The Luftwaffe: Creating the Operational Air War, 1918–1940* (Lawrence, KS, 1997).
2. Bartov, *Hitler's Army*, 107.
3. Gilbert, *Second World War*, 35, 260–61.
4. Wounded soldiers in *Stufe* (level) III had lost an arm, a leg, both feet, or suffered other types of grave injury. BA-MA, RH 12-23/834, 93.
5. Rudolf Absolon, *Wehrgesetz und Wehrdienst 1935–1945: Das Personalwesen in der Wehrmacht* (Boppard, Germany, 1960), 120; BA-B, DZA 62 Ka. 1 83, 91–92, Parteikanzlei, Beförderung von Schwerstbeschädigten, 11 October 1941.
6. BA-B, DZA 62 Ka. 1 83, 34, Der Reichsminister des Inneren (Schönfeldt) to Rust, 20 February 1942, and OKW to Kanzlei des Führers, 16 September 1943, and 67b, "Jüdische Mischlinge im Wehrdienst," von Blankenburg.
7. BA-B, DZA 62 Ka. 1 83, 73, OKW an KdF, 16 September 1943; BA-MA, BMRS, G. F. Müller, 52; BA-MA, BMRS, Haller.
8. The author published a similar article on Milch in *World War II Magazine*, January 2004.
9. BA-MA, BMRS, Erhard Milch, James Corum to Michael Briggs, March 2001; Corum, *Luftwaffe*, 125.
10. Corum, *Roots of Blitzkrieg*, 150–51, 153; Corum, *Luftwaffe*, 60.
11. Corum, *Roots of Blitzkrieg*, 150–51; Corum, *Luftwaffe*, 77, 125; Anthony Read, *The Devil's Disciples: Hitler's Inner Circle* (New York, 2004), 176–78, 205. Corum to Rigg, 28 July 2004.
12. BA-MA, N 179, Milchs Tagebücher, entry from 31 January 1933; Corum to Rigg, 17 July 2004.
13. "U.S.A. Military Tribunals: Case No. 1-2, Nuremberg Trials," 1776, in Office of the U.S. Chief Counsel for Prosecution of Axis Criminality, ed., *Nazi Conspiracy and Aggression*, Vol. 2; BA-MA, N 179, Milchs Tagebücher, entry from 1 November 1933, 46; BA-B, R 15.09/90, 2, Göring to Leiter der Reichsstelle für Sippenforschung, 7 August 1935; BA-MA, BMRS, File Erhard Milch, Heft 3; BA-MA,

Pers 8–385; Horst Boog, "Erhard Milch," in Ronald Smelser and Enrico Syring, eds., *Die Militärelite des Dritten Reiches* (Berlin, 1995), 351; Robert Wistrich, *Who's Who in Nazi Germany* (New York, 1982), 210; Konrad Heiden, *Der Fuehrer: Hitler's Rise to Power* (London, 1967), 500.

14. BA-MA, BMRS, Erhard Milch, Heft 3, Heinz Fahrenberg (ex-Major in the Generalstab der Luftwaffe) to Rigg, 18 April 1997 and 22 June 1997, and Walter Frank to Rigg, 18 April 1997, and Dr. Ludwig Spangenthal (relative of Milch) to Rigg, 4 July 1997; BA-MA, N 179, 46, Milchs Tagebücher, 1 November 1933; Wheeler-Bennett, *Nemesis of Power*, 342; Manfred Messerschmidt, *Die Wehrmacht im NS-Staat* (Hamburg, 1969), 46; Victor Klemperer, *Ich will Zeugnis ablegen bis zum letzten: Tagebücher, 1933–1945*, Buch 1, 18 October 1936 (Darmstadt, Germany, 1996), 317; BA-MA, BMRS, interviews with Dieter Bergman, 10–16 September 1996; BA-MA, Pers 6/11, 4, "Milchs Vater Anton Milch, Marine-Oberstabs-apotheker"; BA-MA, Pers 8-385; Boog, "Erhard Milch," in Smelser and Syring, *Die Militärelite des Dritten Reiches;* Gerhard L. Weinberg, *Germany, Hitler and World War II* (New York, 1996), 66. Hans Hirsch knew some prominent Jewish Milchs in Germany and asked them about their famous cousin. In reply, they told him they found their cousin embarrassing. Unrecorded interview with Hans Hirsch, 12 July 2005.

15. BA-B, R 15.09/90, 2, Göring to Meyer, 7 August 1935.

16. Unrecorded interview with John E. Dolibois, 22 July 2001. BA-MA, BMRS, John E. Dolibois, Dolibois to Rigg, 23 July 2001. Dolibois worked for the War Crimes Commission and took part in the Ashcan Program. "Ashcan" was the military code word for the Central Continental Prisoners of War Enclosure 32 (CCPWE32), where Göring and many other Nazi officials were incarcerated from May to August 1945.

17. Robert Gellately, ed., *The Nuremberg Interviews: Conducted by Leon Golden-sohn* (New York, 2004), 364.

18. BA-MA, BMRS, Erhard Milch, Heft 2, Klaus Hermann to Rigg, 14 October 1994 and 30 March 1995.

19. BA-MA, BMRS, Erhard Milch, Klaus Hermann to David Irving, 26 October 1997; BA-MA, ZA 3/648, Personal-Nachweis über Erhard Alfred Richard Oskar Milch; BA-MA, RL 3/3271, Personal-Nachweis über Erhard Milch; Gilbert, *Second World War*, 11–12, 20, 32, 70, 105, 228; Michael Burleigh, *The Third Reich: A New History* (New York, 2000), 383.

20. Williamson Murray, *Luftwaffe* (Baltimore, 1985), 6–7.

21. Matthew Cooper, *The German Air-Force 1933–1945* (New York, 1981), 13; Corum, *Luftwaffe*, 125.

22. Corum, *Luftwaffe*, 161–62, 181; Cooper, *German Air-Force*, 13. See also Murray, *Luftwaffe*, 9.

23. Leonard Mosley, *The Reich Marshal* (London, 1974), 306; Murray, *Luftwaffe*, 100–103.

24. Adam R. A. Claasen, *Hitler's Northern War: The Luftwaffe's Ill-Fated Campaign, 1940–1945* (Lawrence, KS, 2001), 99–100, 121, 140.

25. Joel S. A. Hayward, *Stopped at Stalingrad: The Luftwaffe and Hitler's Defeat in the East, 1942–1943* (Lawrence, KS, 1998), 286–310; Murray, *Luftwaffe*, 148.

26. Cooper, *German Air-Force.*

27. Corum to Rigg, 17 July 2004.

28. Interviews by Colin Heaton with Johannes Steinhoff, 26–28 January 1984.

29. Heiden, *Der Fuehrer,* 352; BA-MA, N 179, Telegramm Milchs an Hitler, 21 July 1944.

30. "U.S.A. Military Tribunals: Case No. 1-2, Nuremberg Trials," 2524.

31. Office of the U.S. Chief Counsel for Prosecution of Axis Criminality, ed., *Nazi Conspiracy and Aggression,* Vol. 2 (Washington, DC, 1946).

32. Robert Jay Lifton, *The Nazi Doctors* (New York, 1986), 286; Joseph E. Persico, *Nuremberg: Infamy on Trial* (New York, 1994), 370; Office of the U.S. Chief Counsel, *Nazi Conspiracy and Aggression,* 445–46; James Corum, "Die Luftwaffe, ihre Führung und Doktrin und die Frage der Kriegsverbrechen," in Gerd Ueberschaer and Wolfram Wette, eds., *Kriegsverbrechen im 20 Jahrhundert* (Darmstadt, Germany, 2001), 288–302.

33. "U.S.A. Military Tribunals: Case No. 1-2, Nuremberg Trials," 77.

34. Hilberg, *Destruction of the European Jews,* 599; Corum to Rigg, 17 July 2004.

35. "U.S.A. Military Tribunals: Case No. 12, Nuremberg Trials," 10261.

36. Discussion with author on 28 October 1998.

37. Liddell Hart, *The German Generals' Talk* (New York, 1979), 198; Behler, *German Library,* Vol. 13, *Kant,* 291.

38. Cooper, *German Army,* 4.

39. Corum, *Roots of Blitzkrieg,* 151–53.

40. Ibid., 151–53; Corum to Rigg, 17 July 2004.

41. Corum, *Roots of Blitzkrieg,* 144–68; Corum, *Luftwaffe,* 30–34, 52, 59–61, 125–27, 142–46, 180; James S. Corum, "The Old Eagle as Phoenix: The Luftstreitkräfte Creates an Operational Air War Doctrine, 1919–1920," *Air Power History* 14 (Spring 1992), 13–21; Cooper, *German Air-Force,* 39, 379–89; A. Baeumker, *Ein Beitrag zur Geschichte der Führung der deutschen Luftfahrttechnik im ersten halben Jahrhundert 1900–1945,* Langfristiges Planen der Forschung und Entwicklung No. 44 (July 1971); Helmut Wilberg, Abschliessender Flieger-Erfahrungsbericht über die Schlacht in Flandern (Buch- und Steindruckerei der Artillerie-Fliegerschule Ost 1), 1923; Karl Friedrich Hildebrand, ed., *Die Generale der deutschen Luftwaffe, 1935-1945,* 3 vols. (Osnabrück, 1990–1992), 3: 513–14.

42. Corum, *Roots of Blitzkrieg,* 151–53, 162.

43. Ibid., 167–68; Corum to Rigg, 17 July 2004.

44. Corum, *Roots of Blitzkrieg,* 167–68; Corum to Rigg, 17 July 2004.

45. BA-MA, N 761/7, 2, Generaloberst a.D. Erwin Jaenecke, Erinnerungen aus dem spanischen Bürgerkrieg, Typoskript, o.D. (nach 1955); Herbert Molly Mason, Jr., *The Rise of the Luftwaffe* (New York, 1973), 168–71, 218–21; Corum, *Luftwaffe,* 147, 183–84, 219–21; Corum to Rigg, 17 July 2004.

46. BA-MA, N 761/7, 2, Bericht Jaenecke, 1–2.

47. BA-MA, N 761/7, 1–2; BA-MA, BMRS, Helmut Wilberg, Boog to Rigg, 31 July 2005.

48. BA-MA, N 761/7, 1–2.

49. Bartov, *Hitler's Army,* 39.

50. Sajer, *Forgotten Soldier*, 111.
51. BA-MA, BMRS, Arthur Becker, 5.
52. Berlin, *Four Essays on Liberty*, 170.
53. Much of the material presented here about Rogge is drawn from BA-MA, BMRS, File Rogge, Heft 1-3; Institut für Schiffahrts und Marinegeschichte in Hamburg, File Rogge; August Karl Muggenthaler, *German Raiders of World War II* (London, 1980); Wolfgang Frank and Bernhard Rogge, *The German Raider Atlantis* (New York, 1956); Ulrich Mohr and A. V. Sellwood, *Atlantis: The Story of the German Surface Raider* (London, 1955); Edward P. von der Porten, *The German Navy in World War II* (London, 1970).
54. Gellately, *Nuremberg Interviews*, 13; Muggenthaler, *German Raiders*, 29.
55. *Weisse Segel Weite Meere* by Fritz Otto Busch (Berlin, 1939) chronicled a cruise of the *Albert Leo Schlageter* under Rogge's command.
56. Muggenthaler, *German Raiders*, 10.
57. Geoffrey P. Jones, *Under Three Flags: The Story of Nordmark and the Armed Supply Ships of the German Navy* (London, 1973), 144.
58. Koburger, Charles W., *Steel Ships, Iron Crosses, and Refugees: The German Navy in the Baltic, 1939–1945* (New York, 1989), 45–48; Bidermann, *In Deadly Combat*, 237; Muggenthaler, *German Raiders*, 140.
59. Sajer, *Forgotten Soldier*, 428.
60. Werth, *Russia at War 1941–1945*, 961.
61. Joseph Slavick, *The Cruise of the German Raider Atlantis* (Annapolis, 2003), 229.
62. BA-B, R 43 II/599, Bormann an Lammers, 2 November 1944; BA-B, 43 II/603b.
63. Remarque, *All Quiet on the Western Front*, 10.

CHAPTER 4. *MISCHLINGE* AND THE PROCESS
OF GETTING A *GENEHMIGUNG*

1. IfZ, N71–73, "Herrn Minister auf dem Dienstwege," Zu I e Ei 1 IV/40–5017a, 22 May 1940.
2. This information about Erwin Fischer comes from Amelis von Mettenheim. Jürgen Fischer, Erwin's grandson, says that many family members doubt this story and he disagrees with the version from his aunt Amelis. He states that Erwin later married again. However, at the time, many homosexuals married to hide their sexual orientation, so marrying again did not necessarily prove he was a heterosexual. BA-MA, BMRS, Dieter Fischer, Jürgen Fischer to Rigg, 3 August 2005.
3. Although interviewees have mentioned that *Ostjuden* participated in street crimes, this may be more a reflection of their prejudices than what really happened.
4. Fritz, *Frontsoldaten*, 71–72.
5. Rigg, *Hitler's Jewish Soldiers*, 114.
6. BA-B (Bundesarchiv-Berlin), DZA 62 Ka. 1 83, 198, "Aktennotiz für Reichsamtsleiter Brack."
7. BA-MA, N 328/45, Ehrhardt an Förste, 14 November 1956; *Heeresadjutant bei Hitler 1938–1943. Aufzeichnungen des Majors Gerhard Engel*, ed. and with commentary by Hildegard von Kotze (Schriftenreihe der Vierteljahreshefte für Zeitgeschichte no. 29), 32; Noakes, "Development of Nazi Policy," 316, 333.

8. BA-B, NS 19, 3134, 1–2.
9. Ericksen, *Theologians under Hitler,* 164–65.
10. Hilberg, *Destruction of the European Jews,* 12.
11. Ibid., 7; BA-B, NS 19/3134, 1–2; Werner Maser, *Adolf Hitler: Legende Mythos Wirklichkeit* (Munich, 1971), 282; Henry Picker, *Hitlers Tischgespräche im Führerhauptquartier 1941–1942,* Percy Ernst Schramm, ed. (Stuttgart, 1976), 45; Jochen von Lang, *The Secretary: Martin Bormann* (New York, 1979), 156; Max I. Dimont, *Jews, God and History* (New York, 1994), 331–32.
12. Horst von McGraw, *The Evolution of Hitler's Germany* (New York, 1973), 56; Jochmann, Werner, ed., *Adolf Hitler Monologe im Führerhauptquartier 1941–1944* (Hamburg, 1980), 96–99, 412–13; Fritz Redlich, *Hitler: Diagnosis of a Destructive Prophet* (Oxford, 1998), 309; Saul Friedländer, *Nazi Germany and the Jews,* Vol. 1, *The Years of Persecution, 1933–1939* (New York, 1997), 102, 177; Norman H. Baynes, ed., *The Speeches of Adolf Hitler,* Vols. 1–2, *April 1922–August 1939* (Oxford, 1942), 19.
13. Yehuda Bauer, *A History of the Holocaust* (New York, 1982), 133; Redlich, *Hitler,* 302; Burleigh, *Third Reich,* 13–14, 259–60; Friedländer, *Nazi Germany and the Jews,* 326–27; Jonathan Steinberg, "Croatians, Serbs and Jews, 1941–5," in David Cesarani, ed., *Final Solution: Origins and Implementation* (New York, 1994), 190.
14. Sajer, *Forgotten Soldier,* 334; Cooper, *German Army,* 333.
15. Fritz, *Frontsoldaten,* 90.

CHAPTER 5. *MISCHLINGE* AND UNCOMMON RESCUE STORIES

1. Wilhelm Deist, *The Wehrmacht and German Rearmament* (Toronto, 1981), 70–81.
2. Tent, *In the Shadow of the Holocaust,* 87.
3. A full account of the rescue was published by Yale University Press in 2004 as *Rescued from the Reich: How One of Hitler's Soldiers Saved the Lubavitcher Rebbe.*
4. Bauer, *History of the Holocaust,* 142–43; Keegan, *Second World War,* 44–47; Gilbert, *Holocaust,* 87, 99; Rossino, *Hitler Strikes Poland: Blitzkrieg, Ideology, and Atrocity* (Lawrence, KS, 2003), 1–4.
5. André Brissaud, *Canaris* (London, 1986), 157.
6. WNRCSM, 811.111.
7. WNRCSM, 811.111, Lubavitch promotional tract; WNRCSM, 15/1, secondary data on the Rebbe; Di Yiddische Heim, "Journey to America," Israel Jacobson (1956), 3.
8. Rachel Altein, *Out of the Inferno: The Efforts That Led to the Rescue of Rabbi Yosef Y. Schneersohn of Lubavitch from War-Torn Europe in 1939–40,* Eliezer Y. Zaklikovsky, ed. (New York, 2002), 298–302.
9. *The Rebbes,* Vol. 2: *Rabbi Yosef Yitzchak Schneersohn of Lubavitch* (Israel, 1994), 149. One must use the *Rebbes* book carefully because it is written for a young audience and its sources are not listed. Nonetheless the book tells the story most Lubavitchers accept.
10. Cooper, *German Air-Force,* 101; Altein, *Out of the Inferno,* 298–302; Gilbert, *Second World War,* 19.

11. WNRCSM, 15/1, Hull to Wagner, 23 September 1939.
12. Ibid., 15/2, Wagner to Hull, 26 September 1939, 15/7, Packer to Hull, 30 September 1939.
13. Ibid., 15/2, Rabinovitz to Brandeis, 29 September 1939, 15/3, Cohen to Pell, State Department, 2 October 1939; Di Yiddische Heim, "Journey to America," 3.
14. WNRCSM, 15/4, memorandum from Pell, 2 October 1939, 1–2.
15. Ibid., 15/6, Hull to Farley, 2 October 1939; BA-MA, BMRS, CLD (Chabad Library Documents), Kleinfield to Farley, 27 September 1939, Chanin to Bloom, 27 September 1939; WNRCSM, 811.111, Department of State to American Legation in Riga, 13 January 1940.
16. WNRCSM, 15/3.
17. Brissaud, *Canaris,* 158; Karl Heinz Abshagen, *Canaris* (London, 1956), 150; WNRCSM, 15/5, Geist and Kirck to Hull.
18. Abshagen, *Canaris,* 150.
19. Rolf Vogel, *Ein Stück von uns* (Bonn, 1973), 306–7; Nachhut, 15 February 1971, Heft no. 11 S. 12; BA-MA, Msg 3-22/1; Michel Bar-Zohar, *Hitler's Jewish Spy: The Most Extraordinary True Spy Story of World War II* (London, 1985).
20. NWHSAD, 100021/49193, 55F, Bürkner to Wohlthat, 15 January 1948; Brissaud, *Canaris,* 158.
21. Brissaud, *Canaris,* 153; Bauer, *History of the Holocaust,* 147; Kershaw, *Profiles in Power,* 152.
22. NWHSAD, 100021/49193, 55, Bürkner to Wohlthat, 15 January 1948; BA-MA, BMRS, interview with Martin Bloch, 13 October 1996.
23. BA-MA, BMRS, interview with Martin Bloch, 13 October 1996.
24. BA-MA, BMRS, interview with Ursula Cadenbach, 15 October 1996; BA-MA, Pers 6/9887.
25. BA-MA, Pers 6/9887; BA-MA, BMRS, Ernst Bloch; Vogel, *Ein Stück von uns,* 308–9.
26. BA-MA, BMRS, CLD, Jacobson to Liebermann, 24 October 1939, Pell to Cohen, 28 October 1939; WNRCSM, 15/7, Kirck to Pell, 19 November 1939.
27. BA-MA, BMRS, Schneersohn Folder 2, Rhoade to Cohen, 4 November 1939.
28. BA-MA, BMRS, interview with Klaus Schenk, 18 November 1996; NWHSAD, 56, Bürkner to Wohlthat, 15 January 1948.
29. Raphael N. Cohen, *Shmuos Vsipurim* (Israel, 1977), 235; Di Yiddische Heim, "Journey to America," 5.
30. BA-MA, BMRS, Schneersohn folder 2, Rhoade to Kramer, 27 November 1939.
31. WNRCSM, 15/25, Rhoade to Pell, 4 December 1939.
32. WNRCSM, 15/19, Kirck to Pell, 22 December 1939; Isaac Levinson, *The Untold Story* (Johannesburg, 1958), 121.
33. *Rebbes,* 154.
34. Ibid.; Vogel, *Ein Stück von uns,* 311.
35. WNRCSM, 15/20, Rhoade to Rissman, 13 January 1940.
36. Di Yiddische Heim, "Journey to America," 6; WNRCSM, 15/20; *Time,* 1 April 1940, 46; *Newsweek,* 1 April 1940, 31; *Rebbes,* 157.
37. WNRCSM, 811.111, Schneersohn to Hull, 25 March 1940.
38. Uri Kaploun, ed., *Likkutei Dibburim: An Anthology of Talks by Rabbi Yosef*

Yitzchak Schneersohn of Lubavitch, Vol. 3 (Brooklyn, NY, 1987–1990), 40, 56–57, 62–64, 79, 81–86.

39. Discussion with Norman Lamm, 18 December 2004; Norman Lamm, *The Face of God: Thoughts on the Holocaust*, Yeshiva University, Department of Holocaust Studies, 1986, 121; John Troyer, "Hatemongers Try to Cleanse History. Gays: Forgotten Heroes of 9/11," *Counter Punch*, 3 May 2002 (http://www .counterpunch.org/troyer0503.html; accessed 16 September 2008); Mitchell Plitnick, "Reclaiming Antisemitism," Jews for Global Justice, 20 July 2003; Anti-Defamation League, "Rev. Falwell's Statement That the Antichrist Is a Jew Borders on Antisemitism and Is Rooted in Christian Theological Extremism" (press release), 19 January 1999 (http://www.adl.org/PresRele/asus_12/3311_12.asp; accessed 16 September 2008).

40. Interview with Kenneth Roseman, 25 August 2003.

41. Karen Armstrong, *A History of God: A 4,000-Year Quest of Judaism, Christianity and Islam* (New York, 1993), 376.

42. Harold S. Kushner, *When Bad Things Happen to Good People* (New York, 1981), 10; BA-MA, BMRS, interview with Chaskel Besser.

43. Discussion with Lamm, 18 December 2004; Lamm, "Face of God," 120–32.

44. Discussion with Weisfogel, 18 November 2004.

45. Di Yiddische Heim, "Journey to America," 10; *Rebbes*, 14.

46. BA-MA, Pers 6/9887, 19; Julius Mader, *Hitlers Spionagegenerale sagen aus* (Berlin, 1971), 57–66; BA-MA, BMRS, interview with Ursula Cadenbach, 15 October 1996.

47. BA-MA, Pers 6/9887, 35, 42; BA-MA, BMRS, interview with Martin Bloch; BA-MA, BMRS, interview with Ursula Cadenbach, 15 October 1996.

48. BA-MA, BMRS, interviews with Martin Bloch, 13 October 1996 and 4 December 1996, interview with Ursula Cadenbach, 15 October 1996; BA-MA, BMRS, Ernst Bloch, Bloch to Bloch, 10 April 1945.

49. BA-MA, Pers 6/9887, 41–43.

50. BA-MA, BMRS, Ernst Bloch, interview with Ursula Cadenbach, 15 October 1996, Register's Officer to Preis, 1 November 1946.

51. Louis P. Lochner, ed., *Goebbels Diaries* (New York, 1948), 241.

52. Brissaud, *Canaris*, 153.

53. Walter Laqueur, "The Failure to Comprehend," in Donald L. Niewyk, ed., *The Holocaust: Problems and Perspectives of Interpretation* (New York, 2003), 260–62.

54. Talmudic Tractate *Sanhedrin* 37a and *Baba Batra*, 11-a.

55. See Rigg, *Rescued from the Reich*.

56. Letter to author, 12 March 2003.

CONCLUSION

1. BA-MA, BMRS, interviews with Dieter Bergman, 10–16 September 1996.

2. David Wyman, *The Abandonment of the Jews: America and the Holocaust 1941–1945* (New York, 1989), 5.

3. Bauer, *American Jewry and the Holocaust*, 19, 58.

BIBLIOGRAPHY

PRIMARY SOURCES
Bundesarchiv Berlin, Germany
Akten der Parteikanzlei der NSDAP, microfiches, Part 1, Vol. 1.
BA-B, 43 II/603b
BA-B, DZA 62 Ka. 1 83
BA-B, NS 19/453
BA-B, NS 19/3134
BA-B, R 43 II/599
DZA 62 Ka. 1 83
R 15.09/90
R 21-448

Bundesarchiv/Militärarchiv Freiburg (BA-MA), Germany
MSG 1/1570
MSG 3-22/1
N 39/62
N 179
N 328/45
N 761/7
NS 19/1772
Pers 6/11
Pers 6/9887
Pers 8-385
Reichsgesetzblatt (RGBL), I (1935)
RH 12-23/834
RW 6/56
RW 6/73
W 01-6/359

BA-MA, BMRS (Bryan Mark Rigg Collection), Freiburg, Germany
Files
Arthur Becker
Dieter Bergman
Heinz Bleicher
Ernst Bloch
John E. Dolibois
Dieter Fischer
Horst Geitner
Heinz Gerlach
Hans Günzel
Paul-Ludwig Hirschfeld
Edgar Jacoby

Helmut Krüger
Herbert Lefèvre
Moshe Mantelmacher
Hans Meissinger
Walter Melchior
Franz Mendelssohn
Erhard Milch
G. F. Müller
Horst von Oppenfeld
Ernst Prager
Bernhard Rogge
Karl-Heinz Scheffler
Konrad Schenck
Friedrich Wilhelm Schlesinger
Klaus Peter Scholz
Arno Spitz
Florian Stahmer
Karl-Arnd Techel
Helmut Wilberg

CLD (Chabad Library Documents), Folders 1–4
Schneersohn Folders 1–4

Interviews, Recorded
Eleonore Barz-Mendelssohn, 17 March 1995
Dieter Bergman, 10–16 September 1996
Chaskel Besser, 15 July 2003
Heinz Bleicher, 10 February 1995
Martin Bloch, 13 October 1996 and 4 December 1996
Ursula Cadenbach, 15 October 1996
Eva-Irene Eder-Mendelssohn, 26 February 1995
Dieter Fischer, 12 December 1996
Hugo Fuchs, 8 July 1995
Horst Geitner, 18 March 1997
Barry Gourary, 8 May 2003
Meyer Greenberg, 18 August 1996
Colin Heaton, 13–14 September 2004
Paul-Ludwig Hirschfeld, 15–16 August 1994 and 22 November 1996
Barbara Jacoby, 17 November 1994
Marianne Jacoby, 1 November 1994 and 19 November 1996
Helmuth Kopp, 27 September 1994
Helmut Krüger, 31 August 1994
Heinz-Günther Löwy, 12 January 1996
Hans Meissinger, 17 September 1996
Walter Melchior, 10 December 1994

Amelis von Mettenheim, 3 December 1996
Horst von Oppenfeld, 5 January 1995
Shlomo Perel, 10 September 1994
Stephan Prager, 11 October 1997
Richard Reiss, 15 October 1994
Rudolf Sachs, 20 November 1995
Günther Scheffler, 10 March 1995 and 14 December 1996
Karl-Heinz Scheffler, 9 March 1995 and 19 May 1996
Klaus Schenk (not his real name), 18 November 1996
Friedrich Wilhelm Schlesinger, 10 December 1994
Joachim Schmidt, 11 March 1995
Klaus Peter Scholz, 7 January 1995
Arno Spitz, 17 June 1996
Irmgard Techel, 29 May 1997
Karl-Arnd Techel, 29 May 1997
Joseph Wineberg, 4 May 2003

Interviews, Unrecorded
John E. Dolibois, 22 July 2001
Simon Gossel, 11 January 2005 and 27 January 2005
Hans Hirsch, 12 July 2005
Frau Karl-Heinz Löwy, 25 August 2005 and 10 September 2005
Gerhard Weinberg, 2 September 2005
Interviews by Colin Heaton with Johannes Steinhoff, 26–28 January 1984

Nordrhein-Westfälisches Hauptstaatsarchiv Düsseldorf, Germany
NWHSAD 100021/49193.

Institut für Schiffahrts- und Marinegeschichte in Hamburg, Germany
File Bernhard Rogge

Institut für Zeitgeschichte—Munich, Germany
N 71-73.

National Archives and Records Administration—Suitland, Maryland
Box 329, File AE 501661, Fritz Bayerlein
WNRCSM 360 C.60P
WNRCSM RG 59, CDF 811.111

SECONDARY SOURCES
Abshagen, Karl Heinz. *Canaris.* London, 1956.
Absolon, Rudolf. *Wehrgesetz und Wehrdienst 1935–1945: Das Personalwesen in der Wehrmacht.* Boppard, Germany, 1960.
Adler, H. G. *Der verwaltete Mensch: Studien zur Deportation der Juden aus Deutschland.* Tübingen, 1974.

Altein, Rachel. *Out of the Inferno: The Efforts That Led to the Rescue of Rabbi Yosef Y. Schneersohn of Lubavitch from War-Torn Europe in 1939–40*. Eliezer Y. Zaklikovsky, ed. New York, 2002.

Armstrong, Karen. *A History of God: A 4,000-Year Quest of Judaism, Christianity and Islam*. New York, 1993.

Bartov, Omer. *Hitler's Army: Soldiers, Nazis, and War in the Third Reich*. New York, 1991.

Bar-Zohar, Michel. *Hitler's Jewish Spy: The Most Extraordinary True Spy Story of World War II*. London, 1985.

Bauer, Yehuda. *American Jewry and the Holocaust: The American Jewish Joint Distribution Committee 1939–1945*. Detroit, 1981.

———. *A History of the Holocaust*. New York, 1982.

Baynes, Norman H., ed. *The Speeches of Adolf Hitler*. Vols. 1–2, *April 1922–August 1939*. Oxford, 1942.

Behler, Ernst, ed. *The German Library*. Vol. 13, *Kant, Philosophical Writings*. New York, 1986.

Bergman, Dieter. *Between Two Benches*. Hayward, CA, 1995.

Berlin, Isaiah. *Four Essays on Liberty*. Oxford, 1969.

Bidermann, Gottlob Herbert. *In Deadly Combat: A German Soldier's Memoir of the Eastern Front*. Lawrence, KS, 2000.

Bradley, James. *Flags of Our Fathers*. New York, 2000.

Brissaud, André. *Canaris*. London, 1986.

Burleigh, Michael. *Ethics and Extermination: Reflections on Nazi Genocide*. New York, 1997.

———. *The Third Reich: A New History*. New York, 2000.

Campbell, Joseph. *The Power of Myth with Bill Moyers*. New York, 1991.

Cesarani, David, ed. *The Final Solution: Origins and Implementation*. New York, 1994.

Claasen, Adam R. A. *Hitler's Northern War: The Luftwaffe's Ill-Fated Campaign, 1940–1945*. Lawrence, KS, 2001.

Clark, Alan. *Barbarossa: The Russo-German Conflict, 1941–1945*. New York, 1985.

Cohen, Raphael N. *Shmuos Vsipurim*. Israel, 1977.

Cooper, Matthew. *The German Air-Force, 1933–1945*. New York, 1981.

———. *The German Army, 1933–1945: Its Political and Military Failure*. New York, 1978.

Corum, James S. *The Luftwaffe: Creating the Operational Air War, 1918–1940*. Lawrence, KS, 1997.

———. "The Old Eagle as Phoenix: The Luftstreitkräfte Creates an Operational Air War Doctrine, 1919–1920." *Air Power History* 14 (Spring 1992), 13–21.

———. *The Roots of Blitzkrieg: Hans von Seeckt and German Military Reform*. Lawrence, KS, 1992.

Craig, Gordon. *Germany 1866–1945*. New York, 1978.

Deist, Wilhelm. *Militär, Staat und Gesellschaft. Studien zur preussisch-deutschen Militärgeschichte*. München, 1991.

———. *The Wehrmacht and German Rearmament*. Toronto, 1981.

Dimont, Max I. *Jews, God and History*. New York, 1994.

Dower, John W. *War without Mercy: Race and Power in the Pacific War.* New York, 1986.

Elon, Amos. *The Pity of It All: A History of Jews in Germany, 1743–1933.* New York, 2002.

Ericksen, Robert. *Theologians under Hitler.* New Haven, CT, 1985.

Farar-Hockley, Anthony. *Student.* New York, 1973.

Frank, Wolfgang, and Bernhard Rogge. *The German Raider Atlantis.* New York, 1956.

Frankl, Victor. *Man's Search for Meaning.* New York, 1990.

Friedländer, Saul. *Nazi Germany and the Jews.* Vol. 1, *The Years of Persecution, 1933–1939.* New York, 1997.

Friedman, Saul. *No Haven for the Oppressed: United States Policy toward Jewish Refugees, 1938–1945.* Detroit, 1973.

Fritz, Stephen G. *Frontsoldaten: The German Soldier in World War II.* Lexington, KY, 1995.

Gay, Ruth. *The Jews of Germany.* New Haven, CT, 1992.

Gellately, Robert, ed. *The Nuremberg Interviews: Conducted by Leon Goldensohn.* New York, 2004.

Gilbert, Martin. *The Holocaust.* New York, 1985.

———. *The Second World War.* New York, 1989.

Goethe, Johann Wolfgang von. *Faust.* Franklin Center, PA, 1979.

Goldin, Judah, ed. and trans. *The Living Talmud: The Wisdom of the Fathers.* New York, 1957.

Hart, Liddell. *The German Generals' Talk.* New York, 1979.

Hartman, Geoffrey, ed. *Holocaust Remembrance: The Shapes of Memory.* New York, 1994.

Hausner, Gideon. *Justice in Jerusalem.* New York, 1966.

Hayward, Joel S. A. *Stopped at Stalingrad: The Luftwaffe and Hitler's Defeat in the East, 1942–1943.* Lawrence, KS, 1998.

Heeresadjutant bei Hitler 1938–1943. Aufzeichnungen des Majors Gerhard Engel. Ed. and with commentary by Hildegard von Kotze. Schriftenreihe der Vierteljahreshefte für Zeitgeschichte no. 29. Stuttgart, 1974.

Heiden, Konrad. *Der Fuehrer: Hitler's Rise to Power.* London, 1967.

Hertz, Deborah, "The Genealogy Bureaucracy in the Third Reich." *Jewish History* (Fall 1997).

Hilberg, Raul. *Destruction of the European Jews.* New York, 1961.

Hildebrand, Karl Friedrich. *Die Generale der deutschen Luftwaffe, 1935–1945.* 3 vols. Osnabrück, 1990–1992.

Hitler, Adolf. *Mein Kampf.* Boston, 1971.

The Holocaust. Vol. 1, *Legalizing the Holocaust—The Early Phase, 1933–1939.* Introduction by John Mendelsohn. New York, 1982.

Jacobson, Rabbi Israel. "Journey to America." *Di Yiddische Heim.* 1956.

Jochmann, Werner, ed. *Adolf Hitler Monologe im Führerhauptquartier, 1941–1944.* Hamburg, 1980.

Jones, Geoffrey P. *Under Three Flags: The Story of Nordmark and the Armed Supply Ships of the German Navy.* London, 1973.

Kahn, David. *Hitler's Spies: German Military Intelligence in World War II.* New York, 1977.

Kammer, Hilde, and Elisabet Bartsch, with Manon Eppenstein-Baukhage. *National-sozialismus. Begriffe aus der Zeit der Gewaltherrschaft, 1933–1945.* Reinbek bei Hamburg, 1992.

Kaplan, Chaim A. *Scroll of Agony: The Warsaw Diary of Chaim A. Kaplan.* New York, 1965.

Kaplan, Marion A. *Between Dignity and Despair: Jewish Life in Nazi Germany.* New York, 1998.

Kaploun, Uri, ed. *Likkutei Dibburim: An Anthology of Talks by Rabbi Yosef Yitzchak Schneersohn of Lubavitch,* Vols. 1–3, 5. Brooklyn, NY, 1987–1990.

Katsuichi, Honda. *The Nanjing Massacre: A Japanese Journalist Confronts Japan's National Shame.* London, 1999.

Keegan, John. *The Second World War.* New York, 1989.

———. *War and Our World.* New York, 1998.

Kershaw, Ian. *Hitler: 1889–1936: Hubris.* New York, 1999.

———. *Hitler: 1936–1945: Nemesis.* New York, 2000.

———. *The Hitler Myth: Image and Reality in the Third Reich.* Oxford, 1990.

———. *Profiles in Power: Hitler.* London, 1991.

Klemperer, Victor. *Ich will Zeugnis ablegen bis zum letzten: Tagebücher, 1933–1945.* Darmstadt, Germany, 1996.

Koburger, Charles W. *Steel Ships, Iron Crosses, and Refugees: The German Navy in the Baltic, 1939–1945.* New York, 1989.

Kushner, Harold S. *When Bad Things Happen to Good People.* New York, 1981.

Lang, Jochen von. *The Secretary: Martin Bormann.* New York, 1979.

Lessing, Gotthold Ephraim. *Nathan the Wise, Minna von Barnhelm, and Other Plays and Writings.* Peter Demetz, ed. New York, 1991.

Levinson, Isaac. *The Untold Story.* Johannesburg, 1958.

Lifton, Robert Jay. *The Nazi Doctors.* New York, 1986.

Lochner, Louis P., ed. *Goebbels Diaries.* New York, 1948.

Lösener, Bernhard. "Als Rassereferent im Reichsministerium des Innern." In *Das Reichsministerium des Innern und die Judengesetzgebung.* Vierteljahreshefte für Zeitgeschichte no. 6 (1961).

Mader, Julius. *Hitler Spionagegenerale sagen aus.* Berlin, 1971.

Maier, Karl-Heinz. *Und höret niemals auf zu kämpfen.* Berlin, 1994.

Maser, Werner. *Adolf Hitler: Legende Mythos Wirklichkeit.* Munich, 1971.

Mason, Herbert Molly, Jr. *The Rise of the Luftwaffe.* New York, 1973.

McGraw, Horst von. *The Evolution of Hitler's Germany.* New York, 1973.

Merten, Karl-Friedrich. *Nach Kompass.* Cloppenburg, 1994.

Messerschmidt, Manfred. *Die Wehrmacht im NS-Staat.* Hamburg, 1969.

Meyer, Beate. *Jüdische Mischlinge: Rassenpolitik und Verfolgungserfahrung 1933–1945.* Hamburg, 1999.

Meyer, Winfried. *Unternehmen Sieben. Eine Rettungsaktion für vom Holocaust Bedrohte aus dem Amt Ausland-Abwehr im Oberkommando der Wehrmacht.* Frankfurt, 1993.

Mill, John Stuart. *On Liberty, with the Subjection of Women and Chapters on Socialism.* Stefan Collini, ed. Cambridge, UK, 1991.

Mohr, Ulrich, and A. V. Sellwood. *Ship 16: The Story of the Secret German Raider Atlantis.* New York, 1956.

Morgan, Roger. "Hitler's 'Jewish Soldiers.'" *History Today* (November 2007), 45–51.

Mosley, Leonard. *The Reich Marshal.* London, 1974.

Muggenthaler, August Karl. *German Raiders of World War II.* London, 1980.

Müller, Rolf-Dieter, and Hans-Erich Volkmann, eds. *Die Wehrmacht: Mythos und Realität.* Stuttgart, 1999.

Murray, Williamson. *Luftwaffe.* Baltimore, 1985.

Nachhut, 15 February 1971, no. 11.

Niewyk, Donald L., ed. *The Holocaust: Problems and Perspectives of Interpretation.* New York, 2003.

Noakes, Jeremy. "The Development of Nazi Policy towards the German-Jewish 'Mischlinge' 1933–1945." *Leo Baeck Yearbook* 34 (1989).

Office of the U.S. Chief Counsel for Prosecution of Axis Criminality, ed. *Nazi Conspiracy and Aggression,* Vol. 2. Washington, DC, 1946.

Paret, Peter, ed. *Makers of Modern Strategy from Machiavelli to the Nuclear Age.* Princeton, NJ, 1986.

Pätzold, Kurt, ed. *Verfolgung, Vertreibung, Vernichtung: Dokumente des faschistischen Antisemitismus, 1933 bis 1942.* Leipzig, 1984.

Persico, Joseph E. *Nuremberg: Infamy on Trial.* New York, 1994.

Picker, Henry. *Hitlers Tischgespräche im Führerhauptquartier, 1941–1942.* Percy Ernst Schramm, ed. Stuttgart, 1976.

Raeder, Erich. *My Life: Grand Admiral Erich Raeder.* Annapolis, MD, 1960.

Rautkallio, Hannu. *Finland and the Holocaust: The Rescue of Finland's Jews.* Helsinki, 1989.

Read, Anthony. *The Devil's Disciples: Hitler's Inner Circle.* New York, 2004.

The Rebbes, Vol. 2: *Rabbi Yosef Yitzchak Schneersohn of Lubavitch.* Israel, 1994.

Redlich, Fritz. *Hitler: Diagnosis of a Destructive Prophet.* Oxford, 1998.

Remarque, Erich Maria. *All Quiet on the Western Front.* New York, 1982.

Rich, Norman. *Hitler's War Aims.* New York, 1974.

Rigg, Bryan Mark. *Hitler's Jewish Soldiers: The Untold Story of Nazi Racial Laws and Men of Jewish Descent in the German Military.* Lawrence, KS, 2002.

———. *Rescued from the Reich: How One of Hitler's Soldiers Saved the Lubavitcher Rebbe.* New Haven, CT, 2004.

Rossino, Alexander. *Hitler Strikes Poland: Blitzkrieg, Ideology, and Atrocity.* Lawrence, KS, 2003.

Rudel, Hans Ulrich. *Stuka Pilot.* New York, 1979.

Ruppin, Arthur. *The Jews in the Modern World.* London, 1934.

Sajer, Guy. *The Forgotten Soldier.* New York, 1971.

Seaton, Albert. *The Russo-German War, 1941–1945.* London, 1971.

Shelton, Dinah, ed. *Encyclopedia of Genocide and Crimes against Humanity.* New York, 2005.

Slavick, Joseph. *The Cruise of the German Raider Atlantis.* Annapolis, 2003.

Smelser, Ronald, and Enrico Syring, eds. *Die Militärelite des Dritten Reiches.* Berlin, 1995.

State of Israel Ministry of Justice, ed. *The Trial of Adolf Eichmann: Record of Proceedings in the District Court of Jerusalem,* Vol. 7. Jerusalem, 1992.

Steinberg, Jonathan. *All or Nothing: The Axis and the Holocaust, 1941–43.* New York, 2002.

Stoltzfus, Nathan. *Resistance of the Heart: Intermarriage and the Rosenstrasse Protest in Nazi Germany.* New York, 1996.

Sydnor, Charles. *Soldiers of Destruction: The SS Death's Head Division, 1933–1945.* Princeton, NJ, 1977.

Tanaka, Yuki. *Hidden Horrors: Japanese War Crimes in World War II.* New York, 1996.

Tent, James F. *In the Shadow of the Holocaust: Nazi Persecution of Jewish-Christian Germans.* Lawrence, KS, 2003.

Ueberschaer, Gerd, and Wolfram Wette, eds. *Kriegsverbrechen im 20 Jahrhundert.* Darmstadt, Germany, 2001.

Vogel, Rolf. *Ein Stück von uns.* Bonn, 1973.

Von der Porten, Edward P. *The German Navy in World War II.* London, 1970.

Voss, Johann. *Black Edelweiss: A Memoir of Combat and Conscience by a Soldier of the Waffen-SS.* Bedford, PA, 2002.

Vuletic, Aleksandar-Saša. *Christen Jüdischer Herkunft im Dritten Reich: Verfolgung und organisierte Selbsthilfe 1933–1939.* Mainz, 1999.

Walk, Joseph, ed. *Sonderrecht für den Juden im NS-Staat: Eine Sammlung der gesetzlichen Massnahmen und Richtlinien: Inhalt und Bedeutung.* Heidelberg, 1981.

Weinberg, Gerhard L. *Germany, Hitler and World War II.* New York, 1996.

———. *A World at Arms: A Global History of World War II.* New York, 1994.

Werth, Alexander. *Russia at War: 1941–1945.* New York, 1964.

Wheeler-Bennett, John. *The Nemesis of Power.* New York, 1980.

Wilberg, Helmut. *Abschliessender Flieger-Erfahrungsbericht über die Schlacht in Flandern.* Buch- und Steindruckerei der Artillerie-Fliegerschule Ost 1, 1923.

Wistrich, Robert. *Who's Who in Nazi Germany.* New York, 1982.

Wyman, David. *The Abandonment of the Jews: America and the Holocaust, 1941–1945.* New York, 1989.

Yahil, Leni. *The Holocaust: The Fate of European Jewry.* New York, 1990.

Zoepf, Wolf. *Seven Days in January: With the 6th SS-Mountain Division in Operation NORDWIND.* Bedford, PA, 2001.

INDEX